D1431613

Developing Human Capital

Wiley & SAS Business Series

The Wiley & SAS Business Series presents books that help senior-level managers with their critical management decisions.

Titles in the Wiley & SAS Business Series include:

Activity-Based Management for Financial Institutions: Driving Bottom-Line Results by Brent Bahnub

Analytics in a Big Data World: The Essential Guide to Data Science and Its Applications by Bart Baesens

Bank Fraud: Using Technology to Combat Losses by Revathi Subramanian

Big Data Analytics: Turning Big Data into Big Money by Frank Ohlhorst

Big Data, Big Innovation: Enabling Competitive Differentiation through Business Analytics by Evan Stubbs

Branded! How Retailers Engage Consumers with Social Media and Mobility by Bernie Brennan and Lori Schafer

Business Analytics for Customer Intelligence by Gert Laursen

Business Analytics for Managers: Taking Business Intelligence beyond Reporting by Gert Laursen and Jesper Thorlund

The Business Forecasting Deal: Exposing Bad Practices and Providing Practical Solutions by Michael Gilliland

Business Intelligence and the Cloud: Strategic Implementation Guide by Michael S. Gendron

Business Intelligence Applied: Implementing an Effective Information and Communications Technology Infrastructure by Michael S. Gendron

Business Intelligence Success Factors: Tools for Aligning Your Business in the Global Economy by Olivia Parr Rud

Harness Oil and Gas Big Data with Analytics: Optimize Exploration and Production with Data Driven Models by Keith Holdaway

Health Analytics: Gaining the Insights to Transform Health Care by Jason Burke

Heuristics in Analytics: A Practical Perspective of What Influences Our Analytical World by Carlos Andre Reis Pinheiro and Fiona McNeill

Human Capital Analytics: How to Harness the Potential of Your Organization's Greatest Asset by Gene Pease, Boyce Byerly, and Jac Fitz-enz

Implement, Improve and Expand Your Statewide Longitudinal Data System: Creating a Culture of Data in Education by Jamie McQuiggan and Armistead Sapp

Information Revolution: Using the Information Evolution Model to Grow Your Business by Jim Davis, Gloria J. Miller, and Allan Russell

Killer Analytics: Top 20 Metrics Missing from your Balance Sheet by Mark Brown

Manufacturing Best Practices: Optimizing Productivity and Product Quality by Bobby Hull

Marketing Automation: Practical Steps to More Effective Direct Marketing by Jeff LeSueur

Mastering Organizational Knowledge Flow: How to Make Knowledge Sharing Work by Frank Leistner

The New Know: Innovation Powered by Analytics by Thornton May

Performance Management: Integrating Strategy Execution, Methodologies, Risk, and Analytics by Gary Cokins

Predictive Analytics for Human Resources by Jac Fitz-enz and John Mattox II

Predictive Business Analytics: Forward-Looking Capabilities to Improve Business Performance by Lawrence Maisel and Gary Cokins

Retail Analytics: The Secret Weapon by Emmett Cox

Social Network Analysis in Telecommunications by Carlos Andre Reis Pinheiro

For more information on any of the above titles, please visit www.wiley.com.

Developing Human Capital

Using Analytics to Plan and Optimize Your Learning and Development Investments

Gene Pease
Bonnie Beresford
Lew Walker

WILEY

Published by John Wiley & Sons, Inc., Hoboken, New Jersey.
Published simultaneously in Canada.

For general information on our other products and services or for technical support, please contact our Customer Care Department within the United States at (800) 762-2974, outside the United States at (317) 572-3993 or fax (317) 572-4002.

Wiley publishes in a variety of print and electronic formats and by print-on-demand. Some material included with standard print versions of this book may not be included in e-books or in print-on-demand. If this book refers to media such as a CD or DVD that is not included in the version you purchased, you may download this material at http://booksupport.wiley.com. For more information about Wiley products, visit www.wiley.com.

Library of Congress Cataloging-in-Publication Data:

Pease, Gene, 1950-
   Developing human capital : using analytics to plan and optimize your learning and
development investments / Gene Pease, Barbara (Bonnie) Beresford, Lew Walker.
   1 online resource. — (Wiley & SAS business series)
   Includes bibliographical references and index.
   Description based on print version record and CIP data provided by publisher; resource
not viewed.
   ISBN 978-1-118-91088-7 (ebk); ISBN 978-1-118-91098-6 (ebk);
   ISBN 978-1-118-75350-7 (hardback)
     1. Manpower planning. 2. Human capital—Management. 3. Employees—
Training of. 4. Personnel management. I. Beresford, Barbara, 1957- II. Walker, Lew,
1957- III. Title.
   HF5549.5.M3
   658.3'01—dc23
                                                                              2014011509

Printed in the United States of America.

10 9 8 7 6 5 4 3 2 1

Contents

Foreword

I think of myself as an information management and analytics expert, not a human resources (HR) or learning expert. However, I am a sociologist by educational background, and I have frequently dabbled in HR topics—specifically in the HR analytics area. I am occasionally told that someone likes my book, *Human Capital: What It Is and Why People Invest in It*. I thank them graciously. The only problem is that I didn't write that book—Thomas O. Davenport did (I have a different middle initial). But I take the fact that people attribute it to me as an indication that I have fooled some people about my human capital expertise.

In any case, in this foreword I will focus primarily on the broader trend to think more analytically about almost everything, and what that means for HR. Almost every industry is becoming more analytical these days. Retail, banking, and other consumer businesses have long been analytical, and they are becoming more so. Even the holdouts, such as the entertainment industry and business-to-business firms, are starting to make more analytical decisions. Traditional manufacturing firms have gotten the "big data" message, and are popping sensors into their "big iron" devices to measure and optimize their performance.

Virtually every business function is adopting more analytical approaches to management as well. Supply chain optimization and manufacturing quality assessment (Six Sigma) have been going on for decades. But now the softer functions are increasingly using hard metrics and statistics. Marketing, for example, is undergoing dramatic change. Once satirized by *Dilbert* as the department that requires a "two-drink minimum," marketers are increasingly generating targeted and personalized offers, making decisions about which digital ads to place where in milliseconds, and optimizing their investment decisions on a monthly basis.

The implications for HR are obvious. HR was the other soft function in terms of using analytics. Decisions in that function were typically among the most intuition- and experience-based ones you could find in a company. Whether it was whom to hire, whom to fire, what to pay, and how to develop, HR and line managers relied on their gut or the seat of their pants. As Lew Walker notes in the Introduction to this book, "HR was not an area where analytical minds came to launch a career."

But if every industry and every function are becoming more analytical, HR will too. In fact, this has been going on for a while. HR thought leaders like Jac Fitz-enz, John Boudreau, and Gene Pease himself have written books on analytical HR several years ago. Laurie Bassi has related human capital orientation to stock prices. Companies like Google have transformed how they hire and evaluate their people—HR analytics have replaced time-honored wisdom.

In fact, HR and marketing are alike in some key ways. Just as marketing's view of customers has become more individualized and personalized, HR's view of employees is more oriented to the individual as well. Just as the goal of marketing has become "one to one," the goal of HR has become to address a "workforce of one," as my former colleagues Sue Cantrell and David Smith put it in a book by that name. This means more metrics, more analysis, and more automated recommendations for HR as we go forward.

However, learning analytics is perhaps the last frontier for HR analytics. As the authors note later on in this book, learning and knowledge were historically perceived to be good things for their own sake, and there was precious little evaluation of the effects of learning in the workplace. Just as with marketing investments, however, we can now determine whether a firm's learning investments are paying off.

This book is well-timed. It comes at a point, as the authors note in the first chapter, when there is enormous generational change in organizations, and great change as well in what people want from their jobs. Learning is more important than ever. It also comes at a time when we can equip almost any HR and learning process with instruments for measuring and recording data. Modern HR information systems keep track of employee assignments, evaluations, and even productivity. The dependent variables—those factors we are attempting to explain and predict—are well taken care of.

The independent variables around learning that drive business outcomes are also increasingly measurable. In the old days, we could know only that a person was sitting in a classroom or was not. Low-level employees might be asked to take a test to measure recall. Now, however, with increasingly online learning materials, we can measure all sorts of factors as learning inputs: how much time the learner spent with the content, whether he or she lingered over a particular section, and even whether linked websites were investigated for further learning. And of course it's very easy to test whether something was learned—not only right after the studying, but later on as well.

All this means that there will soon be models that explain and predict what business benefits have accrued from what learning content. The models will be at the individual, departmental, business unit, and organizational level. They will ultimately prescribe a set of learning materials that optimize performance for each learner. In short, analytics will tell us how each employee can achieve his or her ultimate performance potential.

I will leave it to these highly capable and experienced authors to relate the details of how to apply analytics to learning. They have plenty of evidence and examples of such application. As I read the book, it seemed highly likely to me that corporate learning would have a much more analytical future. If you want to be ahead of—or at least fully aware of—that trend, you've come to the right place. Keep reading, and remember that we are monitoring each word you read. (Just kidding!)

THOMAS H. DAVENPORT
President's Distinguished Professor, Babson College
Fellow, MIT Center for Digital Business
Cofounder and Director of Research,
International Institute for Analytics
Author of *Competing on Analytics* and *Big Data at Work*

Preface

When I collaborated on our first book, *Human Capital Analytics: How to Harness the Potential of Your Organization's Greatest Asset* (John Wiley & Sons, 2012), big data and the power of analytics were hot topics in a wide variety of circles. Yet not much had been written on predictive analytics, and almost nothing on applying predictive analytics to human capital. The same can be said for learning and development (L&D) investments. Quite a bit has been written about measuring learning investments, primarily using assumptive methodologies that have been around for more than 50 years. But very little, if any, literature applies predictive analytics to L&D investments. As I come to the culmination of a decade of work in this field, I'm focused on how you can apply advanced methodologies and statistics to the organization's largest investment: its people.

I am fortunate to have collaborated on this book with two thought leaders who have decades of experience in corporate learning: Bonnie Beresford, PhD, and Lew Walker. Bonnie and I collaborated for more than four years at Capital Analytics (now Vestrics), where she oversaw the delivery of our analytical services. Lew is the Vice President of Learning Services at AT&T and responsible for one of the world's largest learning organizations. AT&T, under Lew's stewardship, has won numerous awards for its corporate learning.

Business leaders recognize that the value of a modern company is in the intangibles, most of which consist of some form of human capital: expertise, customer relationships, employer brand, intellectual property, and business processes. The companies that thrive and prosper are those that get the most out of their human capital, which requires a deep understanding of what is going on with their workforce, how investments affect it, and how to communicate changes effectively with all parts of the enterprise. The human resources (HR) industry is just beginning to grasp the value of understanding human capital, and is evolving to make a strategic contribution to business goals. Rigorous analysis that uncovers the true impact of investments, thereby showing how to optimize those investments, is necessary for organizations to outperform their competitors in today's unsparing environment.

This book shows how to accomplish the holy grail of learning analysis: optimizing investments using predictive analytics. The book imparts the major lessons we have learned from many years doing this work. We begin by summarizing the forces changing the workforce, and then jump into building a measurement strategy and framework. From here we discuss how to align the curriculum with business outcomes. The last chapters show how to improve upon the reporting basics and get beyond return on investment (ROI) to predictive analytics. It's here that we introduce our Level 6 of the Kirkpatrick/Phillips model, which we call optimization. Many of the chapters are accompanied by a case study from a world-leading company that illustrates the chapter topic to show how our lessons are applied in complex environments.

We hope this book will be read by the leaders of human resources, leaders in L&D, and their colleagues outside of HR. We believe it will inspire you to apply the same tools used to evaluate and improve finance, marketing, and operations investments to human capital investments. We also hope to show practitioners that the lessons learned in this book, and lots of hard work, will result in better L&D investments that ultimately drive organizational strategic goals.

GENE PEASE

Acknowledgments

I am blessed to have my mother, Deanne Pease, and my wife, Pamela Pease, for their continued love and support. They make me strive to be the man my dog, Bailey, thinks I am. I also want to acknowledge a few pioneers who have inspired me in this journey of optimizing human capital: Donald Kirkpatrick, Jack Phillips, Jac Fitz-enz, Tom Davenport, Ed Lawler, John Boudreau, Mike Echols, Jeffrey Pfeffer, and Marshall Goldsmith.

—Gene Pease

I extend much gratitude to my parents, Molly and Bill, who have forever encouraged me to persevere and chase my dreams. I also thank my wonderful clients over the years who have provided me with the opportunities to push the measurement envelope. Many thanks, too, to my colleagues at BBDO Detroit and Capital Analytics who fed my enthusiasm for uncovering the mysteries hiding within the data. Finally, and most important, this journey of a first book would have been impossible without the unending support and understanding of my partner Lee, who stood by my side while I chased this dream. Thank you, Lee.

—Bonnie Beresford

I want to thank my wife, Karen, who is not only my life partner but has been a coach, mentor, and cheer leader. To my three sons, Greg, Corey, and Colin, by looking through their eyes I continue to see a whole different world. Lastly to all the people I have worked with, I will always be grateful to the relationships and camaraderie as they have helped shape me as a person.

—Lew Walker

Introduction

Lew Walker

Not long ago I had the opportunity to meet with Gene Pease from his organization, Capital Analytics, Inc., now Vestrics. As our discussion was concluding, Gene left me a copy of his first book, *Human Capital Analytics: How to Harness the Potential of Your Organization's Greatest Asset*. When Gene asked if I would be interested in collaborating on this book, I was excited to be given the chance to offer a perspective from the front lines. If you are like me, it's a challenge to find time to update your skills or read a book with more than 200 pages, but as I had a few minutes here and there, I started reading. After quickly coming to the conclusion that I was not doing the book justice by only reading pieces and parts—and being very interested in the subject—I dedicated time to read it cover to cover. I found that it offers a road map to measure human capital, but more important, how to derive business value via measurement and calculation. From a practitioner's perspective it showed a clear and comprehensible point of connection between the arcane world of measurement and statistics and the "what have you done for me lately?" mind-set that learning professionals deal with day in and day out today.

Over my professional career I have led every function within a human resources (HR) organization, and some outside it. From that vantage point, I've discovered that measuring the impact that training and development have on learners and organizations is the most critical measurement performed within HR.

Organizations make significant investments in their workforces. Compensation, benefits, and opportunities for career growth are all used to engage the workforce and motivate employees to be successful. The essential goal of any organization is for its employees to perform at their highest level. Yet do we really understand the impact of this investment in training? This book left me with a clear picture of how to provide even greater value through training. We have to continue to educate ourselves relative to the importance of measurement, and we need to ensure that business stakeholders see value beyond the less sophisticated ways to measure such as simply asking, "Did they like the training?"

The book resonates with the word *optimization*. The world is changing, the ways people communicate are changing, and business models are changing. While technology continues to make us more productive, are we optimizing our productivity? Change is difficult, but it keeps us focused on the need to visit and revisit our models and assumptions. The value of optimization is to provide a framework in which to isolate the impact, improve the outcome, and make better decisions.

SHOW ME THE MONEY

Working with business leaders, I've found they are most concerned with outcomes. How often do we hear them say, "Sounds great, but how is this going to help me solve my problem?" or "increase sales?" or "provide better customer service?"

I remember some years ago having a discussion with a senior executive about investing in training for a group of high-potential managers. After reviewing the proposal and cost, he said, "I believe the best way to develop skills is by placing people into stretch jobs. The ability to manage adversity by stretching them is the best skill builder you can use. But Lew, if you can show me that by sending them to training they will perform better, then I will consider funding it." Of course, I had no way to prove this other than by relying on the traditional belief that training is the way to raise people's skills.

This leads me to one of the most important steps we have taken in the field of learning: widespread use of statistically relevant metrics and analytics. CEOs, CFOs, CMOs, and other C-level executives are driven by metrics and analytics. For these roles there is a history of standard metrics that help shape decisions. But do we in the field of learning make it a point to speak the metrics and analytics language? Or do we use *learning*-speak?

LEARNING METRICS ARE BUSINESS METRICS

When I started my HR career in the mid-1980s as a personnel representative, HR was not an area where analytical minds came to launch a career. In fact, when I started working as the head of HR for a small wireless start-up in the early 1990s, I reported to the CFO. The CEO believed that HR needed the guiding hand of someone who understood the numbers. I am not a numbers person by nature, but I have always been an eager student, with a strong desire to understand how data can be used to help businesses succeed.

The wireless start-up I was working for was acquired in 1994 and shortly thereafter I was fortunate to be named the head of HR of the acquiring company. I was determined to show the president the power of HR data—turnover, cost per hire, and time to fill—all good standard stuff that I had used with leadership in my previous role. I guess those leaders either didn't understand the data or perhaps weren't terribly interested in how it could be utilized. In any event, the president asked me two simple questions in one of our first meetings: "What is actionable about this data?" and "Will these actions translate into helping me meet and exceed my business objectives?" Suffice it to say I had not really thought through the action part, and quite frankly had not thought much further than the fact that I had produced data.

Generally speaking, HR professionals and business leaders see the value in HR data, but considering data versus outcomes requires different mind-sets. I have always applied these two simple questions asked of me so many years ago: "What is actionable?" and "How will it help my client meet and exceed objectives?" It is a strong argument in support of measuring and analyzing.

I have led training organizations for different companies as part of my responsibilities. Like many, I struggled to provide realistic measurements of the impact of training. Yes, generally everyone agrees you need to train new hires, you need to raise skills of your workforce, and in some cases you need to reskill your workers to take on new jobs. It always reminds me of the motto of Faber College from the movie *Animal House*: "Knowledge is good." However, as learning professionals, we should add, "But even better when we measure and optimize its impact."

UNDERSTAND THE BUSINESS

Through feedback from many clients, we know that most agree that training is critical to an organization's success. Most also agree that measurement is important. We possess systems that can provide data on training impact. What then is missing? The ingredient that brings this all together is not only a strong knowledge of the needs of the business, but an intimate knowledge of how the business operates. This knowledge ensures you can speak the language of the business, understand how it operates, and serve as a credible adviser. When combining knowledge of the client's business with the skill set of a learning professional, learning interventions can be identified that will impact the client's key business metrics.

BE THE BUSINESS

A few years ago I was discussing learning metrics with a senior client whose organization I supported. When I concluded, he said, "This is all great, but what I want to know is: What have you done to improve my AHT [average handling time] in my call centers?" Having learned my lesson over the years, I was prepared to reinforce the importance of leading with business-impacting metrics. For this and most business leaders, if you're not delivering the training they need, your other learning metrics are meaningless.

So, are learning metrics meaningless? Of course not. A balanced approach—one where you are utilizing metrics that measure the operational actions of your learning team along with those that reflect the learning impact on the client's goals and objectives—is important to you and your client.

In order to maximize your learning outcome and to measure the impact to the client's objectives, it is critical to understand what the measurable impact will be on the learner. First, what are we looking for—increased sales, better call quality, reduced installation time? Second, can the business unit provide the data we need to assess impact—or in some cases, is there a will to provide the data in the time frame in which the measurement is taking place? Finally, are there other initiatives being introduced that may affect the outcome—for example, a new compensation plan, or new processes that reduce installation time?

I have observed, and I think most HR professionals would agree, that business objectives are a critical piece of learning metrics. A few years ago, our company initiated a strong focus on NPS (Net Promoter® Score).[1] NPS measures your customers' willingness to recommend your products and services.

In order to reflect the training objectives, the Level 1 survey must ask learners to weight their *willingness to recommend* the training and the instructor, rather than how much they liked them. Accordingly, we recently changed the statements to "I would recommend this course to coworkers" and "I would recommend this instructor to a coworker." This simple change from "like" to "would recommend" shifted the scores downward. The most significant outcome from making this change was that it provided a different (lower) result than what we'd seen in the past. We believe that using "would recommend" unmasked deficiencies in our content and delivery. This allowed us to do more investigation and make the appropriate changes. Our overall measurement philosophy is centered on NPS.

ON THE HORIZON AND BEYOND

What I find fascinating about the Digital Age is the vast amount of information that can be used to improve our daily lives and make us more productive. Take playing a video game, for example. The objective generally is to win. I remember in the late 1970s and early 1980s there was an arcade game called Asteroids. The tools used to play the game were pretty simple: one button to rotate the spaceship, one button to move it, one button to fire missiles at the asteroids, and one last button to escape when you had no other alternative but to be crushed by the asteroids. I spent a small fortune trying to master that game (which, by the way, I never did). Fast-forward to the present; video games today are more complex. I could not even begin to explain to you what each button does on an Xbox controller, but my players (i.e., students) manipulate those buttons as if they were extensions of their hands.

We can say that the tools to play the game have remained generally consistent (buttons, joysticks, etc.), but the ability to learn and measure the player's skill has allowed game creators to increase the level of complexity; participants are now motivated to play and therefore buy new games because they can measure and improve their performance. Internet sites, message boards, and YouTube videos all provide pathways that will improve the players' skill.

In addition, with today's games you can play online and test your skills against strangers. This provides an opportunity to measure your progress. That asteroid game had two players. If your score was good enough you entered your initials on the top 10 board. These measurements surely fueled the competition among all of us who played.

This simple example reinforces the value of measuring progress when we learn. Learning professionals are not alone in their need to utilize predictive measurement. We are all conditioned to expect such feedback. Perhaps more uncertainty leads to a greater need for certainty. From report cards in elementary school to performance appraisals, we live in a world that (whether formally or informally, whether within ourselves or provided by others) measures what we learn.

From what I have observed, learning professionals are simply looking for a reliable way to measure behavior change and how that change impacts business. Implementation of a measurement strategy has to be balanced with the understanding that it needs to evolve as the business evolves.

Supporting our goal to provide continuing value to the business, this book will enable you to gain insight from case studies, providing real-world examples of how to apply and optimize your analytics.

I have observed people calling analytics revolutionary, extraordinary, evolutionary, or all of these. I would rather categorize it as expeditionary: used in an ongoing journey to provide better outcomes for learning professionals, business partners, and ultimately our students who count on us to provide training to improve their skills. This book will serve as a great companion on your expedition.

NOTE

1. Net Promoter® is a registered trademark of Bain & Company, Inc., Fred Reichheld, and Satmetrix Systems, Inc.

CHAPTER **1**

The New Workforce

The Millennials are coming!

—CBS News, February 11, 2009

Learning and development (L&D) generally represents an organization's single largest investment in its people. The American Society for Training & Development (ASTD) estimates that U.S. organizations spent over $150 billion on training in 2011.[1] Our intent with this book is to show you how you can use analytics to better manage the learning and development needs of a thriving organization in a rapidly changing environment. It is no coincidence that the field of human capital analytics is growing in popularity at a time when organizations are managing up to five generational cohorts in the workplace. These generational groups represent different backgrounds, ideals, challenges, and opportunities, many of which can be better understood through the various analytical tactics presented in this book. It's going to take the evidence and insights from analytics for organizations to effectively manage their workforces—and their human capital—for competitive advantage.

DEFINING THE GENERATIONS

Despite what the buzz around the Baby Boomers and the Millennials may have you believe, there are five generations in the current workforce:

1. Traditionalists (born prior to 1946)
2. Baby Boomers (born between 1946 and 1964)
3. Generation X (born between 1965 and 1976)
4. Millennials (born between 1977 and 1997)
5. Generation 2020 (born after 1997)[2]

For the purposes of our discussion, in this chapter we focus on the three generations with the largest employee presences at the majority of organizations: Boomers, Xers, and Millennials, as well as some of the attendant changes and significant issues facing the workforce. For a more detailed discussion of the future workplace, we highly recommend Jeanne Meister and Karie Willyerd's book, *The 2020 Workplace*.[3]

Figure 1.1 shows how these workforce populations have shifted (and are projected to shift) over time.

While each generation is made up of individuals with unique belief systems and life experiences, we can assume a number of generalizations about each generation based on their collective experiences. As the generation of drugs, sex, and rock 'n' roll, the Baby Boomers came of age during the era of the Vietnam War and Watergate. In their youth, they took to the streets for human rights and the women's movement. They are said to be optimistic, competitive, and questioners of authority. At work, they're motivated by money, they work long hours at the expense of their personal lives, and they pursue upward career mobility.

Generation X is the skeptical generation. They saw the divorce rate triple as they grew up, with parents working long hours at the expense of family life. Experiencing life in a single-parent household became commonplace. Gen Xers were often latchkey children, left to their own devices after school. As adults, they tend to distrust institutions and be highly adaptive to change. In the office, Xers are known

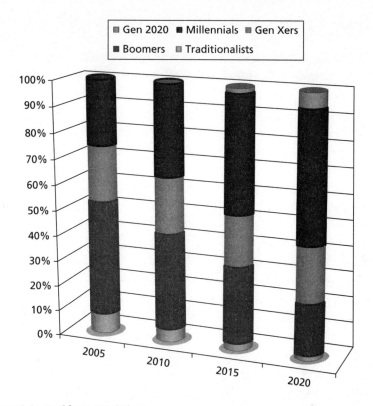

Figure 1.1 Workforce Populations

for following their hearts. They're motivated by freedom and prefer to be judged on their output instead of the number of hours spent at their desks. Their families are just as important as their careers, and they're unconcerned about lateral moves and career plateaus.

Millennials were the first generation raised from day one with technology, experiencing the expansion of its capabilities and reach into everyday life as they grew up. They've been influenced by a diversifying population, violence ranging from gang activity to terrorist attacks, and large-scale natural disasters. Millennials are known for their technological savvy, their concern for global affairs, and their short attention spans. In the workplace, they crave feedback, fulfillment, and flexibility. They've echoed Generation X's equal-parts emphasis on career and family.[4]

PROJECTED GAPS AS THE GENERATIONS SHIFT

As with any changing of the guard, there are institutional concerns accompanying the generational shift. One is the loss of institutional knowledge. While many Boomers have built their careers within one organization or industry, the younger generations tend to jump from company to company as opportunities arise. Many learning leaders are grappling with the challenges of retaining the institutional knowledge that departs with the retiring Boomers, not to mention the transient workforces that are the hallmark of so many organizations today (more on this later).

Certain industries are also suffering from a shortage of skilled workers in particular job roles. These jobs tend to be on the ends of the educational spectrum: highly specialized sectors and labor-intensive positions. High schools have shifted their emphasis from vocational skills to preparation for four-year colleges, which is one factor in the shortfall of laborers. For example, the aging population of skilled-trade workers (e.g., welders or machine operators) is not being replaced by younger workers. In 2012, 53 percent of skilled-trade workers were over the age of 44; by contrast, in the overall workforce only 44 percent of workers were over age 44.[5] On the other end, the health care, manufacturing, and technology industries are struggling to fill open job positions. The Bureau of Labor Statistics counts 3.5 million job openings at a paradoxical time of high unemployment, reflecting the difficulty of filling certain types of positions.[6]

CHASING DOWN RETIREMENT

Retirement was once a shining beacon at the end of one's career path; today, it's a shifting, elusive state that some mature workers may never attain. For many Boomers, retirement is simply not economically feasible. Others aren't interested in facing another 20-plus years of life without gainful employment. A Deloitte study found that 48 percent of Baby Boomers plan to keep working past age 65.[7] As life expectancies increase, wealth declines, and government policy shifts, the definition of retirement for the Boomers has changed.

When the Boomers leave the workplace primarily through retirement, they leave with significant institutional knowledge, most of which is in their heads from years of on-the-job experience. So the question is: How do you capture this knowledge?

On one hand, the gap in numbers of skilled workers is helped by delayed retirements. Many workers are entering a state of semiretirement, in which they work part-time or as independent consultants.[8] These types of arrangements buy time for organizations to shift institutional knowledge to the younger generations, particularly when the older workers are encouraged to serve as mentors to their younger colleagues. On the other hand, delayed retirements can create frustrating roadblocks to career advancement for younger workers, particularly those in Generation X.

To assist in this knowledge transfer, organizations are investing in knowledge management systems, centralized repositories of knowledge and history that can be accessed. Millennials are comfortable and well versed in using platforms such as Google and Wikipedia to search for information; however, implementing an internal knowledge management system is an expensive and complicated undertaking.

CHANGING THE WAY WE WORK

There's no question that the generational shift from Boomers to Millennials is changing the way we work. While many of these changes are driven by the inherent differences between the generations, there are a number of other factors impacting—and impacted by—the generational shift. One of the biggest changes to impact corporate America in the twenty-first century is the flexible workplace, often referred to as mobile working. While the flexible workplace began as an initiative to retain and accommodate working mothers, it has become a lynchpin in the race to attract and retain top talent. Almost every organization has its own rules for flexible work arrangements; generally these include variable working hours and the ability to perform work outside of the office.

Millennials may voice the loudest demands for flexible work arrangements, but the Boomers have embraced flexibility as they've taken on the care of aging parents. One in five employees cares for elderly parents, and that statistic is projected to increase to one in two in the coming years.[9] Many other factors are driving the trend toward the flexible workplace: technology, economic forces, and globalization, to name a few. These are hallmarks of the early twenty-first-century workforce. As the generations transition, we see a workforce that is increasingly connected, diverse, and fluid. In this chapter, we consider the flexible workplace as both instigator and consequence; flexible workplaces are driving change every bit as much as they are driven by it.

TECHNOLOGY

Many workplace theorists point to technology as the biggest difference between the Boomers and the Millennials. The Baby Boomers "encountered new technologies in the smoke-filled workplaces of the 1980s. [They] came in the forms of the IBM Selectric III, word processors, and dot matrix printers," notes i4cp's Lorrie Lykins.[10] But, she points out, "Technology didn't dominate [Boomers'] lives."

Advances in technology (particularly mobile technology) have spurred a cultural revolution in which we are always connected. Fax machines and cell phones began breaking down the barriers between home and office in the 1990s, and today's smartphones keep employees connected 24/7. Employees see many benefits as a result. Work isn't tied to a physical office space; workers take a conference call while picking up the kids, or keep up with e-mails in the doctor's waiting room. Of course, there are trade-offs. Lykins says, "Life before cell phones meant going home at the end of the day fully disconnected from work. There were no emails to check, no intrusive mobile devices buzzing during little league games."[11]

The Millennial generation has never experienced a workplace that shuts down at the end of the day. In this case, developing technologies have shaped the way Millennials work and have fueled the demand for flexible workplaces. After all, the Millennials reason, if they are expected to answer e-mails from home in the evenings or take the boss's calls on vacation, what is the rationale behind the "butts in seats" mentality of measuring corporate productivity?

Furthermore, technology has enabled virtual collaboration across the globe. Using videoconferencing, online collaboration tools (e.g., Google Docs, Sharepoint, Skype, etc.), and corporate social platforms, teams can transcend distance and tap nearly limitless subject matter expertise. These types of technologies have spurred the rise of virtual teams, and it's no longer a given that an employee will have a manager in the same office, or even in the same country. Millennials have led the charge to build virtual communication skills, and Boomers have seen their tried-and-true leadership styles fall by the wayside as they navigate the challenges of, and adapt to, virtual management.

From a learning perspective, technology has changed learners' expectations when they approach a training event. While instructor-led training is still the preferred modality for many learning topics, shrinking budgets have pushed learning leaders to seek more cost-effective solutions. Asynchronous and synchronous distance learning and e-learning have rocketed in popularity, but even those are evolving in response to mobile and video game technology. Mobile learning allows employees to access training at the point of need, and it also offers opportunities to digitize training for employee populations that don't typically have computer access (such as retail or food service employees). So-called gamification seeks to engage a generation that has "essentially grown up digital." Gamification also drives performance and offers opportunities to highlight achievement.[12]

Technology and social media in the workplace have also given rise to informal learning. Learning leaders use the term *informal learning* to refer to a variety of different types of activities, and it has become a catchall for everything from watercooler conversations to company wiki pages and social learning platforms. Its hallmarks include user-created content and learning that occurs at the point of need.

ECONOMY

The 2008 recession hit and hurt all of the generations, but they have been impacted in different ways. The Baby Boomers have seen an unprecedented loss of wealth, which has caused many to push back (or forgo) their retirements. As noted earlier in this chapter, the Boomers continue to linger in the workplace and occupy leadership positions that many Generation Xers thought they would assume.

The older Millennials were just establishing their careers or finishing college in 2008. Those who were newer to the workforce were, in many cases, the first to be laid off as companies began trimming their payrolls. Those graduating from college saw once-promising futures become uncertain as they struggled to find job opportunities. College graduates snatched up jobs for which they were overqualified, leaving the high school graduates with fewer openings. College grads struggled to keep up with hefty student loan payments, and record numbers defaulted on student debt.

Changes to the shape of the professional career began well before the 2008 recession, but that event brings the new resume into sharp relief. Many Boomers began their careers with a clear path to follow, often climbing the corporate ladder within one or two companies and feeling secure in the knowledge of promised pensions that would allow them to enjoy their retirements. By contrast, Millennials' career paths tend to zigzag all over the map. The U.S. Department of Labor predicts that the average Millennial will have had 10 to 14 jobs by the time he or she reaches age 38. Millennials, by and large, do not feel a sense of employer loyalty and in turn tend to be disengaged at work. Millennials make many lateral moves, jumping from company to company, and build their skill sets through contract positions and freelance work.

GLOBALIZATION

Technology enables a global workforce, and the global market economy demands it. For an increasing number of organizations, the ability to compete on a global scale is vital to success. As communication across continents has become commonplace, time zones, language barriers, and cultural mores are now the biggest barriers to global collaboration. Furthermore, offshore development models have fueled developing economies and enabled new players in the global competition.

Deloitte calls this new model "the open talent economy." Most companies are mixtures of "full-time employees, contractors, and freelancers, and—increasingly—people with no formal ties to [the] enterprise at all. People move more freely than ever from role to role and across organizational and geographic boundaries." These conditions developed in response to the global marketplace, which "demand[s] new talent models that can be rapidly configured and reconfigured."[13]

DEMOGRAPHICS

The Millennial generation's demographic makeup reflects the shifting demographics of the United States as a whole. Forty percent of Millennials are nonwhite, and 20 percent have at least one immigrant parent.[14] The U.S. Census Bureau projects that white children will become the minority in the public school systems by 2020.[15] As the United States continues to diversify, the needs of the upcoming generation of workers (including the younger cohort of Millennials and on to the next generation) will shift.

Brookings Institution demographer William Frey points out that "a lot of immigrants that have come in over the last 20 years, especially from parts of Latin America, haven't had the same levels of education as middle-class Americans do, or did. That puts even more pressure on making sure that their children are getting the right kind of movement into the middle class."[16] Frey's point highlights one cause of the talent gap being created by retiring Boomers. There's a crucial need for training to prepare future leaders, as well as to ensure adequate numbers of workers to fill various professions.

ARE VIRTUAL WORKPLACES HERE TO STAY?

Virtual workplaces are by no means a done deal in corporate America. Yahoo! CEO Marissa Mayer was simultaneously maligned and applauded when she announced that Yahoo! employees could no longer telecommute. In fact, Mayer's pronouncement sparked a fierce debate about whether flexible workplaces are beneficial or detrimental to a company's overall success. Google, Mayer's previous employer and a workplace revolutionary in its own right, views working from home as a detriment to productivity.[17] Best Buy, one of the pioneers of flexible working hours, also reined in its policy in response to its struggles in the marketplace.[18]

WHAT CAN LEARNING LEADERS DO?

Generations have always been in the process of entering and exiting the workforce. The difference today is in the method of value creation of organizations. The majority of value in companies has shifted from traditional revenue-generating balance-sheet assets (e.g., facilities, equipment, raw materials, etc.) to intangible assets—including people and intellectual capital. To compete and succeed in today's market-place, it is absolutely critical for companies to inspire, develop, and engage their employees. Investing in people isn't a new concept. But knowing where those investments are working—and where they aren't—is the new competitive advantage.

The age of big data has created opportunities for learning leaders to drive change in their organizations. In this book, we'll equip you with a variety of analytical methods—from the basic to the advanced—to improve your ability to make effective investments in people. This book will make the case for a strategy around designing and evaluating your investments in people to strategically align learning to the business. We will look at the tried-and-true methods of evaluation, then take you to the next frontier—predictive analytics.

SUMMARY

It's no coincidence that interest in the field of human capital analytics is growing at a time when organizations are managing five generational cohorts in the workplace. The Baby Boomers, Generation X, and the Millennials represent different backgrounds, ideals, challenges, and opportunities. Analytics can help learning leaders make informed decisions about how to tackle the looming human capital challenges. One of these challenges is retaining institutional knowledge as the generations shift and employee populations become more transient. Another is the projected worker shortfall in a number of industries.

As the generations transition, the acquisition and development of talent becomes a fundamental driver of business success. To compete and succeed in today's marketplace, it's absolutely critical for companies to build their human capital intelligently and effectively. Investing in people isn't a new concept. But knowing where those investments are working—and where they aren't—is the new competitive advantage.

NOTES

1. *Training* magazine's annual Industry Report and ASTD annual survey.

2. Jeanne C. Meister and Karie Willyerd, *The 2020 Workplace: How Innovative Companies Attract, Develop, and Keep Tomorrow's Employees Today* (New York: HarperCollins, 2010), 19.

3. Ibid.

4. Cathy A. Trower, "Traditionalists, Boomers, Xers, and Millennials: Giving and Getting the Mentoring You Want," Brown University, October 16, 2009, 11–13, www.brown.edu/Administration/Provost/Advance/Trower%20Generations%20and%20Mentoring.pdf.

5. Joshua Wright, "America's Skilled Trades Dilemma: Shortages Loom as Most-in-Demand Group of Workers Ages," *Forbes* March 7, 2013, www.forbes.com/sites/emsi/2013/03/07/americas-skilled-trades-dilemma-shortages-loom-as-most-in-demand-group-of-workers-ages/.

6. Darrell West, "The Paradox of Worker Shortages at a Time of High National Unemployment," *Brookings*, April 10, 2013, www.brookings.edu/research/papers/2013/04/11-worker-shortage-immigration-west.

7. "Human Capital Trends 2013: Leading Indicators," Deloitte, 17.

8. Ibid., 17.

9. Ibid., 14.

10. Lorrie Lykins, "OMG: The Time to Invest in Millennials Is Now," *i4cp Trend Watcher*. May 8, 2013, www.i4cp.com/trendwatchers/2013/05/07/omg-the-time-to-invest-in-millennials-is-now.

11. Ibid.

12. Whitney Cook, "Five Reasons You Can't Ignore Gamification," *Chief Learning Officer*, May 8, 2013, http://clomedia.com/articles/view/five-reasons-you-can-t-ignore-gamification/1.

13. "Human Capital Trends 2013: Leading Indicators," Deloitte, 8.

14. Holden Thorp and Buck Goldstein, *Engines of Innovation: The Entrepreneurial University in the Twenty-First Century* (Chapel Hill: University of North Carolina Press, 2010).

15. Jennifer Kahn, "The Face of the Future Workforce," *Talent Management*, May 2013, 48–49.

16. Ibid.

17. Julianne Pepitone, "Marissa Mayer: Yahoos Can No Longer Work from Home," *CNN Money*, February 25, 2013, http://money.cnn.com/2013/02/25/technology/yahoo-work-from-home/index.html.

18. Julianne Pepitone, "Best Buy Ends Work-from-Home Program," *CNN Money*, March 5, 2013, http://money.cnn.com/2013/03/05/technology/best-buy-work-from-home/index.html.

19. "Human Capital Trends 2013: Leading Indicators," Deloitte, 8.

CHAPTER **2**

The Need for
a Strategy

If you don't know where you are headed,
you'll probably end up someplace else.

—Douglas J. Eder, PhD

N ow that you understand the major forces affecting your changing workforce, you should see how crucial it is to have a strategy
for investing in, understanding, and inspiring your most valuable
asset—your people. Organizations are stepping up to the challenge
with more deliberate and intentional strategies for talent development.
The best of these learning strategies include a measurement strategy as
well. Such learning leaders recognize the importance of the guidance
and feedback that measurement can provide. Useful measurement
grows out of alignment with business goals, which are critical from the
outset of planning curricula and designing courseware. Each phase of
measurement serves a unique purpose, following the progression of
the learning initiative from design to launch and all the way through
to its impact on the business.

Initial measures of utilization or throughput help to determine
completion rates and compliance. Measure progress through student
determine reactions and learning transfer to determine if learners
are applying their training once they get back on the job. Ultimately,

measurement leads to isolating training's impact, both to prove and to improve the value of the initiative.

By implementing a measurement strategy, learning organizations are able to integrate the intelligence gained through measurement into their planning. This provides the framework that enables learning and development departments to:

- Drive alignment with business goals right from the start.
- Establish business measures of success.
- Guide the development of content that is aligned with business needs.
- Provide in-process measures for continuous improvement.
- Prove and improve the impact and value of learning.

A well-designed measurement strategy will make the explicit connection between learning and the business goals.

Numerous studies from the American Society for Training & Development (ASTD) and Bersin by Deloitte have shown that most organizations are doing very little in the way of using any advanced techniques to measure their human capital investments. Despite low usage, there are numerous benefits available to those who systematically measure their learning. Here are a few examples of the insights leading organizations have gleaned by using sophisticated analytical techniques:

- Google suspected that many of its low-performing employees were either misplaced or poorly managed. Employee performance data bore that out and was used to determine the most appropriate intervention to help both high- and low-performing employees succeed.[1]
- Harrah's used metrics to evaluate the effects of its health and wellness programs on employee engagement and the bottom line.[2]
- Supervisors at ConAgra who were enrolled in a leadership development program had a significantly higher rate of retention than associates not enrolled in the program, resulting in a multimillion-dollar savings in turnover costs.[3]

- Starbucks can precisely calculate the value of a 0.1 percent increase in engagement among employees at a particular store.[4]

- JetBlue analysts developed a metric, the "crew member net promoter score," that monitors employee engagement and predicts financial performance.[5]

- Chrysler understood that training was directly responsible for a fully trained salesperson selling on average 16 more vehicles per year than an untrained salesperson.[6]

Google's Vice President of People Operations, Laszlo Bork, says, "It's not the company-provided lunch that keeps people here. Googlers tell us that there are three reasons why they stay: the mission, the quality of the people, and the chance to build the skill set of a better leader or entrepreneur. And all our analytics are built around these reasons."[7]

These are only a few examples, but as you can see, some of the world's leading companies are using advanced analytics to better understand their workforce, their investments, and ways to improve employee retention, engagement, and productivity. All of these ultimately tie back to improving the bottom line. Can you imagine the results if you applied that level of analysis to your learning and development investments? That is what this book will teach you.

MEASUREMENT AS AN INTENTIONAL PROCESS

What gets measured gets managed.

—Peter Drucker

We know that companies spend millions of dollars annually on employee training and development, usually with no concrete evidence that those dollars are generating bottom-line results. Fortunately, more and more human resources (HR) and learning and development (L&D) functions are aligning with their company's overall business metrics. However, being able to *demonstrate and quantify* the linkage between training and results is not a simple task, and it's where many learning leaders fall short.

Simply showing that trained employees outperform their untrained colleagues is generally met with skepticism outside the HR and training departments—"the trained people were better performers to start with," "people who sign up for training are more motivated," and so on. To counter these doubts, the learning industry needs to isolate the impact of its interventions.

Accurately isolating and quantifying the impact of learning interventions requires a good study design and statistical analysis to determine just how much of a performance gain can be attributed to the learning. By understanding where and how an initiative is making an impact, organizations will be able to show the value of the investment and, perhaps even more important, continuously improve the impact of their offerings. Showing how investments in human capital pay off with business results can guide strategic planning when it comes to employee development and a high-quality workforce.

Dean Spitzer, an expert on performance measurement and management, in 2005 wrote: "For a long time, training and development was accepted as something that was inherently good, and measures of success were the number of programs, number of participants, number of course days, training costs, end-of-course satisfaction survey ratings, and sometimes learning test scores. This situation is slowly changing. Today there is a new call for accountability in the business of learning. Organizational stakeholders are increasingly asking for proof instead of assumption of bottom-line effectiveness."[8]

Several years later, McKinsey stated basically the same thing. All organizations train their people, and most spend significant sums doing so. Yet they generally don't have any idea whether they're getting any business value from the training. Beyond teaching new employees the specifics of their jobs, many companies train staff in areas such as leadership, communications, performance management, or lean organizations. But they typically measure training's impact by conducting surveys of attendees or counting how many employees complete courses, rather than by assessing whether those employees learned and applied anything that improved business performance.[9]

This book is not for those who merely want to justify their learning and development investments, but for those who want to improve them.

Consider these scenarios:

- Suppose your Customer First program was increasing overall same-store revenue, but it was not working in the Northeast. Would you adjust anything?

- Would you change anything if your leadership development initiative was successfully building the management pipeline, but you discovered it was working only for men?

- What if your new onboarding program showed an increase in initial performance, but the benefit disappeared after the first six months? Would the program still be worthwhile?

- Suppose your new call center training program successfully increased sales, but also increased call handling time. What would you need to know in order to see if the training was responsible and whether the overall return was worthwhile?

If you could answer these questions, of course you would make changes to your programs. This is the power of optimization. When you apply analytics, you no longer need to deploy programs using anecdotes and gut instincts. You have evidence.

CONTINUUM OF ANALYTICS

In our first book, *Human Capital Analytics: How to Harness the Potential of Your Organization's Greatest Asset*, we introduced the human capital analytics continuum—a look at how organizations collect and report data. Figure 2.1 shows our paradigm of human capital analysis. The continuum is based on what we have seen in our work, starting with simple, commonly used techniques. Viewing the continuum as a mountain, we suggest that, like mountain climbing, things become both more difficult and more rewarding as you move to higher ground.

Anecdotes

The ascent begins with anecdotes or storytelling. Every organization has its own version of anecdotal evidence of the effectiveness of training. While anecdotes can help to tell the story of a training program's impact, they fall short in delivering actionable intelligence.

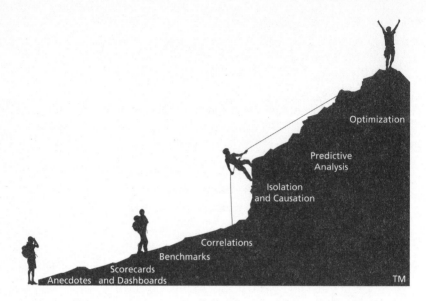

Figure 2.1 Continuum of Human Capital Analytics

Scorecards and Dashboards

Scorecards and dashboards are other important areas. Scorecards are performance management tools that can leverage automated surveys to track how an organization executes strategy and the consequences arising from business processes, most commonly referred to as activity metrics. They are an important step on the continuum, because this step is where you must lay out the basic assumptions: What are your strategies, and what are the various ways you will measure them?

Dashboards share those characteristics. A dashboard is a distillation of the most important key performance indicators of a company that an executive can view at a glance. Dashboards might be an ad hoc effort put together on spreadsheets or even lower-tech tools, or they may involve special-purpose programming. Basic descriptive statistics can be derived from dashboards and are rich sources of data and new views of your organization.

Benchmarks

Benchmarks are the next step on the continuum. Benchmarking has long been used as a standard tool; the idea is that studying the best-run companies in a specific area can be very beneficial in terms of setting things like salary, training levels, desired turnover rates, and so forth. Our first book detailed why we are not great fans of benchmarking. In a nutshell, there's just something intrinsically contradictory to us about aspiring to greatness by doing the same thing as everyone else.

Correlations and Causation

Correlations and causation are the next two stages in the continuum. We use these phrases in a way that we find comfortable, but may not entirely agree with standard usage. Correlations are the descriptive statistics that might occur on a sophisticated dashboard. They show relationships between different data elements, such as sales and region. Where are sales highest? Did the trained employees outperform the untrained ones? Correlations are rich data mines for understanding business resources and human capital.

Causation is the next level beyond correlation. "Correlation does not imply causation" is commonly said but rarely applied. We like Cascio and Boudreau's three-part criteria for causation:

1. One event must precede the other.
2. Two events must show a clear and statistically significant connection.
3. All other plausible causes must be ruled out.[10]

Predictive Analytics and Optimization

The final stages on the continuum are predictive analytics and optimization, the holy grail of learning measurement. Predictive analytics answers the question: If we make changes, what will happen? Optimization allows you to determine what actions can be taken to generate the best future impact. Optimization is having the intelligence to understand where the impact is occurring; it is intimately wrapped up with causation. Without understanding all the factors that are driving impact, it is impossible to be sure that you have correctly assessed that impact. The positive side of having assessed and measured the different factors that control and mediate impact is that you can use them to control future impact and improve outcomes.

If you have controlled and assessed the impact of the various other influencers, you are able to use them prescriptively. For example, if you know how much tenure controls performance and how the various tenure levels benefit from training, the logical consequence is that you can now specify where training should be focused and what new programs need to be created for populations that do not show the benefits.

CONTINUUM OF LEARNING AND DEVELOPMENT ANALYTICS

There is another, better-known continuum of learning and development analytics: the Kirkpatrick scale.[11] It, like ours, makes the assumption that measurement complexity and usefulness increase as you go along. Kirkpatrick's four levels have been augmented over the years, and we identify six levels here:

- *Level 0: Usage.* Usage is how many people take advantage of a training program. This was not in the original Kirkpatrick scale (as you might guess by the numbering), and it recently became popular in the learning management system (LMS) community.

- *Level 1: Satisfaction.* Satisfaction is the learners' perception of the course's quality. It is usually measured via a survey after training.

- *Level 2: Learning Gain.* Learning is how much of the course content was absorbed by the trainee. It is measured by some sort of posttraining test. Though infrequent in practice, a pretest should also be given so that learning gain can be calculated.

- *Level 3: Transfer (Behavior Change).* Do trainees actually do their jobs differently (i.e., transfer the new learned behaviors to the workplace)? Transfer is preferably measured by direct observation, or by surveys of students and their supervisors.

- *Level 4: Business impact.* What is the change in key performance indicators caused by the training program? This book is largely about Level 4, so we will not discuss it much here.

- *Level 5: Return on investment (ROI).* This important addition was added by Jack Phillips.[12] Phillips has long been the spokesman for ROI, and his contribution to learning measurement has been significant. The extra math and effort required to calculate ROI are not profound, but the change in focus is. Level 5 circles us back to the idea of *business* impact.

Figure 2.2 applies our view of the analytics continuum to Kirkpatrick/Phillips's commonly used learning measurement system.

In the figure, you may notice an additional level to the Kirkpatrick/ Phillips scale: Level 6, Optimization. Chapter 9 is devoted entirely to this subject, so we'll be brief here. In a nutshell, when you isolate the business impact from all of the other variables, you can understand where your investments are working and predictively make improvements as you deploy them (i.e., optimize).

So where is your organization on this analytics continuum?

This book will show you how to leverage each of the levels to better understand how your investments in people are working, and to encourage you to make the climb.

In the next chapter we will introduce the Measurement Framework for Learning and how having such a model for thinking

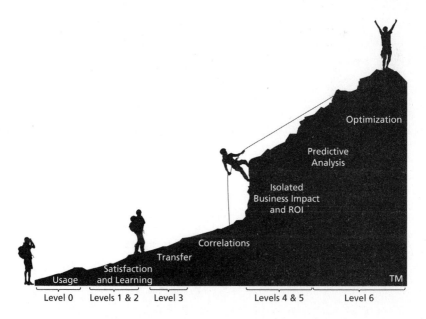

Figure 2.2 Continuum of Human Capital Analytics with the Kirkpatrick/Phillips Scale

about measurement can help make evaluation and analysis part of your learning culture. And it all starts with alignment to the business.

SUMMARY

The best learning strategies include a measurement strategy as well. Such learning leaders recognize the importance of the guidance and feedback measurement can provide. Useful measurement grows out of alignment with business goals, which is critical from the outset of planning curriculum and designing courseware. Each phase of measurement serves a unique purpose, following the progression of the learning initiative from design to launch and all the way through to its impact on the business.

We presented the continuum of analytics, based on what we see in practice, and showed how it applies to the Kirkpatrick/Phillips scale. We introduced Level 6 to that scale: Optimization. All forms of measurement can be useful: Data ranges from anecdotes to hard operational data interpreted with statistics. Anecdotes add stories and context to your reports. More rigorous analysis provides deeper and more actionable insights; showing impact and optimization opportunities enables you to make evidence-based decisions about the development of your organization's human capital. This is the kind of analysis that it takes to make your organization competitive in today's environment.

NOTES

1. Thomas Davenport, Jeanne Harris, and Jeremy Shapiro, "Competing on Talent Analytics," *Harvard Business Review*, October 2010.
2. Ibid.
3. Pease, Byerly, and Fitz-enz, *Human Capital Analytics*.
4. Davenport, Harris, and Shapiro, "Competing on Talent Analytics."
5. Ibid.
6. Gene Pease, Boyce Byerly, and Jac Fitz-enz, *Human Capital Analytics: How to Harness the Potential of Your Organization's Greatest* (Hoboken, NJ: John Wiley & Sons, 2012).
7. Ibid.
8. Dean R. Spitzer, "Learning Effectiveness Measurement: A New Approach for Measuring and Managing Learning to Achieve Business Results," *Advances in Developing Human Resources* 7, no. 1 (February 2005): 55.

9. Jenny Cermak and Monica McGurk, "Putting a Value on Training," *McKinsey Quarterly*, July 2010.

10. W.F. Cascio and J.W. Boudreau, *Investing in People: Financial Impact of Human Resource Initiatives* (Upper Saddle River, NJ: Pearson, 2008.)

11. D. L. Kirkpatrick, "Evaluating Training Programs: Evidence vs. Proof," *Training & Development Journal* (1977).

12. J. J. Phillips, *Return on Investment in Training and Performance Improvement Programs* (Houston, TX: Gulf Publishing Company, 1997).

A Measurement Strategy in Action: Pfizer

BACKGROUND

Pfizer is the world's largest research-based pharmaceutical company. Its global portfolio includes medicines and vaccines, as well as many of the world's best-known consumer health care products. Every day, Pfizer's employees work across developed and emerging markets to advance wellness, prevention, treatments, and cures that challenge the most feared diseases of our time.

Pfizer recognizes the crucial role its employees play in keeping the company at the forefront of the industry and in compliance with Food and Drug Administration (FDA) safety standards. Each division of the company has its own small learning organization to support the diverse body of technical skills required of Pfizer employees. At Pfizer's main campus in Groton, Connecticut, the divisional learning organizations collaborated to form the Groton Community of Practice (CoP). Valerie Gamble, Education and Performance-Enhancement Lead for Pfizer's Drug Safety Research and Development Group (DSRD), is coleader of the CoP.

Gamble's team is charged with preparing and enabling laboratory technicians, researchers, and scientists to safely and efficiently conduct research and analysis that lead to good decisions during

24

drug development. The variety of training programs reflects Pfizer's diverse portfolio; training ranges from teaching laboratory technicians how to dose animals to equipping drug safety team leaders with project management skills. One of Gamble's goals was to set the bar for high-quality learning. In order to do so, Gamble recognized the need to measure training in a way that matched the caliber of data collection and analysis occurring in other parts of the company.

THE NEED FOR A STRATEGY

In a challenging economy, learning leaders across a variety of industries have to do more with less. Those who show alignment with the business are often a step ahead of their unaligned peers. Gamble knew that Pfizer's training budgets were often tight and under scrutiny. DSRD's job-specific training was generally thought to be on target, yet she was unsure how to demonstrate its alignment and quantify its impact on broader organizational outcomes.

"As I started to think about how I could show that I add value to the organization, I decided that some sort of measurement would be helpful to show the organization that my role is important and training is important," Gamble said. To date, her team had the occasional Level 1 survey as evidence of training's value. She determined she needed an explicit plan—a measurement strategy—to be able to proactively show how training contributed to the business. "The hope was that we could start to measure learner understanding, which had never been done before," Gamble said. "We had no idea how well the learners were doing once they left us."

Gamble's team developed the following goals for its measurement strategy:

- Drive alignment right from the start.
- Establish business measures of success.
- Guide the development of aligned content.
- Provide in-process measures for continuous improvement.
- Prove and improve the impact and value of learning.

CREATING A STRATEGY

The team began by adopting a measurement framework that starts with alignment and incorporates Kirkpatrick's four levels of evaluation (similar to the one detailed in Chapter 3). Guided by Capital Analytics (now Vestrics), the team reviewed each phase and took inventory of the skills and technology they had available. "It was a great process to go through," Gamble said, "and helped me to look at what questions still needed to be answered." This process helped the team create near-term goals to improve current measurement efforts. It also framed longer-term actions and uncovered technology investments that would be required to fully implement Gamble's vision for actionable measurement.

TAKING ACTION

The measurement strategy identified four areas for initial focus:

1. Ensure that each initiative is aligned with the organization's goals.
2. Build a culture of measurement and create a measurement plan for every initiative.
3. Improve postcourse evaluations (Level 1).
4. Improve course assessments (Level 2).

Alignment

Being able to show that training is aligned to the business was one of Gamble's key goals. Capital Analytics taught a measurement mapping process to the team. A Measurement Map (fully explored in Chapter 6) is a visual depiction of the causal links between a learning initiative and business goals. Not only does the mapping create a picture of success, but it also defines how to measure success. "Showing the start-to-finish process of how training can help drug safety meet its goals has been helpful," Gamble said. "We work with scientists, so it's structured and data-driven, which they like. I think that's why we've been able to get the message across."

A Culture of Measurement

Gamble wanted the CoP members to think about alignment and measurement as an intentional part of any learning development activity. To ensure measurement was top of mind for her team, Gamble added it to the launch agenda of new training initiatives. Doing so ensured that the team discussed alignment right from the start and made a conscious decision about how far to take measurement on each initiative. "When I go to meet with my customers and I start talking about the measurement process as part of the design process, originally people were taken aback because they thought it would add more time and they couldn't see the value it would add to the end result," Gamble said. "Now that I've done it a couple of times with repeat customers, they see the value in it and it's been an easier sell."

Part of the strategy included measurement plan templates for each phase. The templates specify the purpose of the measurement, as well as data collection and reporting methods. Gamble knew that even if the answer was "We only need to track completions," at least her team would have discussed measurement and made a collective decision about it.

Improve Postcourse Evaluations

Gamble's team recognized that its current Level 1 process was inconsistent both in its format and in its administration, which made it difficult to aggregate results and compare courses and trends over time. The new strategy called for standardizing the approach to postcourse evaluations. To get members of the CoP on the same page, Gamble hosted a workshop called "Improving Level 1 Evaluations." Together, the group developed their standards, including everything from common questions to what scale to use. The new Level 1 evaluations provided specific, actionable data. The shorter, more targeted evaluations also encouraged more end users to actually complete them.

The evaluations have two parts: a section on content and a section on the trainer. The team hadn't previously asked learners to evaluate their trainers, and the new evaluations helped refine the pool of trainers. On the content side, the learners evaluate whether the content was targeted, whether it had clear objectives, and how they could use the information in their jobs. "I think the end users can actually see now why we would ask the questions," Gamble said. "Honestly, we didn't take into account whether the end user really got something out of it. We're starting to see that information and use the information to make changes in the program going forward."

Improve Course Assessments

Due to the nature of the business, many of Pfizer's courses are designed to ensure that employees are compliant with Pfizer's standard operating procedures (SOPs) and with FDA requirements. While completion records used to suffice, the FDA is beginning to ask, "How do you know that the student really knows the rules and can do the tasks?" These questions require a more sophisticated level of measurement to ensure compliance.

To address this, Gamble expanded the measurement strategy to include a detailed assessment strategy. SOPs are often written by researchers and scientists, making it challenging for technicians to extract the required actions. The assessment strategy called for adding performance-based learning objectives to the SOPs. "Before, we were guilty of using words like *understand* instead of focusing on some actionable objective," Gamble said. With the new learning objectives, each course could include performance-based assessments, designed to be rich with real-life scenarios that test for knowledge and application.

NEXT STEPS

The measurement strategy has added credibility to the drug safety training program. "If you look at it from a qualitative point of view," Gamble said, "we're getting a lot of positive comments around starting to measure and look at actual data. The other piece we're starting to see, which is more quantitative, is that because I can show the value and impact of these programs for drug safety, I've been able to maintain a training budget." Getting the team on board with measurement mapping and the use of Levels 1 and 2 were critical in building a culture of measurement. "The organization can wrap its head around why we do what we do and what the results are," Gamble said.

Gamble knows that, even with a solid strategy in place, building a culture of measurement is ongoing work. "I hope we can continue to provide programs for our staff that are having an impact, helping them to do their jobs more efficiently and more effectively," Gamble said. Her team is now focused on how training can impact quality throughout drug safety, making "necessary changes and recommendations that will ultimately help our colleagues get their jobs done faster, better, and with higher quality."

For other learning leaders embarking on a measurement journey, Gamble said that although it isn't easy, they should not get discouraged. "You're going to think, 'I can't do it, the organization will never buy in,'" Gamble said. "See it through. I felt that way in the beginning, but I'm so happy we got this started. Being able to measure things has made my life easier."

CHAPTER **3**

Establishing a
Measurement
Framework

*The loftier the building, the deeper must the
foundation be laid.*

—Thomas à Kempis

appily, the days of learning leaders measuring simply to justify
one's budget seem to be fading, and are being replaced by a desire
to gain actionable intelligence that can be used for continuously
improving the organization's learning and development initiatives.
This shift from *prove* to *improve* is a significant one for learning leaders.
It signifies that, rather than being reactionary at budget time, they are
intentionally measuring to proactively ensure that they are delivering value to the business. It represents a shift from defensive (having
to prove) to strategic (continuously seeking ways to contribute to the
organization's success).

Most learning organizations have a formal learning strategy; however, most do not have an explicit measurement strategy. In fact, some
experts believe that less than 5 percent of learning organizations have
a true strategy for measurement.[1] Increasingly, learning leaders are

acknowledging the importance of measurement, but are often confounded by where to start and what to measure. The heart is there, but the specifics for its development and execution often aren't.

When thinking about designing and implementing a measurement strategy, the image of the messy room of a four-year-old comes to mind. Yes, there is an analogy here. If you ask that four-year-old to tidy up his (or her) room, he may stare at the toys, books, clothes, and crayons, and then simply pull another toy off the shelf and start playing. Why? He has no mental model for how to actually do it. He doesn't know whether to start with the toys or the clothes. Instead, he is paralyzed, and then goes back to what he's good at—playing! As adults, when we face situations that are unfamiliar, we are very much like that four-year-old—lacking confidence to take action, paralyzed by the unknown, so we put it off for another day. This chapter is about creating that mental model—a framework around which we can build the confidence to embark on the measurement journey.

MEASUREMENT FRAMEWORKS

Measurement just doesn't happen. It's a very intentional process, and organizations that get it right create a culture of measurement. They embrace it rather than fear it. And it starts with having that mental model of just what "it" is. In Chapter 2, we presented a "Continuum of Human Capital Analytics." The development of the continuum was informed by the work of several seminal thinkers who have provided a variety of frameworks for thinking about measurement.

The best-known in learning circles is Kirkpatrick's four levels,[2] first introduced by Donald Kirkpatrick in 1959, and expanded upon with a fifth level by Jack Phillips[3] (see Figure 3.1). Commonly referred to as satisfaction (Level 1), learning gain (Level 2), transfer or behavior change (Level 3), business impact (Level 4), and return on investment (ROI) (Level 5), this framework has guided many learning leaders in gaining wonderful insights into their learning initiatives. Later, an initial level (Level 0) was added to capture the basics that are tracked by most learning management systems (LMSs)—utilization. (As noted in Chapter 2, these levels also form the basis for a continuum of analytics.)

Level	Measure
Level 0	Utilization
Level 1	Satisfaction
Level 2	Learning gain
Level 3	Behavior change
Level 4	Impact
Level 5	ROI

Figure 3.1 Kirkpatrick/Phillips Levels of Evaluation

The recent introduction of the Talent Development Reporting principles (TDRp) by the Center for Talent Reporting shifted these measures to a scorecard that may resonate more with businesspeople by categorizing the traditional Levels 1 through 5 into efficiency, effectiveness, and outcome categories[4] (see Figure 3.2). (See Appendix D for sample reports.) TDRp enhanced traditional measures by incorporating targets against which to measure progress. Importantly, these targets are jointly agreed upon by the learning team and the business owners.

The learning effectiveness measurement (LEM) methodology,[5] developed at IBM by Dean Spitzer, took a broader perspective of measurement. This five-phase model was developed not only to evaluate learning initiatives, but to explicitly improve their effectiveness (see

Type	Measures
Efficiency	- Cost - Utilization
Effectiveness	- Satisfaction - Learning - Application
Impact	- Organizational business outcomes

Figure 3.2 Talent Development Reporting Principles (TDRp)

Figure 3.3). To do this, the LEM suggests that measurement actually starts well before the delivery of training with what Spitzer calls the "predictive measurement phase."

Similar to a front-end analysis, this phase ensures that training is aligned with business results by explicitly mapping out the desired outcomes and organizational and individual performance indicators, and then defining the required behaviors and the knowledge and skills to achieve them. The LEM's second phase, baseline measurement, similar to the TDRp, includes an up-front determination of what to measure and desired target values. The third phase, formative measurement, is a bit of a variation from formative evaluation familiar to instructional designers. In the context of the LEM, its purpose is to check readiness (of students and content) and verify that the business alignment is maintained throughout the design and development of the intervention. The remaining two phases, in-process measurement and retrospective measurement, are akin to Kirkpatrick's Levels 1 through 3 and Level 4, respectively.

Bersin by Deloitte, a well-regarded learning and human resources consultancy, offers a framework for measuring business impact that presents nine driving forces, shown in Figure 3.4. This framework is wide enough to take into account the Kirkpatrick and Phillips hierarchies, as well as Spitzer's alignment and individual and organizational performance distinctions.

Phase	Measures
1. Predictive	- Alignment
2. Baseline	- Prior performance
3. Formative	- Readiness
4. In-process	- Satisfaction - Learning - Application
5. Retrospective	- Impact (individual and organizational)

Figure 3.3 Learning Effectiveness Measurement (LEM) Methodology

Measures
1. Satisfaction
2. Learning
3. Adoption
4. Utility
5. Efficiency
6. Alignment
7. Attainment of customer objectives
8. Individual performance
9. Organizational performance

Figure 3.4 Bersin by Deloitte Impact Measurement Framework

A PRACTICAL MEASUREMENT FRAMEWORK FOR LEARNING

Based on our own experiences as consultants and as learning leaders, we have seen many variations on these general themes. We have also seen what gets successfully implemented in organizations (yes, often simpler is better, especially when just starting on a measurement journey). We enthusiastically welcome the inclusion of alignment into the up-front process of measurement; without it, measuring true business impact can be a misguided effort. Based on these experiences and building on the groundwork of others, we created the Measurement Framework for Learning (see Figure 3.5), a straightforward framework that integrates the good work described earlier together with our experience of what works in practice.

Each phase of measurement serves a unique purpose, following the progression of the learning initiative from design to launch and all the way through to its impact on the business. Measurement—and course design—starts with alignment. With the learning initiative in place, measurement shifts to the in-process measures of engagement, learning, and transfer. Ultimately, measurement leads to the impact phase to isolate training's impact on the business.

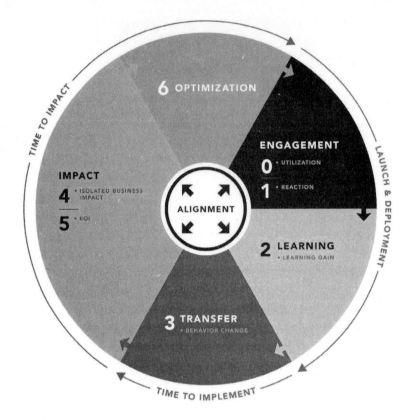

Figure 3.5 Measurement Framework for Learning

While these phases are presented in a sequential format (as with Kirkpatrick's four levels), there is no prerequisite to execute measures at each and every phase. As with most things in life, it depends! While we will argue that alignment should be mandatory on all interventions (after all, we need to define why we are doing this in the first place), it is simply impractical from a cost and effort perspective to conduct all phases of measurement on all interventions. Ultimately, it will be up to each learning leader and each project team to determine the value of each phase and how far to take measurement on any given initiative.

The *alignment phase*, missing from many measurement strategies and frameworks, is intended to ensure that you are aligned to the business and know what needles you are trying to move. Sometimes the link between training and business results is clear (e.g., sales training should increase sales). However, more often than not that link is less clear, as in the case of leadership development or soft skills training. Establishing this linkage is where measurement starts—by creating the causal link between business goals and investments in people. It defines those behaviors and outputs in quantifiable terms so instructors, students, and business leaders all know the expected outcomes of a learning investment before the investment is made—and can track progress toward those goals.

The framework includes two types of alignment: curriculum alignment and initiative alignment. We believe that alignment is so important, and too often shortchanged in the planning process, that we dedicate two chapters to the topic, introducing the Performance Map in Chapter 5 (for creating an aligned curriculum) and the Measurement Map in Chapter 6 (for identifying the specific metrics to track in measuring the business impact of an intervention).

The *engagement phase* provides early indications of the acceptance of a learning intervention. Are students partaking of the offerings? Good utilization measures reflect not just how many people are signing up, but what percentage of the audience has been trained, alerting the learning organization to any potential throughput or compliance issues. Similarly, student reactions captured through post course surveys provide an early indication of the perceived quality of the training and the likelihood of its application back on the job. A well-designed Level 1 evaluation can provide insights that uncover issues with content and delivery, enabling the learning organization to take prompt corrective action to improve the quality of training. Poor Level 1 results provide an early alert that the expected business outcomes are unlikely to come to fruition.

The *learning phase* is an in-process phase that mirrors Kirkpatrick's Level 2. Are students learning anything? Are they retaining it in ways that enable them to actually apply it on the job? The value of measurement done at this phase is dependent on the quality of the design of the instruments and methods used to capture the data. In other words, simply having everyone pass a posttest does not mean that learning has actually occurred.

Akin to Kirkpatrick's Level 3, the ***transfer phase*** is often one of the hardest measures to capture. Is learned information actually being applied back on the job? Did the learning transfer? That is, did behavior change? From surveys of students and their managers to observation checklists and mystery shopping, the methods are numerous. The method selected depends on the desired level of rigor (and available budget, of course).

These in-process efficiency and effectiveness measures are typically easier to capture than the impact measures, as they are generally within the control of the learning organization and its learning management system. However, that does not imply that measuring efficiency and effectiveness is easy. Fully leveraging the value of in-process measures requires two critical details: good data from well-designed instruments (surveys, tests, etc.) and good analysis. Both of these will be addressed in Chapter 7, Improving on the Basics.

In the ***impact phase***, business data is king. The purpose is to identify the business impact of a learning intervention, or Kirkpatrick's Level 4. In order for such an analysis to be credible to the business stakeholders, impact measures come from actual business data that is collected in the course of daily business operations. The Measurement Map from the alignment phase defines the metrics to be examined. The evaluation should use performance data from both before and after the learning intervention and for both the trained and untrained populations in order to examine and isolate changes in performance due to the intervention. By using actual business data, results are made credible to your business stakeholders. These results may then be used to calculate return on investment (ROI, or Level 5). The use of statistical techniques like isolation, optimization, and predictive analytics takes a traditional Level 4 analysis to a whole new level.[6] Advances in technology such as improved collection and access to data and PC-based statistical tools make it possible. To acknowledge this broader view of impact, in Chapter 2 we introduced this idea as Level 6. (Chapters 8 and 9 covers this methodology in greater detail.)

In practice, many organizations have adopted the Kirkpatrick/ Phillips framework. Others have started with it, and then integrated various other models and concepts to align with their learning cultures. Case studies presented throughout this book demonstrate how organizations are adopting, implementing, and succeeding with measurement. This chapter's case study tells the story of AT&T Learning Services and how, starting with alignment, the organization designed a curriculum to address a specific business problem. The story presents the measurement plan—following Kirkpatrick's four levels—and the results.

Ultimately, the value of adopting a framework is that it gives the learning organization that mental model for thinking about—and implementing—measurement. Make it explicit. Create a diagram of it. By providing a common language around measurement, you start to demystify it and make it accessible and doable. Put measurement on the agenda of every new initiative, and use the framework to guide the discussion. Start with describing its alignment, and then consciously determine, right at the start, how you want to measure it. Even if the answer is simply to evaluate efficiency measures, you've made that a conscious decision. Talking about measurement within the context of a commonly understood framework is a key step in building a culture of measurement.

SUMMARY

Deciding to implement a measurement strategy can be a daunting task. Having a measurement framework provides an organization with a mental model for tackling the measurement challenge. There is no single right framework, though many use Kirkpatrick's basic four levels as a foundation. The inclusion of alignment expands the strategic value of the framework and integrates business stakeholders into the process. Implementing measurement is more of an evolution than a revolution. You simply cannot do everything all at once. Start small. Identify a few key areas for your initial focus. Learn from them and celebrate successes. Soon you'll be on your way to leveraging measurement to:

- Drive alignment right from the start.
- Establish business measures of success.
- Guide the development of aligned content.
- Provide in-process measures for continuous improvement.
- Prove and improve the impact and value of learning

NOTES

1. Interview with Dean R. Spitzer.
2. D. L. Kirkpatrick, "Evaluating Training Programs: Evidence vs. Proof," *Training & Development Journal* (1977).
3. J. J. Phillips, *Return on Investment in Training and Performance Improvement Programs* (Houston, TX: Gulf Publishing Company, 1997).
4. Center for Talent Reporting: TDRp Measures Library, www.centerfortalentreporting.org/tdrp-measures-library/.
5. Dean R. Spitzer, "Learning Effectiveness Measurement: A New Approach for Measuring and Managing Learning to Achieve Business Results," *Advances in Developing Human Resources* 7, no. 1 (February 2005): 55–70.
6. D. Van Tiem, J. Moseley, and J. Dessinger, *Fundamentals of Performance Improvement: Optimizing Results through People, Process, and Organizations* (San Francisco: Pfeiffer/John Wiley & Sons, 2012).

Improving Collectors' Skills: AT&T

Disclaimer: Throughout these materials, persons who are involved in training are referred to as trainees, instructors, or administrators (also students, conferees, candidates, etc., as appropriate). In addition, personal pronouns are used to refer to trainees, instructors, and any other individuals. This was done to improve readability and is in no way intended to discriminate against persons of either gender. Nothing in this material should be construed to indicate any discrimination based on race, color, religion, creed, national origin, sex, age, disability, sexual orientation, gender, gender identity, marital status, citizenship status, military status, veteran status, or any other protected characteristic.

BUSINESS ISSUE

Business Situation

Two distinct organizations, Wireline Collections and Wireless Collections, united into one after a merger. Each organization had its own priorities, best practices, and visions of success.

The Wireline Collections organization excelled in collection results by using the vision of as much as possible, as soon as possible (AMAP/ASAP).

The Wireless Collections organization excelled in customer satisfaction results by focusing on the human side of a customer conversation rather than on collections.

Business Goals

Credit & Collections (C&C) sought to bridge the two cultures, uniting employees into a shared vision and mission.

The aim was to determine organizational priorities, key business drivers, and best practices so they could shape the new Credit & Collections organization.

The business goal was to align priorities, champion change, and build essential skills in the workforce to impact two Credit & Collections bottom-line results:

1. Improve customer satisfaction results.
2. Increase dollars collected results.

The overall goal of the initiative was to improve the bench strength of the entire Credit & Collections organization, producing collectors highly skilled in connecting with customers and solving their collection needs.

Consequences of Inaction

By failing to unite the new organizations, each organization would pursue its own priorities, best practices, and visions of success.

Collectors' skills would be skewed toward negotiation at the expense of customer satisfaction for one half of the organization, and would neglect negotiation in favor of customer satisfaction for the other half.

By aligning priorities, both organizations could excel in collection skills, thus improving customer satisfaction on each call and impacting bottom-line results significantly.

CHALLENGE FOR AT&T LEARNING SERVICES

Learning Services Goals

Credit & Collections (C&C) Learning Services was asked to assist its client in merging these cultures. The goals established for the initiative included:

- Leverage each organization's strengths to develop a new organization vision.
- Provide learning solutions to align priorities and build essential skills in the workforce.
- Gain buy-in, champion change, and minimize resistance to a new vision of success.
- Improve two key Credit & Collections metrics:
  1. Customer satisfaction results
  2. Dollars collected results

Develop New Vision

Learning Services partnered with the C&C Senior Leadership to determine organizational priorities, key business drivers, and best practices to shape the new Credit & Collections organization.

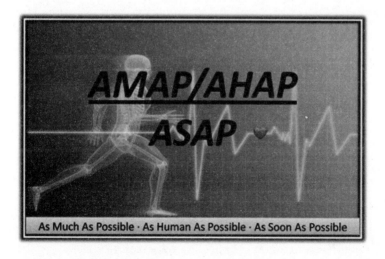

Through these planning sessions, a new vision of success emerged: AMAP/AHAP/ASAP (as much as possible, as human as possible, as soon as possible).

This vision united the Wireline Collections organization's excellence in collection results with the Wireless Collections organization's excellence in customer satisfaction results.

Determine Skill Needs

After setting the vision with C&C senior leadership, Credit & Collections Learning Services conducted additional needs analysis across the organization.

Learning Services led the Human Connection task team, facilitating discussions, listening to customer contacts, analyzing reports, and conducting additional research with C&C managers and collection representatives.

This needs analysis revealed which new skills needed to be built and which existing best practices could be leveraged to achieve the new vision.

In addition, instructors and designers with previous experience performing collection roles provided insight into the challenges faced by collection representatives and managers.

Determine Measures of Success

Learning Services analyzed the customer satisfaction and dollars collected metrics as well as the call observation form data conducted on performers to determine the metrics and behaviors that would need to be impacted to drive results.

These behaviors were instrumental in designing a training solution that focused on improving collectors' skills. The same behaviors and metrics would be reevaluated at the end of the initiative to determine its success.

Collector skills to measure for success included:

- Capitalizing on opportunities to make human connections with customers
- Capitalizing on opportunities to transition human connections with customers into collection opportunities

Manager skills to measure for success included:

- Drilling down to collector behavior root causes
- Developing improvement strategies for their performers
- Giving timely, specific feedback and recognition

Metrics included:

- Customer satisfaction results
- Dollars collected per call

TRAINING DESIGN APPROACH

Address Two Populations through Life Cycle of Change

Learning Services outlined a two-pronged approach to build collections skills in the core audiences: call center representatives and management.

- Human Connection (HC) workshops would build collection skills and unite the representatives in a shared definition of success.
- Developing Extraordinary Performers (DeEP) workshops would build managers' coaching skills, ensuring alignment and promoting effectiveness in their roles.

For each audience, Learning Services targeted the life cycle of change, from implementing the vision to delivering skill-focused training and ending with coaching and reinforcement.

Focus on One Vision

Learning Services targeted the strengths from both organizations to design a new vision of success called AMAP/AHAP/ASAP (as much as possible, as human as possible, as soon as possible) in the Human Connection workshops.

Human Connection (HC) workshop series goals:

- Unite collection representatives into a shared vision of success.
- Build skills in balancing the human and business sides of collection conversations.

■ Improve customer satisfaction results.

■ Increase dollars collected results.

The first module of the Human Connection workshop series leveraged the customer satisfaction strength of the Wireless Collections organization.

The second module capitalized on the collection strength of the Wireline Collections organization.

The third and fourth modules took these best practices to the next level by infusing additional external tools to continue to build skills.

Focus on Management Skills

Learning Services designed the Developing Extraordinary Performers workshops to teach managers how to coach and motivate collectors, hold them accountable, and plan for success.

Developing Extraordinary Performers (DeEP) workshop series goals:

■ Develop the bench strength of the Credit & Collections organization.

■ Reinforce key ideas from corporate-wide training initiatives (e.g., Promoting AT&T Values, Building Trust, Creating an Effortless Customer Experience, and Innovating), translating concepts into real-world skill building and hands-on application.

■ Facilitate sharing of best practices across the enterprise.

■ Promote employee engagement.

Ensure Buy-In and Engagement

Learning Services focused on making training fun, interactive, real-world, and timely to increase learner engagement, minimize resistance to change, and improve retention of skills learned.

C&C Learning Services incorporated new learning strategies in the design of both workshops to engage students in highly interactive events, appealing to all learning styles:

- Scenario-based learning (immerse students in real-word experiences that require decision making to resolve the situation).
- Story-based/theme-based learning (create a unique setting for the workshops, such as a Hawaiian destination, and provide a storyline that the students follow from beginning to end).
- Group activities and problem solving (groups work together to discuss an objective and present their solutions).

Modules included the following:

- Customer Contact Audio Examples
- Theme and Music
- Accelerated Learning Activities (e.g., appeal to all learning styles, collaborative, scenario-based)
- Role-Play Practice

Focus on the Learners

Throughout the design of both the Human Connection and Developing Extraordinary Performers workshops, Learning Services kept the learner's perspective at the forefront.

Providing these workshops to employees from two different organizational cultures required analyzing what previous training they had received, determining what they needed next, and positioning the new content in a way that would logically flow for either culture.

Address Life Cycle of Change

C&C Learning Services paid attention to the full life cycle of change (defining vision with leaders, marketing and executing the plan, and reinforcing afterward) to ensure success.

To address the full life cycle of change, Learning Services focused on the following:

- Gaining sponsorship from C&C senior leadership
- Establishing a shared vision
- Defining desired outcomes and success measures

- Leveraging best practices from both organizations
- Providing real-world examples in the workshops
- Ensuring hands-on application in the sessions
- Incentivizing collectors to implement new collection skills
- Equipping managers with coaching skills to support execution of the vision
- Implementing a plan for coaching and reinforcement on the job

TRAINING DESIGN CONTENT

Human Connection Workshops

Learning Services designed the Human Connection workshops to build representatives' skills in implementing the AMAP/AHAP/ASAP (as much as possible, as human as possible, as soon as possible) vision.

Customer satisfaction (as human as possible) was chosen for the first Human Connection module for two reasons:

1. The Wireless representatives already demonstrated some skill in making human connections; the first workshop would build on their current success. By valuing their strength in customer satisfaction in the first module, Learning Services paved the way for them to accept future collections-focused workshops as the newly formed Credit & Collections organization continued to evolve.
2. The Wireline representatives, although already focused on collections, were able to see the value in enhancing the customers' experience throughout the negotiation process.

After gaining that buy-in, the second, third, and fourth modules took a deeper dive into the core of collections.

Human Connection

Module 1: Connect to Collect

This 2½-hour workshop focused on building collectors' skills in making human connections with their customers, improving customer satisfaction results.

Module 2: Negotiating to Win

This 3½-hour workshop focused on transitioning human connections with customers into collection opportunities. Key concepts included collecting with confidence, avoiding prejudging a customer's ability to pay, overcoming objections by turning a reason for delay into a reason to pay, and negotiating to create a win-win solution.

Module 3: Negotiating with Style

This 3½-hour workshop focused on improving cooperative negotiation skills and increasing dollars collected. Throughout the Negotiating with Style workshop, representatives completed the Kraybill Conflict Style Inventory to identify their own negotiation style out of five possible styles (Avoiding, Harmonizing, Directing, Compromising, and Cooperating).

This Conflict Style Inventory tool was created by Dr. Ron Kraybill, the Peace and Development Advisor for the United Nations in Lesotho, who has dedicated his life to promoting peace through cooperative communication at senior leadership levels in countries such as South Africa, Israel, and Iraq.

Fully validated through academic research and studies, the Kraybill Conflict Style Inventory was used in Human Connection Modules 3 and 4 to help collectors identify their own styles, their customers' styles, and techniques to promote cooperative negotiation throughout collection conversations with customers.

Module 4: Collection Experts: Solving with Style

This one-day training (which included 3½ hours of hands-on application) focused on creating the mind-set of a collection expert to lower days sales outstanding.

A choose-your-own-adventure learning strategy promoted employee engagement by offering scenarios based on locations students visited on the island. Each location provided an experience that highlighted a key collection expert behavior. Students were served by an expert waiter at a local restaurant, presolved customers' future needs at a beach rental booth, negotiated top dollar at a pawnshop, and asked guided questions and motivated customers to pay at a surf shop.

By the end of the trip, they had put into action the behaviors of a collection expert in negotiating more money faster.

Developing Extraordinary Performers (DeEP)

Learning Services designed the DeEP workshops to build coaches' skills in coaching and motivating representatives to implement the AMAP/ AHAP/ASAP (as much as possible, as human as possible, as soon as possible) vision.

Due to the diversity of managerial roles in Credit & Collections, the Developing Extraordinary Performers workshop series was designed for delivery in three phases.

DeEP Phase 1. Target audience: 500 first- and second-level C&C operations managers.

This 3½-day workshop focused on improving operations managers' abilities to improve performance with their representatives through skill building, motivational techniques, and effective accountability discussions.

DeEP Phase 2. Target audience: 100 C&C support managers who supervise first- and second-level support managers.

This 1½-day workshop focused on improving support managers' abilities to improve performance with their direct reports through mentoring, guiding self-development, motivational techniques, and effective accountability discussions.

DeEP Phase 3. Target Audience: 300 first- and second-level individual contributing support managers.

This 1½-day workshop focused on how to apply personal mentoring moments for improved results and performance, how to understand personal motivators and implement motivational strategies to promote engagement, how to improve communications by setting expectations and holding others and self accountable, and how to plan for success.

DeEP Engagement Techniques

This workshop followed a similar three-phase approach, tailoring content to operations managers, support managers with direct reports, and individual contributing support managers, respectively.

This workshop focused on how to engage performers and build trust, grow performers in their roles, drive innovation, and coach for higher performance.

Managers committed to fulfilling their own Engagement Promise, centered around driving employee engagement and ensuring an effortless customer experience.

DeEP Engagement Techniques Design

DeEP workshops included in-class learning and hands-on application within the session.

For example, operations managers received classroom training in the mornings and applied the coaching techniques they learned in the afternoons by coaching their own representatives. This approach enhanced the effectiveness of the training, building skills and ensuring real-world relevance.

It also provided an opportunity for managers to share best practices and coaching techniques with their peers.

EXECUTION

Preview Workshops

Learning Services conducted preview workshops via TelePresence with the C&C senior leadership to gain sponsorship and promote accountability throughout the organization, a key driver to transforming the C&C culture.

Learning Services partnered with C&C executives to gain support and buy-in. Their sponsorship played a critical role in ensuring the success of these initiatives.

The C&C vice president and executive directors set expectations and communicated the "why's" behind these initiatives to their organization, ensuring participation enterprise-wide, effective coaching and reinforcement post-training, and execution of the vision.

Delivery

Instructors delivered the Human Connection series to approximately 9,000 collection representatives and the DeEP workshops to approximately 900 managers.

Half of the representatives believed that customer service was a higher priority than negotiation, and the other half believed the opposite.

By valuing both perspectives and merging them into a shared vision, the Human Connection workshops built skills and set expectations for future success.

Cultural Considerations

Both initiatives were global, training representatives and managers both domestically and internationally across more than 50 offices. In addition to training in the United States, workshops were also conducted for employees in India, Hong Kong, Philippines, Mexico, Costa Rica, Panama, El Salvador, Canada, and England.

The main challenge of globalization was ensuring that the themes, analogies, and examples were applicable across various cultures. For example, Learning Services redesigned Human Connection Module 2 to enhance cultural relevance. The original module was designed around the concept of negotiating the purchase of a car.

In the Philippines, most collection representatives will not buy a car in their lifetime, but they will likely buy a house and a lot. For this audience, Learning Services redesigned Module 2 using this negotiation example to make it more real-world and relatable.

Instructor Delivery Skills

Through the delivery of these initiatives, C&C Learning Services built instructors' skills in facilitating highly interactive events to maximize learning.

Examples include:

- Intense mentoring of high-performing instructors to deliver leadership training to managers (a new skill set for them)
- Ramping up instructors in face-to-face weeklong sessions where they were able to teach back and refine facilitation techniques
- Coaching instructors to incorporate engaging and active learning events in other courses they deliver in the future

Coaching and Reinforcement

To reinforce the training, Credit & Collections instructors led virtual follow-up sessions with the management teams to facilitate best practice sharing across offices and promote the coaching and reinforcement of the Human Connection and Developing Extraordinary Performers concepts.

Learning Services designed Connection Rallies as an additional reinforcement strategy.

- These ongoing Connection Rallies were 30-minute to one-hour biweekly sessions between the manager and his or her team to focus on goals and priorities for the month.
- While conducting the rally, coaches facilitated the sharing of success stories, identified the priorities for the week, and helped their teams see how their results ranked within their center and across other centers.
- The goals of the Connection Rallies were to reinforce the Human Connection and DeEP concepts, motivate performance, and drive business results.

Reinforcement Tools

During the Human Connection workshop, representatives received a job aid laminate highlighting the human and business sides of a customer contact to use as a reinforcement tool.

Students used the laminates and dry-erase markers to plot stages of their customer contacts and to role-play in the workshops. Managers and representatives then used them on the job to coach and reinforce key learnings from the Human Connection training.

This tool helped sustain the focus on both human and business goals on every call.

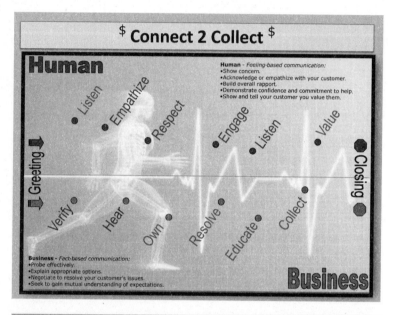

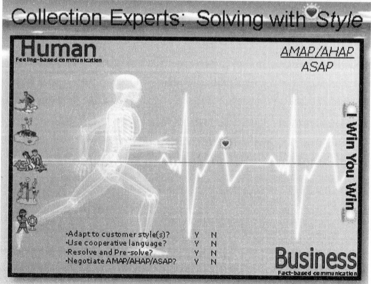

Learning Services expanded this reinforcement tool for each module of the Human Connection workshop to emphasize key skills learned.

Students used the laminate in the preceeding figures and dry-erase markers to identify the customer's initial communication style (represented by the icons on the left) and plotted the human/business stages of the contact.

Managers then used the laminate on the job to coach and reinforce cooperative communication and negotiation skills.

RESULTS

Human Connection: Levels 1 to 4 Evaluations

For the Human Connection initiative, Learning Services conducted Levels 1 to 4 evaluations based on the Kirkpatrick model.

Level 1 Student Surveys:

- Level 1 surveys evaluated the students' reactions to the workshop at the end of each session.
- Students answered 19 questions about their reactions to the overall program, the instructor, the topics included, and the design of training.
- The surveys used a rating scale from 1 (Totally Disagree) to 10 (Totally Agree) to evaluate each item.

Level 2 Learning Assessments:

- Level 2 knowledge checks evaluated the transfer of learning at the end of each session through multiple choice questions.
- The goal for each Level 2 was at least an 80 percent score.

Level 3 Pre- and Post-Behavioral Surveys:

- The Level 3 behavioral survey evaluated the changes in the representatives' behavior after attending the workshop.
- Level 3 surveys were given to managers before and one month after their representatives attended each workshop to evaluate to what extent the representatives had applied the skills learned in the workshop.

Level 4 Business Impact Evaluations:

- The Level 4 evaluations measured business impact to Credit & Collections results after each module was completed.
  - Measurements for Module 1 were customer satisfaction results.
  - Measurements for Modules 2 to 4 were collection effectiveness results.

See the appendix for further details about measuring behavioral changes and business impacts.

DeEP: Levels 1 to 3 Evaluations

For the Developing Extraordinary Performers workshop, Levels 1 to 3 evaluations were conducted.

- Level 1 Student Surveys and Level 2 Assessments were administered at the end of each session.
- Level 3 surveys were given to managers and their supervisors one month after they attended a session. This Level 3 evaluation was a behavioral survey that identified how the managers applied the skills learned in the workshop.

Human Connection Results (Levels 1 to 3)

Level 1 Student Surveys: 99 percent (students expressed 99 percent satisfaction with workshop)

Level 2 Assessments: 97 percent

Level 3 Highlights:

- Exceeded Level 3 evaluation goals.
- There was a 12 percent increase in capitalizing on opportunities to make human connections with customers.
- There was a 13 percent increase in capitalizing on opportunities to transition human connections with customers into collection opportunities.
- There was a 15 percent increase in using controlling questions to ask for more money sooner.

Human Connection Results (Level 4)

Level 4 Highlights:

Module 1: Connect to Collect

- There was a 3.5 percent increase in customer satisfaction results.
- Credit & Collections' results moved from below customer satisfaction targets to exceeding targets post-training.

Module 2: Negotiating to Win

- There was a 6 percent increase in dollars collected per call.
- Consumer Wireless Collections: 4 percent increase in dollars collected per call.
- U-verse Collections: 9 percent increase in dollars collected per call.
- Southwest & West Small Business Collections: 14 percent increase in dollars collected per call.

Module 3: Negotiating with Style

- There was a 5 percent increase in dollars collected per call.

Module 4: Collection Experts: Solving with Style

- There was a 24 percent increase in dollars collected per call. (*Note:* Results were based on delivery to 25 percent of planned audience.)

DeEP Results (Levels 1 to 3)

Level 1 Student Surveys: 99.8 percent

Level 2 Assessments: 96 percent

Level 3 Highlights:

- Exceeded Level 3 evaluation goals.
- 92 percent of managers improved their job performance by more than 20 percent.
- 69 percent of managers improved by more than 40 percent.

- 91 percent of managers were able to develop specific improvement strategies for their performers based on current motivation levels and performance.
- 94 percent of managers were able to effectively implement the Game Plans they created in the workshop.

DeEP Engagement Techniques Results (Levels 1 to 3)

Phase 1 Results (Phases 2 and 3 in progress):

Level 1 Net Promoter Score: 97 percent

Level 2 Assessments: 100 percent

Level 3 Highlights:

- Exceeded Level 3 evaluation goals.
- 96 percent of managers applied the skills learned in the workshop.
- There was a 5 percentage point increase in giving all performers an opportunity to use their strengths and skills.
- There was an 8 percentage point increase in drilling down to root causes using self-discovery techniques.
- There was an 11 percentage point increase in giving performers timely, specific feedback and recognition.

DeEP: Manager Comments

"Having the opportunity to practice what was presented with my reps and then discuss the good/bad of that development session enabled me to put material into action."

"As my managers and I talk about necessary coaching for specific individuals, the content of this class is at the forefront of their plan to improve performance."

"I must say that I've never before been in a training class where I was totally involved, eager to hear and learn, as well as completing a training module with complete understanding. Before your class I thought I was a great communicator, coach, and motivator, but in your class I learned how to *effectively* communicate, coach, and motivate my employees and my peers!"

DeEP Engagement Techniques: Manager Comments

"I thought I had good innovative techniques, but the class gave me so many more ideas. I realized I could be a lot more creative with my team. I especially liked that it showed me how to get my team and individual reps more involved with the Innovation Stations."

"I always felt good with change, and I can adapt to anything, but this class helped me self-identify my own personal acceptance during a change. It made me realize how hard it is to help others when I may be reluctant. It also showed me that you have to use different approaches for those who may be in a different stage of the change."

"My team and I took away a lot of tools and resources that will help increase the level of engagement in our center. Thanks again for your support and level of engagement. You made a difference with my team."

CONCLUSION

Learning Services Achievements

Credit & Collections Learning Services assisted its client in merging two distinct cultures by leveraging each organization's strengths and providing learning solutions to align priorities, champion change, and build essential skills in the workforce.

Learning Services designed two workshop series, Human Connection for representatives and Developing Extraordinary Performers for managers, to build collection skills within two core audiences.

Making training engaging, real-world, and timely improved retention and impacted bottom-line results.

A full life-cycle design strategy united employees into a shared vision and mission and reinforced that vision even after the completion of each training event.

By keeping a finger on the pulse of the client organization, Learning Services demonstrated business agility, responding quickly and purposefully to implement solutions to have a positive and significant impact on the bench strength of the entire Credit & Collections organization and bottom-line results.

Overall Results

Aligning cultures and delivering targeted skill-building training with immediate real-world application realized the following results:

- There was a 3.5 percent improvement in customer satisfaction results.
- There was an 11 percent overall average increase in dollars collected per call.

The two workshop series produced the following overall Levels 1 to 3 results for training content:

- Overall Level 1 results: Greater than 97 percent customer satisfaction score.
- Overall Level 2 results: Greater than 96 percent assessment score.
- Overall Level 3 results:
  - There was a 12 percent increase in capitalizing on opportunities to make human connections with customers.
  - There was a greater than 13 percent increase in capitalizing on collection opportunities.
  - 92 percent of managers improved their job performance.
  - 96 percent of managers applied engagement techniques learned in the workshop.

CHAPTER **4**

Planning for Success

Nobody said it was going to be easy, and
nobody is right.

—George H.W. Bush

When it comes to measurement, it's one thing to have a framework and an idea of what you want to do; it's a far more daunting proposition to actually do it. You don't wake up one morning and instantly have the capabilities and resources to measure. Much as any learning leader would love to have a robust data warehouse that collects real-time training data, integrates with human resources (HR) systems, and is synced with the business's operational data, this is a pipe dream for most organizations. But measurement takes more than systems—it also takes people with the right skill sets to devise a strategy for the alignment, to develop surveys and tests, to collect data, to develop and interpret reports, and to conduct rigorous analysis when needed.

We are aware of a few organizations that have made such investments in staff and in systems. Organizations like Google, JetBlue, Harrah's (now Caesars),[1] and others are staffing their learning and HR functions not only with functional specialists but with business and analytics expertise as well. They have also invested in the systems to integrate disparate data. Every day, we hear of organizations embarking on this journey of building internal measurement competency. One client likened her journey to eating an elephant, noting that you need to deconstruct it and take it one bite at a time; otherwise, you'll get overwhelmed by the magnitude of the task. Have a plan, start small, and gain buy-in and traction by picking some low-hanging fruit. Once you start making data-based decisions, you'll want more. Your questions will become more sophisticated, and your analysis will become richer. Then you'll know you're well on your way with your measurement journey.

But first, with framework in hand, you must prepare for that journey. Where are you today? Where do you want to go? What are your priorities? What kind of investments will be needed? How long will it take to get there? This chapter is not about developing an action plan—you most likely already know how to do that. Rather, it is about laying out the details that need to be considered in such a plan if your measurement strategy is to come to fruition. These considerations fall into four areas that need to be explored and assessed:

1. Purpose and political will
2. Skills and capabilities
3. Tools and technology
4. Data

PURPOSE AND POLITICAL WILL

Why are you measuring? We've already discussed the "prove" and "improve" rationales, and both have solid merit. When thinking about why you want to measure, get specific. What is it that you want to prove? What is it you may want to improve? It will be much easier to get a learning team on board if they know why you want to measure. If there are pressures from above to show value, let the team know. If you are taking a proactive position to make sure you're interventions are hitting the mark, let the team know that, too.

The training department of a global sales organization had historically built courses based on directives from senior operations executives. The new director of training was concerned that this top-down approach, while maybe sufficient for new product training, may not be getting at the real performance issues of the sales force. As a passionate learning professional, he wanted to be sure that the time, effort, and money invested in training was going to measurably improve real business outcomes—like sales and customer loyalty. Results to date were inconclusive. But before he could begin challenging executive requests, he had to find out if there really was a gap in the training that was offered versus what was needed. What does good performance look like? How do we measure it? How do we stack up today? His mission was to identify the performance gaps in order to develop a needs-based curriculum, thereby improving the quality and relevance of course offerings. Then he could measure results both for continuous improvement and to demonstrate the relationships between training and sales, profitability, and customer loyalty. He knew it would take data to change the way training dollars were allocated.

Note that this learning leader started with alignment and the desire to ensure that learning connected to business outcomes. He also specifically called out the desire to improve. This may seem obvious, but in many organizations, people may be afraid to measure. What if the results are not good? A culture of fear, where mistakes are punished (versus leveraged as learning opportunities), can greatly hinder measurement efforts. To explicitly state that measurement is for improvement is to accept all results—the good and the bad. To realize the true power of measurement, learning leaders must ensure that poor results are not punished, but analyzed for improvement. Create an explicit goal for measurement and post it; then live by it.

This brings us to political will, which is directly related to the purpose. Measurement takes work; therefore, it's going to consume some amount of time and budget. Justifying this expenditure of resources takes a clear objective—and a clear understanding as to how it will benefit the organization. Making the case takes commitment. It also takes courage. This gets back to the possibility of bad results. Too often we've heard learning leaders hesitate about going beyond Level 1 and Level 2. Frequently, underneath this hesitancy is the secret fear of all learning professionals: What if our wonderful training isn't making any difference to the business? This fear gets right at the fundamental and first phase of measurement—alignment. If training gets designed without first mapping out its intended outcomes, why would it hit the mark? That's why alignment is so critical, not just for measurement (though it surely helps you figure out what to measure), but also for designing and building quality learning solutions that will make a difference.

Even with alignment, there is the risk that the learning might not be having the desired impact, or is maybe effective for only a segment of the audience, such as new hires. Suppose the program were a half-million-dollar investment in leadership development and was only partially successful. How would your organization respond to such news? Would this be an opportunity to slash budgets and staff? Would this be a learning opportunity to make a midcourse adjustment? Perhaps an even better question is: "Would you want to know?" For, without measurement, the program would certainly continue blissfully along until its natural conclusion—and stakeholders might wonder why leadership performance didn't seem much improved.

Results of Levels 1 through 3 are largely of interest only to the learning organization. They can provide good indicators (what we define as leading indicators) of receptivity and applicability of the learning. They offer insights for refinements and adjustments to course content and delivery. It is unlikely that they present much external risk to the learning organization, because these measures are typically not politically charged. Business impact, in contrast, is of interest to all stakeholders.

Some stakeholders may be skeptical about training's value and even more skeptical about the ability to measure it. Measuring impact requires gaining access to operational business data from outside the learning department, so engage these stakeholders in the design of the analysis so their concerns can be heard and addressed. Share your goals for measurement and how findings will be used to improve training's contribution to the business. (See Chapter 6 for more discussion on engaging stakeholders in the measurement process.) By going into an impact analysis as partners, both the business leader and the learning leader can anticipate the invaluable insights that lie ahead, and how together they can work to improve the business.

SKILLS AND CAPABILITIES

The skill sets you need to implement measurement depend on the depth of analyses you want to undertake. All your measurement activities will be wasted without good reporting and analysis. You need to determine the frequency and depth of desired analysis and how results will be reported. Then take inventory of the skill sets you will need versus what you have. Clearly, conducting a rigorous statistical impact analysis takes specialized skills not needed for basic reporting on completion rates. Not all analysis requires statistical prowess, but a logical mind, comfort with numbers, and decent Excel skills are prerequisites for even the most basic analyses. As shown in Chapter 2 with the continuum of analytics, analysis can take on many flavors, from the straightforward (i.e., dashboards and descriptive analyses that can be done with Excel) to the complex (i.e., impact and predictive analyses that require more sophisticated tools and statistical acumen).

To determine what skills you may want on staff, examine each phase of measurement, asking questions such as:

- How often will we pursue this level of measurement?
- What skills are required for this type of measurement?
- What skills do we already have on staff?
- Who may be able to develop these skills?
- Should we build or buy (or contract) for this capability?

Often, measurement functions become part of the jobs of existing employees, though some large learning organizations may dedicate a full-time project manager and staff to measurement. Some of the most common skills that many organizations seek to have on a measurement team include:

- Project manager
- Reporting analyst (commonly referred to as a business analyst)
- Survey designer (often part of an instructional design role)
- Assessment designer (often part of an instructional design role)

On occasion, we have seen organizations either employ or have access to functions that are not traditionally seen in learning and development: data analyst/programmer and statistician. Individuals who possess that entire skill set are becoming known as data scientists (a position likely to soon be in great demand). Those organizations that regularly evaluate impact measures will benefit from having a data analyst, as this function is frequently needed to extract business data and integrate it with your learning data. Larger organizations frequently tap market research departments for statistical acumen, though more and more, sophisticated learning organizations are adding this talent to the learning team.

TOOLS AND TECHNOLOGY

Almost hand in hand with capabilities is the underlying technology. While tools abound for tracking training, surveys, and tests, the license fees and integration into existing systems can stall a measurement initiative. An inventory of what you have versus what you wish you had can shed light on the current feasibility of various levels of measurement and analysis. It can also help you prioritize future technology expenditures. Technology will be the cornerstone of how you collect, integrate, and analyze data. The following questions can guide an assessment of your readiness in regard to the core technology of learning measurement.

- Do you have a learning management system (LMS)?
    - One or many?
    - Is it integrated with your HR systems (for population and demographic data)?
    - What types of reporting on utilization does it offer?
    - How flexible is the reporting?
- What methods do you have for deploying and capturing survey data?
    - Are surveys stand-alone or integrated with your LMS?
    - How flexible is the reporting?
- What methods do you have for deploying and capturing test and assessment data?

- Are assessments stand-alone or integrated with your LMS?
- Does it support item analysis?
- How flexible is the reporting?

- What analysis tools do you have access to?
- What data integration methods or platforms do you have to integrate HR, learning, and business data?

DATA

Data are the underpinning of all measurement activity. Without data, you simply have nothing to measure. Learning organizations serious about measurement must explicitly define their methods and mechanisms for collection, organization, integration, reporting, and analysis of data. Even Levels 0 and 1 will collapse without a process in place for identifying training audiences, tracking completions, and deploying, aggregating, and reporting surveys.

Knowing where your data will come from is critical. Figure 4.1 illustrates the sources of data typically needed by each phase of measurement. Much of the data for Levels 0 through 3 typically resides within the learning organization. The inclusion of HR data with these measures can create wonderful opportunities to segment results by work location, job role, tenure, size of team, and more. We've seen some wonderful LMS implementations that either have a regular feed from the human resources information system (HRIS) or are integrated into a common data warehouse that enables this kind of analysis. Chapter 7, Improving on the Basics, takes a deeper look at segmenting data from the engagement and learning phases for greater insights.

Taking your measurement initiative to the impact phase will require drawing data from at least two or three major sources around the organization. The LMS is the foundational system. When evaluating change in performance, you simply must know who attended and when, and that comes from your LMS. Data from the HRIS typically plays an important role as well. It provides demographics for segmenting results. It also may hold key performance indicators, such as performance ratings, promotions, and turnover.

		Phases of Measurement			
Data Sources	Alignment	Engagement (Levels 0 and 1)	Learning (Level 2)	Transfer (Level 3)	Impact (Levels 4, 5, and 6)
Stakeholder Input	X				
System Extracts					
• LMS		X	X		X
• HRIS		X	X	X	X
• Business/ operational					X
• Financial					X
• Third-party*					X
Surveys		X	X	X	
Performance tests and observation checklists			X	X	
Interviews					
• Exploratory			X	X	
• Success-based					X

Figure 4.1 Sources of Data Needed by Each Phase of Measurement

*Third-party data sources such as payroll services, engagement surveys, or customer satisfaction surveys.

The most influential data will likely be the operational business data and/or financial data. Business systems hold the key to data on real business outcomes like productivity, quality, safety, timeliness, and more. In fact, based on the expected outcomes of the learning initiative, multiple business systems may be involved. For example, a sales training initiative may be intended to increase sales and customer satisfaction. In most organizations, that data will be tracked in two different systems, or it may have to be obtained from a third-party vendor. Getting at this data can be challenging. Building relationships with stakeholders and engaging them in your impact measurement initiative can go a long way toward getting your hands on this powerful data. In Chapter 6, we will discuss engaging stakeholders in the definition of business metrics through a measurement mapping process.

TAKING INVENTORY: WHAT IT TAKES

By now, you know that implementing a measurement strategy takes some serious planning. To help guide discussions around measurement capability, we have developed an inventory checklist. Exploring each phase of measurement in a structured manner can help learning organizations assess the current state of measurement and learning analytics. It can quickly identify strengths on which to build, and help with planning for growing measurement capacity. Figure 4.2 presents a snapshot of this tool for the Engagement and Learning phases. You can review the full tool in Appendix B.

DEVELOPING THE PLAN: MEASUREMENT BLUEPRINTS

Each phase of measurement serves a different purpose and measures different things. As such, each phase requires different methods for collecting, analyzing, and reporting results. To help our clients think through what they expect to gain from each phase and just how they should go about doing it, we developed a series of measurement blueprints. The blueprint is actually a template that identifies the necessary elements of a measurement plan, including:

- Purpose
- Questions to be answered
- Data sources
- Data collection method
- Timing
- Stakeholders (and how they will use the information)
- Reporting requirements
- Implementation considerations

Typically, our clients create a master set of blueprints—one per phase—that specifies their learning organization's planned approach

What It Takes	What We Have	What We Need
Engagement: Reaction		
Skills/Capabilities ▪ Measurement project owner ▪ Reporting/business analyst ▪ Survey designer ▪ Data analyst/programmer*		
Technology/Infrastructure ▪ LMS or other tracking system ▪ Survey development and deployment tool ▪ Data capture and storage method ▪ Reporting tool		
Data ▪ Course file ▪ Survey questions ▪ Survey responses ▪ Student file ▪ Student demographics (from LMS or HR)* ▪ Instructor file*		
Learning: Learning Gain		
Skills/Capabilities ▪ Measurement project owner ▪ Reporting analyst ▪ Assessment developer ▪ Data analyst/programmer*		

Technology/Infrastructure
▪ LMS or other tracking system
▪ Test development and deployment engine
▪ Data capture and storage method—
  final score
▪ Data capture and storage method—item
  responses and initial scores*
▪ Reporting tool		

Figure 4.2 What It Takes

What It Takes	What We Have	What We Need
Data		
▓ Course file		
▓ Question bank and answer grid		
▓ Item responses*		
▓ Initial score*		
▓ Final score		
▓ Student file		
▓ Student demographics (from LMS or HR)*		
▓ Instructor file*		

Figure 4.2 *(Continued)*

*Recommended if LMS does not provide desired data and/or reports or if organization is pursuing more advanced analysis.

to that element of measurement. An organization just getting started with Level 1 may initially focus on only that blueprint. In some cases, multiple blueprints may be needed if, for example, the organization wanted to implement postcourse surveys for both web and instructor-led training. The way the survey gets deployed and how data gets captured and stored may be different, so each of these processes needs to be spelled out. Figure 4.3 illustrates a sample blueprint for reaction measurement within the engagement phase.

To aid you on your measurement journey, a full set of sample blueprints built based on our years of measuring and evaluating learning is provided in Appendix C. Customize these blueprints to suit your learning organization, and leverage them as a starting point for your measurement plans.

Purpose	Data Sources
To ensure that learning is perceived by learners as relevant to their jobs, and worth the time to participate	▓ Learners ▓ Line managers

Figure 4.3 Reaction Blueprint (Engagement Phase)

Questions to Be Answered	Method
■ Do learners value the learning solution? ■ Is it relevant and applicable to their jobs? ■ What parts of the learning are working best or worst? ■ Can it be applied back on the job? ■ Do different demographic groups perceive the value differently? ■ Do learners and managers feel it was a good investment of their time?	**Learner Survey** ■ Administered on-site and scored in LMS (live) ■ At end of web based training (WBT) ■ Use standard questions/standard scale ■ Add custom questions ■ Include open-ended questions **Manager Perspective** ■ Spot phone call/survey to manager

Timing
■ Following launch ■ Continue throughout course life cycle (live) ■ Continue until results stabilize (WBT) ■ Redeploy if audience, content, or environment changes

Stakeholders	Use Info To . . .
■ Design/development team	■ Revise content, if activities or instruction problems occur
■ Instructor/delivery team	■ Revise delivery
■ Learning management team	■ Ensure that solution is positively received by audience, and viewed as relevant ■ Compare courses ■ Monitor improvements to courses ■ Address instructor problems
■ Business sponsors	■ Build confidence in learning solution ■ Assess continuation of investment

Reporting Requirements	
■ Monthly ■ On demand	■ By curriculum/course/instructor/delivery type/org. unit/audience demographics ■ By time frame ■ Report top box percentage to management

Figure 4.3 (*Continued*)

Implementation Considerations
■ Do we have the necessary technology in place?
■ Do we have sufficient in-house expertise?
■ Do we have resources to administer, maintain, and monitor?

Figure 4.3 *(Continued)*

SUMMARY

Good measurement requires knowing the reasons behind the push for measurement. It also takes organizational capacity in the form of:

■ Staff skills and capabilities

■ Technology and tools

■ Access to data

You may not have everything you want or need at the start of your measurement journey. Don't let that stop you. As this chapter's Chrysler case study shows, you simply need to find a place to start. Taking on a robust measurement strategy is rather like eating that elephant. It becomes a feasible endeavor when you deconstruct it and take it one bite at a time. This chapter has provided you with tools to analyze where you are and how to design work plans at every level. Find that low-hanging fruit to build momentum, to ease fears about measurement, and to demonstrate how quantitative evidence can help improve the quality of your offerings. Once you start making data-based decisions, your questions will become more sophisticated, and your analyses will become richer.

Good measurement results are predicated on designing and delivering solid learning solutions that address identified business requirements. That means alignment. Our next two chapters share two powerful techniques for ensuring that those solutions are on target to deliver business results.

NOTE

1. Thomas Davenport, Jeanne Harris, Jeremy Shapiro (2010). *Harvard Business Review Magazine,* http://hbr.org/2010/10/competing-on-talent-analytics/ar/1.

A Culture of Measurement: Chrysler Academy

BACKGROUND

Chrysler Group, LLC is a major automobile manufacturer with a global network of dealerships selling and servicing its Chrysler, Dodge, Jeep, and Ram cars and trucks. Supporting these sales and service efforts is Chrysler Academy, the learning organization responsible for the training and development of the retail dealership workforce, from sales consultants to service technicians. Training is jointly funded by the company and the dealers, and both audiences expect the Academy to deliver high-quality training that will drive business results.

IT STARTED WITH A PLAN

Nearly 10 years ago, Chrysler Academy began a very intentional performance improvement journey that would leverage measurement and evidence-based methods to continuously improve the value and relevancy of its services to Chrysler's retail audience. Through high-quality, aligned courseware, the Academy believed it would be able to drive measurable improvements in dealership performance.

The journey began with a plan of rather humble beginnings, starting with adopting Kirkpatrick's four levels and improving the quality of Level 1 and Level 2 measures. Next, the Academy implemented a true needs-based approach to curriculum development to ensure it would be nimble in responding to the ever-changing needs of the retail automotive environment. By linking curriculum to business outcomes, the Academy began tracking performance of trained and untrained employees, seeking to better understand the drivers of good business outcomes. Systems and tools were put in place to support measurement activities, and curriculum managers began to understand how systematic measurement could improve the quality of their offerings. Soon they were talking about their "Level 1's" and debating how to isolate Level 4 results. A 2008 business impact study showed positive impacts of sales training in regard to sales volume and sales consultant retention, earning the Academy both the American Society for Training and Development's "Excellence in Practice" award and *Chief Learning Officer*'s "Business Impact" award. The shift to a culture of measurement was under way.

FAST-FORWARD

With the financial meltdown and 2009 bankruptcy filings of General Motors and Chrysler, the auto industry has been through turbulent times. Emerging from bankruptcy, the Academy has put a laserlike focus on its mission of delivering performance improvement solutions that will impact real business results, specifically sales, customer satisfaction and loyalty, and employee retention.

MEASUREMENT FRAMEWORK

As measurement thinking, data systems, and analytics tools have become more sophisticated, so too has the Academy's approach to measurement. Its measurement framework has evolved to include measures of operational efficiency (Levels 0 and 1), knowledge evaluation (Level 2), individual performance (Levels 3 and 4), and organizational performance (Levels 4 and 5) (see Figure 4.A).

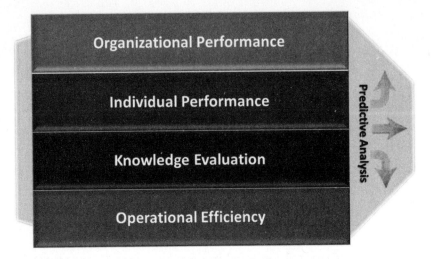

Figure 4.A Chrysler Academy's Measurement Framework for Learning

The Academy has also acknowledged the power of predictive analysis (Level 6) and is incorporating relevant measures from any level in its predictive models. This revised framework provides focus for the Academy's data-driven decision making and informs stakeholders of the intent of its measurement strategy:

- To emphasize our understanding of performance and improving upon it, rather than singularly trying to quantify training's worth

- To continually develop metrics and data collection sources across all dimensions of our business

- To isolate metrics that help us best understand our performance against our business objectives/key performance indicators (KPIs)

Details such as metrics, operational definitions, data collection sources, and reporting are defined within each level. As part of the report design, the Academy collaborates with its various stakeholders to design easy-to-use, actionable dashboards. Dedicated analytics staff is at the ready to mine the data in support of the Academy's strategy, looking for new insights about training, performance, and predictors of success.

RESPONSIVE AND RELEVANT

As the automotive marketplace changes, so too do the needs of the Academy's students. Keeping on top of these changing needs requires both an understanding of new requirements and a frequent calibration of actual performance gaps. The Academy has adopted multiple approaches to maintain its needs-based curriculum, including formal needs and gap analyses, stakeholder surveys and interviews, and knowledge assessments.

Today, Chrysler Academy is still focused on continuous performance improvement—for itself and for its students. Its processes for determining needs, defining gaps, evaluating student satisfaction and learning, and measuring impact have evolved to enable the Academy to be even more responsive. The Academy knows that delivering relevant solutions plays a key role in helping the company, its dealers, and their staffs succeed.

CHAPTER 5

Curriculum Alignment

Once we know something, we find it hard to imagine what it was like not to know it.

—Chip and Dan Heath, authors of *Made to Stick* and *Switch*

Anyone who has ever rowed crew in an eight-man racing shell knows that glorious feeling when the boat is "set up." It means that the boat, or shell, is exactly on keel—every one of the eight oarsmen in the boat is in perfect harmony, perfect balance: eight seats sliding forward together, eight oars squaring up together, eight blades hitting the catch together, 16 legs exploding with power, 16 arms drawing in the stroke, and that final, critical moment—no, instant—when eight oar blades leave the water precisely together and make their way evenly back through the air to the top of the stroke. This is the magical part of the stroke, when only the hull of the boat touches the water. This hull, over 60 feet in length and just over 20 inches wide, is the least stable vessel on the seas at this moment. But when the boat is set up, it's in perfect balance. For the oarsmen, the moment is strangely calm. It's fluid—almost mystical. Everyone and every movement is in perfect alignment to support the goal: to propel the craft through the water with the greatest power and least resistance possible. Unless the boat is set up, you haven't a chance of winning.

What if a learning organization's curriculum was designed in such a way that everything it did was purposefully, knowingly, driving organizational goals? What if the learning function was "set up"? It takes effort to ensure that a curriculum is aligned to organizational goals, but it can be done, and the payback is huge. The specific knowledge and skills that are linked to successful performance can be mapped, and skills gaps can be identified, quantified, and prioritized. A strategy for closing gaps and aligning curriculum can be developed with the twofold benefit of improved employee engagement and improved organizational performance.

GOAL: TO CLOSE THE SKILL GAPS

In every organization there are critical job roles that drive business results. By identifying key performance indicators (KPIs) that link to the business results, we can mine company performance data to identify individuals in these critical job positions who are most successful in advancing the company's business goals. These are the organization's high performers, and they really do drive business results. They might be well-known to their supervisors and peers, but often we find hidden stars out there—unsung heroes. This is especially the case when an organization has not clearly identified its KPIs or properly linked them to business goals, or hasn't tied KPIs to performance management.

Along with these high performers, we have those whose performance is moderate or even low. The reasons for this are varied, from poor performance support by the organization to simple inexperience on the part of the worker. Our goal is to help close the gap between the high performers and their colleagues as quickly and efficiently as possible. Close the gap between the best and the rest, as we say. So, how do we get there?

THE PERFORMANCE MAP

We use a process of performance mapping and performance gap analysis. Let's begin by differentiating it from another popular process, competency modeling.

Many organizations are building competency models that can identify attributes that are shared across many job functions. These models can significantly enhance an organization's career-planning and organizational-development capabilities. Competencies can be linked to organizational goals and, with competency models in place, human resources (HR) professionals and employees can more readily see pathways for career advancement. The list of competencies associated with a job will be general and high-level in nature, often with many competencies being common across multiple job positions. Competencies are not typically enunciated as clear, observable, easily measured, job-specific actions. So, while competency models are highly useful for plotting career paths and identifying the attributes associated with a job, they might not have the precision and agility needed for responding to a specific human performance need.

In key positions where quality of performance can have great impact on the business, a more focused approach may be warranted. Enter the performance map. A performance map begins with a hierarchical task analysis, also known as a job analysis. The job analysis specifies the tasks associated with the targeted job, placing them in logical groupings and identifying how each major task is supported by subtasks. The job analysis, conducted with high performers, produces a list of activities known to be associated with success in that job position. That's the critical point. The tasks are not just tasks—they are the things the high performers actually do, and they might be different and more robust than what is in the job description.

The performance map then goes beyond the job analysis by gathering more information about the conditions needed to perform these activities at a high level. How often are these activities performed? How hard are they to learn? How important are they to the job? What knowledge, inputs, and tools are needed? What is the ultimate output of the activity? And what is the context in which the activities are performed?

The portrait of the job that emerges from a performance map is both detailed and nuanced. It is more than a mere list of tasks: It describes the personal attributes, characteristics, and talents common to the people really driving the company's success in that critical job function. Importantly, the map also describes the conditions needed for exemplary performance. This kind of information, often overlooked in traditional curriculum design, gives the learning and HR departments rich insights into the enablers of high performance that often go well beyond the learning function.

When you have critical positions or if you have a performance problem within a particular job function, performance maps may help you get deeper into the job to uncover what makes high performers so good—and help you determine how to raise everyone else's performance, all aligned with desired business outcomes. If this is what your business needs, a performance map can be an invaluable resource when designing or refining curriculum. Building a map is a bit of a craft, and with practice a good instructional designer can become proficient. It all starts with in-depth interviews with high performers.

HOW WE LEARN FROM HIGH PERFORMERS

It's interesting to discover that high performers often have some difficulty articulating what they do that makes them so successful. Some of the differentiators are obvious, but there are a lot of activities they engage in and attitudes they possess that they wrongly assume are common to everyone. Even when they are aware of differences between what they do on the job and what others do, they often have trouble explaining those differences. We call this phenomenon "unconscious competence," the fourth of the four stages of learning often attributed to the famous psychologist Abraham Maslow.

Unconscious competence comes when a skill has become so much a natural part of us that we don't think about it. Often we don't even know where we learned it. It's like we always knew it. And if we believe we always knew it (which we didn't), it's difficult to explain it to someone else. That's one reason why highly accomplished athletes do not necessarily make good coaches. "I can do it, but I can't explain it." This is true even of everyday activities. Consider the skill of riding a bike. A lot of people can do it, but who can readily describe how it's done?

This is why it's important to have guided interviews with several high performers. The job of the interviewer is to tease out the specifics of what these performers do and to help them articulate the nuances. The interviewer begins to see patterns and similarities from one person to the next, as the map begins to take shape. The complexity of the job will determine the number of high performers needed, but we have found that having 12 to 15 works in most cases.

We interview high performers in groups of two or three to do the job analysis. They play off each other and draw out details that might have gone unspoken had they not been recognized by the other high performers in the room. The facilitators—and participants—use sticky notes to build and iterate the in-progress map (Figure 5.1).

Typically, the interviews run three to four hours, Beyond that, fatigue sets in for the participants and the interviewer. Further, that's about as much information as the interviewer can capture, organize, and absorb at one time. After the session, the interviewer needs sufficient time to recharge and to digest, reflect, and perhaps reorganize the information and sticky notes before conducting the next session. The rough map is then presented to the next group of high performers who can change, reorganize, add, and clarify it as they see fit. From one interview session to the next, the job analysis grows until finally the only changes are on the level of tweaks and word choice. Word choice, and especially the choice of verb, is important. The right verbs will capture what these high performers really *do*. So, if the maps are done well, tasks can later be easily converted into course objectives.

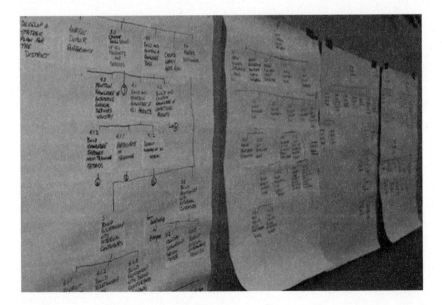

Figure 5.1 Performance Map in Progress

Once the job analysis is stable, it should be validated by two or three people who know the job well and can represent management's perspective. They examine the job analysis to look for omissions, to discuss word choice, and to make sure the organization's goals and values are properly reflected.

QUANTIFYING THE GAP

Once an organization develops a performance map, the next step is to determine the gaps between the high performers and the rest of the people in that job. The foundation of the gap analysis comes from the job analysis part of the map, as it includes the list of tasks or performance items associated with successful performance of the job. These specific activities should be easily recognized by all performers of the job in question—though certainly all performers will not be doing all items on the list, or at least will not be doing them all well.

These performance items are the basis for a survey that is delivered to all occupants of that job position (Figure 5.2). Using a Likert scale, the survey asks two questions about each performance item:

■ How important is this item in the performance of your job?

■ How proficient (competent) are you on this item?

Managers of these performers are also surveyed. They are also asked to rate the importance of each item and to rate the proficiency, per item, of each of their direct reports in this job position.

Needless to say, the survey must be anonymous and confidential. To expect survey takers to give honest answers requires that they are assured that their individual responses will not be reported to the company or used for evaluation purposes. For this reason it's always best to use a third party to conduct the survey and aggregate the data.

1. Identify key decision-makers.					
	Very Low	Low	Average	High	Very High
Importance of Task	○	○	○	○	○
My Proficiency	○	○	○	○	○

Figure 5.2 Sample "Gap Analysis" Survey Question

The data reveal interesting perspectives. If a significant number of performers, say 85 percent, rate a given performance item as important, and if a similar percentage of their managers do the same, then there is concurrence and a pretty strong argument that the item is important. The same goes for items that are rated lower on the importance scale. Even nonconcurrence tells a story. What if managers think something is important but few of their direct reports agree—especially their high performers? What if it's the other way around? That's worth knowing and is a red flag of unclear priorities!

Gaps are identified by looking for those performance items that were rated high in importance but lower in proficiency. For example, if 94 percent of job performers rate "Identify key decision-makers" as high on the importance scale, but only 57 percent rate themselves as high on the proficiency scale, then we have a significant difference between importance and proficiency and thus a performance gap. The really valuable thing about the data, though, is that we can segment the data and divide the performers into high, medium, and low performers using existing company performance data. This cut of the data is highly revealing, for it helps us understand the performance support needs of different audiences within our job position. We can see how high performers rated each item on the importance scale and compare their ratings to those of other performers and of their managers. It's not uncommon to find that high performers see certain activities as important that others don't value as much—even their managers. Sometimes the differentiator in performance is simply a clear understanding of which activities are most important in driving business results. There are many insights to be learned from data as rich as this.

ALIGNING AND PRIORITIZING THE CURRICULUM

Once the performance gaps are identified and quantified, we have a clearer picture of our support needs. If we've segmented our audience into high, medium, and low performers, we have the further luxury of knowing the needs specific to each of these audiences. We are light-years ahead of where we were, but we are not yet ready to design our performance support interventions.

Identifying the performance gaps is not the same as knowing the cause of the gaps. Some gaps will be obvious, for sure, and can be discussed and analyzed by learning and HR personnel and the managers who oversee the job position in question. Some gap causes will have surfaced in the interviews with high performers whose expertise went into making the performance maps. Other gaps may require further investigation to gain understanding of the root cause.

When the gaps and their causes are understood, various stakeholders in the organization, including the learning function, can begin crafting performance support interventions. Curriculum changes will almost always be part of the response. There will be low-hanging fruit—gaps that can easily be addressed by minor changes here or there—retooling, revamping, and repurposing existing material. But sometimes the curriculum is ready for a major refresh or even an overhaul, and the results from the performance gap survey, and the insight into the job that the performance map provides, are extremely valuable in this task.

Whether a major curriculum overhaul is needed or not, the performance map creates a natural structure for the curriculum. Certain performance items will fit together naturally and create a flow to the curriculum. Some items will clearly be for foundational courses whereas others are for more advanced courses. Some items will clearly be knowledge items and can be delivered in web training or self-study. Others will be skills that need to be taught, practiced, and observed. Curriculum designers will see the natural fit and flow as they digest the performance maps and become acquainted with the prioritized performance gaps. Additionally, the performance items themselves frequently translate into both learning objectives and assessment items in the courses in the new curriculum.

BEYOND CURRICULA

Together, the performance map and the gap analysis results provide a multiyear road map for a curriculum plan, but their power goes beyond that, providing tremendous insights for learning and HR decision makers alike. HR can leverage the performance map information to build performance-based job descriptions, to refine or revise recruiting and selection criteria, to create more effective onboarding strategies, and even to reengineer the job functions themselves. Perhaps, though, one of the most powerful noncurricula outcomes of mapping is informing organizational leadership and HR of performance issues that go beyond the responsibility of the learning function. Specifically, the map can highlight specific ways in which performance in the critical job position is both hindered and supported by management decisions about such things as pay plans, technology investment, and communication processes, to name only a few.

One such mapping process uncovered issues with a well-intended corporate communications process, where frequent inaccuracies in communications caused repetitive stops and starts and rework by employees. Upon discovering this and recognizing all the wasted time and effort (not to mention degradation in morale), the organization took corrective action to ensure that directives were finalized before issuing communications about them. With another organization, the interviews and survey results informed decision makers of how much time their district sales managers were spending searching for data to put together reports. Learning and HR executives immediately shared this information with senior leadership, who took steps to fully endorse an information technology (IT) project to create standardized reporting tools for sales staff. If the people charged with driving business results are ill-equipped as in the case of these district sales managers, the organization's decision makers should know it. After all, it's about enabling people, including high performers, to excel. The learning department can provide a great service to the organization by building performance maps for key job positions. After all, who else in the organization has a method and the skills to uncover these support needs and performance blocks?

SUMMARY

For a training curriculum to drive business results, it must be aligned with the tasks that contribute to those results. Performance mapping provides a proven way to systematically align curricula to organizational goals. Through gap analysis, it is possible to identify, quantify, and prioritize performance gaps. These tools can provide the basis for a long-term, performance-based curriculum that targets the most pressing learning and performance needs of the organization.

Performance Analytics for an Aligned Curriculum: VW Credit, Inc.

BACKGROUND

Volkswagen Group is the number-two automobile company in the world, surpassed only by Toyota. In the hypercompetitive automotive industry, Volkswagen Group is focused on 2018, its target year to become the global economic and environmental leader among automobile manufacturers. The 2018 goals include the following:

- Be the world leader in customer satisfaction and quality.
- Increase unit sales to more than 10 million vehicles a year.
- Increase return on sales before tax to at least 8 percent.
- Become the top employer across all brands, companies, and regions.

VW Credit, Inc. (VCI) is the captive finance company to Volkswagen Group of America (VWGoA) and plays an important role in VW's success. VCI serves two important customer bases: buyers and lessees of VW, Audi, Bentley, Lamborghini, and Bugatti products and a 990-dealer network in the US.

VCI recognizes that the quality and commitment of its people are crucial to achieve the 2018 goals. VCI Academy is the company's internal training organization, providing learning and professional development to employees across the company, from credit analysts and collection agents to the business development staff that calls on dealerships to ensure that dealers give their financing business to VCI.

The Academy knows that time in training is time away from the job. Therefore, the Academy wanted to be sure that its offerings addressed real performance gaps. As the senior manager and head of training of VCI Academy, Paige Barrie wanted to define and quantify those performance gaps for one of VCI's most important audiences: the business development managers (BDMs). BDMs are salespeople who compete with banks and other financial institutions to earn the dealers' financing business, which ranges from consumer car loans and leases to dealership construction loans and financing for vehicle and parts inventories. With a nationwide head count of 40 people in the role, BDMs represent VCI's largest presence in the field.

The time BDMs spend with the dealers is critical to their success, so time spent in training needed to be fiercely justified as improving a known performance gap. VCI Academy had an existing certification program in place for BDMs. Prior to taking over leadership of VCI Academy, Barrie had worked closely with the BDMs in another role, giving her a unique appreciation for their position. "Having been with them for a couple of years, I wasn't convinced myself that the things we were training them on were necessarily the things they really needed," Barrie said. "We would ask managers what they thought we should train the BDMs on each year and would get a lot of opinions, so the certification program was rather piecemeal." Barrie wanted to get to the root of what BDMs needed to best do their jobs.

THE APPROACH

VCI Academy recognized that there were many ways to go about a needs assessment. They also knew they had a handful of high performers who could serve as role models for others. "I wanted to objectively determine what behaviors made high performers so good and identify the skill gaps between those performers and the rest,"

Barrie said. To ensure an impartial, third-party view of performance gaps, VCI Academy partnered with Capital Analytics (now Vestrics) to:

- Identify what behaviors made the high performers so effective through performance mapping.
- Identify the skill gaps between the best and the rest through a quantitative gap analysis.

With this information in hand, the Academy could determine how to improve the performance of the rest of the BDMs. "I knew we had a strong base of some solid performers that we could draw from," Barrie said. The first order of business was defining *high performer* using internal performance criteria, largely based on the company's key performance indicators (KPIs). Of the top 10 performers overall, not every high performer was in the top 10 every quarter. However, the 10 BDMs chosen to represent the high performers were consistently in the top 15 from quarter to quarter.

"One thing we discovered when we used the KPIs as the indicator is that it didn't necessarily agree with who the managers thought were high performers," Barrie said. Overall the high performers were eager to help with the project, and some were pleasantly surprised to be chosen at all. "This wasn't based on your relationship with your manager," Barrie said. "It was clearly based on your results, because we want results from our people." The high-performing BDMs' commitment to the project ended up being a key finding: that top performers have a certain personality type. Barrie noted that the top performers were "more sales-oriented. They were more relationship-oriented, people-oriented than numbers-oriented." In a financial services company that is very numbers-focused, this finding has changed the way BDMs are recruited.

BUILDING THE MAP

Starting with a simple "performance statement" or "definition of success," the performance map took form as each group of BDMs, through focused and facilitated discussion, shared the key tasks and behaviors that helped them achieve their KPIs. Using an iterative process, each group built out sections of the map and refined sections that those

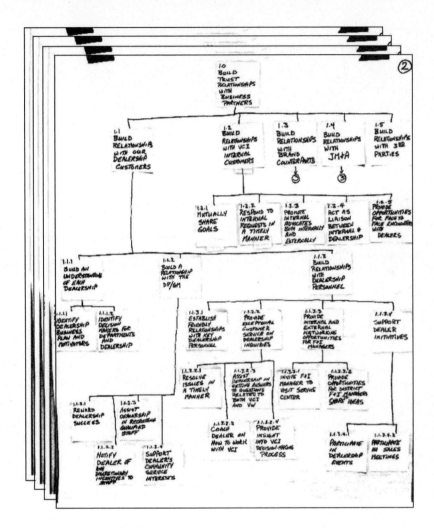

Figure 5.A   Building the Map

before them in the process had built. Barrie likened this approach to tapping the "wisdom of the crowd" (Figure 5.A).

With all the tasks documented, the team began uncovering further details that would later guide instructional designers. This included inputs and outputs as well as tools, reports, and systems that BDMs used, or even created on their own, to get the job done. The interviewers also captured best practices and special situations. Finally, BDMs were asked to estimate the frequency with which they did a task. Was it daily, weekly, monthly, quarterly, or yearly? Barrie knew that something done once a year may be better relegated to a job aid versus training. BDMs also estimated how difficult each task was to learn, how important it was, and what would be the risk if they did not do it or did it poorly. With this picture of what high performers actually do, the Academy was ready to discover what the rest of the BDMs were up to through a Gap Assessment survey.

COMMUNICATING THE GAP ASSESSMENT SURVEY

The Academy and Capital Analytics designed the Gap Assessment survey based on the tasks in the performance map. The survey went out to all BDMs (including those interviewed) and their managers. To encourage honest participation, Barrie engaged the vice president of sales and marketing to announce the survey to the BDMs and their managers. His message reiterated that the survey was all about improving the quality of the Academy and its offerings and not about anyone's individual performance. The announcement noted that the survey would be administered by a third party to maintain confidentiality, and that all results would be presented only in aggregate. BDMs were asked to rate each item for its importance to their job and their proficiency at it. Managers also rated each item for importance, and then rated each of their BDMs for their individual proficiency.

"I'm sure the initial response was a huge groan," Barrie said with a laugh. "It was 62 questions and we didn't give them a lot of time." Barrie said that her team's communication about the survey resulted in a key lesson learned. "Quite honestly, I think that I should've done a better job up front explaining to people what the project was and why we were doing it. There were a lot who didn't have a clue what we were up to." She received a number of e-mails from participants saying that the survey was really interesting and asking to see the results. Some even asked where the questions came from. The BDMs wanted to know: "How did you get this so right?" At that point, Barrie shared the performance map and the process of creating it. "If I could give a tip to someone [doing a similar project], it would be to be more transparent," Barrie said.

QUANTIFYING THE GAPS

The Academy was particularly interested in gaps where both the BDM and the manager agreed there was room for improvement. In the survey, the BDMs rated each item regarding how important it was to successfully fulfilling their job responsibilities, as well as their proficiency at the particular task. The Capital Analytics team aggregated the data and identified gaps based on the differences between those two ratings. Managers also rated the importance of each item and the proficiency of their direct reports, and this aggregate data underwent a similar analysis.

The analysis of results segmented each of the survey items/tasks into one of four categories:

1. Manager and BDM concur there is a gap.
2. Manager sees a gap; BDM does not.
3. BDM sees a gap; manager does not.
4. Neither manager nor BDM sees a gap.

Results were further segmented by high, medium, and low performers based on the internal performance criteria. An immediate finding was that low performers greatly differed from the others in terms of what they thought was important. The Academy recognized that prioritization of tasks was something that should be addressed in initial BDM training. In all, the gap analysis identified eight major categories of opportunities. With the details behind each opportunity, as well as the magnitude of the gap, the Academy could set about prioritizing refinements to the BDM curriculum.

MAKING CHANGES

At the completion of the gap analysis, Barrie focused on her original goal for the project: to improve the BDM curriculum. "We focused on the areas where we saw big skill gaps," Barrie said. "We developed some curriculum to address those, and we're continuing with that curriculum [in subsequent years]." In the past, the curriculum would change from year to year, requiring BDMs to go through the certification process over and over. The new program has offered a more comprehensive training package to help keep BDMs productive in the field.

Performance analyses like this one often provide data to confirm or refute instincts about a particular problem. At VCI, there was a general feeling that BDMs needed an in-depth understanding of the inner workings of dealerships, including how to read and analyze a dealer financial statement. Drawing on her experience working with the BDMs, Barrie felt that five days of training on how to read and analyze financial statements was too much. "In the end, that's not what the high performers told us [they needed]," Barrie said. "The high performers placed greater value on being able to read and interpret [financial statements] than on being able to do deep analysis." As a result of this finding, the training's focus shifted away from in-depth analysis of financial statements to giving BDMs a higher-level familiarity. The new course, called "Through a Dealer's Eyes," teaches BDMs to see a financial statement from the dealer's point of view. Barrie said it's one of the most highly rated classes offered by the Academy.

Once the new curriculum was in place, the BDMs' managers told Barrie, "You're doing the right thing, hitting the right gaps. This is what our people need to know." Barrie said it's the first time in the history of BDM training that management has felt BDMs are getting the training they need to do their jobs well. Once the BDMs are certified, they complete two elective courses each year to keep their certifications current. The result has been a huge cost savings for VCI, not only in terms of not needing to develop new courses each year, but also in keeping the BDMs working in the field instead of in training.

BEYOND TRAINING

Barrie said that the director of human resources (HR), David Bruce, was perhaps even more excited about this project than she was. In fact, while Barrie's overriding goal as the head of training was to improve the BDM curriculum, Bruce saw potential for changes reaching well beyond what training had to offer. The gap assessment survey questions addressed other factors impacting BDMs' performance. For example, one question was: "If we could provide you with one thing that would help you do your job better, what would it be?" Such questions uncovered other areas that needed improvement. These included new reports and tools to help the BDMs save time, working with management to revisit the KPIs, and even a revised program for dealers. Another finding was just how crucial it is for BDMs to have good relationships with their colleagues in other areas of the company. "[BDMs] depend a lot on other people in other areas to help get their jobs done," Barrie said. "The high performers knew people. They had met the people they depended on. So we made that a priority for others as well."

The findings have helped VCI to rewrite job descriptions, change the way they select talent, and create career plans for people who want to move into the BDM role. "Our hope is that what we learned here and how we use it will improve the quality of our hires and improve the retention of talent in this role, as well as the performance of people in this role," Barrie said. "I started out to do one thing and we quickly realized it was so much more. We're already seeing results from that." Bruce, the HR director, shared the project with the executive vice president for VW Group of America, and from there the results spread to the VWGoA's president and CEO. "It just escalated because of his excitement over what it could do from an HR standpoint," Barrie said. As VCI learned, aligning performance with the business improves training and goes far beyond to touch nearly every aspect of a job role.

CHAPTER **6**

Measurement
Alignment

*The greatest value of a picture is when it forces
us to notice what we never expected to see.*

—John Tukey, American mathematician

The leadership development initiative of a global consumer products company was under scrutiny at budget time. The CFO
wanted to know if it was working, and wanted proof beyond surveys from the learning department. With the initiative's goal of "Live
the Vision," the learning department struggled to find any evidence
beyond anecdotal feedback. No one had ever explicitly defined what
"living the vision" would look like in quantifiable, measurable terms.
It felt like leadership development was too squishy to try to quantify.
But was it? This chapter introduces the Measurement Map, a tool for
aligning an initiative to business outcomes using quantifiable measures. We contend that yes, you can measure the squishy stuff.

In the preceding chapter, we talked about curriculum alignment,
where a thorough task analysis could be used to identify the behaviors
of high-performers as they deliver on business goals. In this chapter,
we take alignment to the initiative level, such as a program, course,
or series of courses, to operationalize success so you can quantify and
measure its impact on business outcomes.

ALIGNMENT WANTED

What the consumer products CFO was looking for was a link between the leadership development initiative and its impact in terms of an improvement in business performance. While aligning people strategies with business strategies has become the stated goal of nearly every human resources (HR) and learning practitioner, surveys from the American Society for Training and Development (ASTD), the Conference Board, and others point to the sorry state of actually delivering on that goal. Despite good intentions, the line of sight between investments in people and real business outcomes remains disjointed, which makes it difficult to illustrate the value of those investments.

Organizations intentionally invest in their workforces to build capacity—to become more efficient, to innovate, to grow, and to build a sustainable competitive advantage. For any human capital investment to impact the business, *how* it is expected to contribute needs to be explicitly articulated. Consultants and business leaders are all talking about alignment, but to get beyond the talk and start acting on it, learning leaders need to build the acumen to define the logical relationships between investments in people and the goals of the business. We have found that something called a Measurement Map™ goes a long way in demonstrating that causal chain of evidence. We have also found that building such maps, while challenging at first, is a skill that most learning and development (L&D) people can develop with a little practice. To understand the power of the Measurement Map, we will first explain the details of such a map. We will then explore how to build one, and discuss how the Measurement Map can be leveraged to identify the specific data you need to actually measure impact.

MAPS—AN OLD IDEA, A NEW APPLICATION

The idea of mapping out directions, flows, and relationships is not new. From the earliest Babylonian cartography to Google Maps, travelers have recognized the value of maps in aiding them in getting from point A to point B. A map communicates a lot of complex information in a single image, an image that is understood by all who see it.

Flowcharts are much the same. They clarify complex ideas by deconstructing them into a series of connected shapes. Flowcharts and process maps commonly grace corporate bulletin boards, PowerPoint presentations, and project work plans. Why? Because they communicate complex information in way that is easily understood.

A Measurement Map and a bit of business logic can do this same thing for human capital investments. Imagine all stakeholders agreeing on a picture that shows precisely how leadership development should impact the bottom line. In this scenario, learning practitioners would know how their initiative fits into and supports the organization's strategy. They would also know what to measure.

WHAT IS A MEASUREMENT MAP?

A Measurement Map brings together the concepts of the cartographer's map, the boardroom's flowchart, and the business's need for alignment. Ultimately, it depicts the logical relationships between the people strategies and the business strategies. It communicates in a common language that all stakeholders can understand. And it typically fits on one sheet of paper.

It's important that the links that create this causal chain of evidence are measurable, especially if you want to analyze the impact of an investment. To build this chain, the Measurement Map has four logically connected sections, as shown in Figure 6.1.

In the context of the Measurement Map, we adopt these definitions:

- *Investments in people*. This is the intervention or series of interventions intended to drive the business results. It can be any type of investment in human capital—a training event, a recognition program, a new performance management process, and so on.

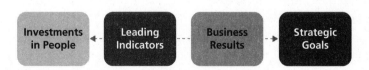

Figure 6.1 Creating a Causal Chain of Evidence.

- *Leading indicators.* Leading indicators are nonfinancial measures that suggest whether you are on the right track. Typically, they appear earlier in the causal chain and provide early evidence of quantifiable business results to come. Common examples include employee engagement scores, performance reviews, number of complaints, number of new accounts opened, promotion rates, and even Level 1 and Level 2 results.

- *Business results.* Often referred to as key performance indicators (KPIs), business impact measures are tied to a financial value. They either are expressed in dollars and cents or can be translated into financial terms. Common examples include turnover rates, customer loyalty, sales volume, revenue per full-time employee, productivity, workers' compensation costs, and cost avoidance.

- *Strategic goals.* These are the desired ultimate end results of the initiative. For most organizations, they boil down to improving financial performance—by increasing revenue, decreasing costs, or both.

Frequently both the investment and the strategic goal are known, but the links between them have not been clearly defined. Sometimes the end goal is known, but the investment is yet to be determined. In this case, the Measurement Map can help shape the nature and content of the intervention by identifying the KPIs that the organization wants to affect. Knowing this is of tremendous help to learning and development staff who are designing performance objectives for a potential intervention.

WHAT DOES A MEASUREMENT MAP LOOK LIKE?

So what does such a map look like? Let's start with the straightforward example in Figure 6.2. This sales training example illustrates how a Measurement Map can deconstruct an initiative into a logical model, showing the expected (and measurable) behaviors that lead to the strategic goal. Just like a road map or a flowchart, a Measurement Map can be read from either end—from the point of origin (investments) to the destination (strategic goals) or vice versa. For this example, we start from the destination, the goal of increasing revenue.

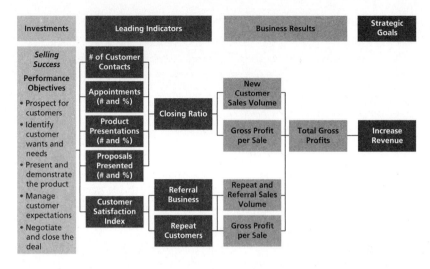

Figure 6.2 Sales Training Measurement Map

Imagine that a sales department wanted to improve bottom-line results by improving the selling skills of its sales force. Before building a sales training course, the learning and development team asked the sales department how they measured success. The answer, and the strategic goal, was "increase revenue." The L&D team probed further, asking what elements of that goal were the responsibilities of the sales force. Now the sales team started getting more detailed, noting that sales volume and of course the gross profit on each sale were critical. They further differentiated that they had different quotas and processes for new versus repeat and referral customers. The L&D team continued digging, asking what evidence there might be that a salesperson was making good progress toward the goal. After identifying the closing ratio, the question was: "How would you know if you might be on track to improve your closing ratio?" In this case, contacts, appointments, presentations, and proposals were all leading indicators for closing ratio.

Notice that there are multiple layers of leading indicators and business results. The leading indicators provide quantifiable evidence of progress toward the goal, but are not financial measures. Sales volume and gross profits are readily identifiable in financial terms. They are all arranged to show the logical links between the performance objectives of the sales training program and the strategic goal of increasing revenue. Now L&D knows what a new sales training program should deliver—and how its success will be evaluated by its stakeholder and sponsor, the sales department. Importantly, the sales department was involved in creating the Measurement Map and defining success—generating buy-in to the causal model.

Let's take another look at the Measurement Map, this time reading it from right to left. For this example, we revisit that squishy thing called leadership development. It is true that these types of initiatives are more difficult to measure than sales training. Simply said, the objectives typically defy what we think of as measurable: develop leadership capabilities, improve company culture, "live the vision," and so on. Yet businesses are investing millions of dollars in leadership. Surely they are hoping for some return! This is where the savvy learning or HR leader can guide stakeholders in connecting the dots by co-creating a Measurement Map with business stakeholders to show those linkages.

Figure 6.3 depicts the causal chain of evidence between a leadership initiative called "Developing People and Teams" and the strategic goal of "improve financial performance." Chances are the vice

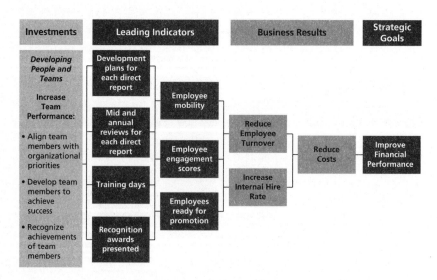

Figure 6.3 Leadership Development Measurement Map

president of operations and the directors of HR and learning agree on these two end points. But how do the two points connect? How can progress be measured? How can the VP and directors determine whether leadership development is having an impact on the business?

Following the Leadership Development Measurement Map, the logic goes like this: If the program objectives are met and the leader implements the lessons learned, it should be evidenced in the leader's behavior. All of her direct reports should have development plans on file. (Often, "quality of plan" is also considered.) The leader should be conducting midyear and annual reviews (also on file). She should be encouraging staff to participate in skill-building training, and she should be taking advantage of the company's recognition program. Data most likely exist for all of these indicators.

If those leading indicators show positive results, it follows that employees (leaders and associates) will have promotional and cross-functional opportunities, engagement scores will rise, and the pipeline of next-generation leaders will begin to fill. Again, many organizations have this data in some fashion.

All of these indicators lead to the business results, where outcomes can be quantified in dollars and cents. Reducing turnover cuts down on expensive turnover costs. Increasing internal hire rates reduces recruiting and onboarding expenses. Both lead to reduced costs, which translate to improved financial performance.

Notice that the Measurement Map starts with leading indicators—things that are quantifiable and are on the path to the ultimate goal. With long-term initiatives like leadership development, agreeing up front on leading indicators can help sustain a program across fiscal years. If those leading indicators show positive results, it logically holds that the business results will follow, and that progress is being made.

These simple examples illustrate how a Measurement Map guides the deconstruction of the strategy down to the observable, on-the-job behaviors that the organization desires. Whether you start with the goal and work toward designing an initiative to achieve it, or start with the investments and work the other way, the Measurement Map provides the logical framework to align your people strategies with your business strategies.

BUILDING A MEASUREMENT MAP

Building a Measurement Map is a cross-functional, creative group effort. The simple act of bringing the various stakeholders together to talk about the expected outcomes of a people initiative creates a powerful message of commitment—both of HR and learning and of the business operations people. After all, the business units are pulling their people off regular work to participate in the sales training or leadership development initiative. Management surely has expectations of a performance change as a result. As described previously in the sales training initiative, the act of co-creating a Measurement Map turns those expectations into explicitly stated leading indicators and business results, and importantly, agreed upon measures of success.

Facilitating a measurement mapping discussion takes some good planning and collaborative brainstorming. A series of open-ended questions can get everyone thinking about what they really expect the targeted initiative to do. The direction of questioning truly depends on whether you are looking to align and measure an existing intervention or if you are trying to deconstruct a performance goal down to its performance objectives. Remember, this is a *Measurement Map*, not a *process map*. You are looking for evidence—things you can see and count. Don't worry yet about whether the data exists. Most likely, some of it will and some of it won't, and that's okay—you're brainstorming. Here are thought-starter questions for each approach.

Align and Measure an Existing Intervention

- What business goal is this intervention intended to impact?
- How do we measure that?
- What are the performance objectives of this intervention?
- What should people be able to do as a result of participating in this program?
- What would be the evidence of that?
- How do we measure that?

Align, Define, and Measure a New Intervention

- What business issue are we trying to address?
- What kind of change do we want to see?
- How do we measure that change?
- What part of that goal is the responsibility of our target audience?
- What does an employee have to do to do that?
- How would you know if employees are doing that?
- What would be the evidence of that?
- How do we measure that?

A proven approach to building a map includes starting by capturing all the brainstormed responses on a flip chart or whiteboard. Encourage participants to think beyond what they measure or formally track today. Keep the group focused on things that are observable and can be counted. Then review your list, getting clarification on items, consolidating others, and eliminating some as needed. Have participants put the remaining items on sticky notes. Now, build your chain of evidence right on the wall. Allow stakeholders to move the notes around and refine the language. When complete, ask for volunteers to tell the story—from right to left and from left to right. The group will quickly determine if the logic holds or if there are gaps, and will guide refinements. Your end product is a collaboratively built Measurement Map.

It is no surprise that conducting a measurement mapping session gives you far more than just a map. Business, HR, and learning stakeholders may, for the first time, be truly working collaboratively toward a clearly articulated common goal. Once the initiative is launched, program participants will sense the unified front and know that the business supports the initiative and has expectations of them upon their return. In fact, some clients include measurement maps right in their courses to highlight for students the connection between their training and the business. This cross-functional mapping also shows other departments that HR and learning have a willingness and a process to work with the business leaders to understand, align, and contribute to the organization's success in a measurable way.

DEFINING THE DATA

The benefits of a Measurement Map don't end here. If you intend to measure business impact, you will need business data. And that data is defined—and agreed upon by your business stakeholders—in the Measurement Map. Because each element of the map is measurable (something you can count), you now have an inventory of desired data elements. Consider each element, from leading indicators like number of appointments to business results like sales volume. Determine if and how each is tracked and what system does the tracking. If an element is tracked manually, is it worth converting it to an electronic format? If it isn't tracked at all, should it be, and would it be worth it to do so?

Once you've identified what data may be available, you can get a sense of how your measurement plan can unfold. Experience has taught us to verify the credibility of the data before we get too excited and start requesting file extracts. A manufacturing organization wanted to include results from an implementation survey to gauge how supervisory training contributed to the adoption of a new process across plants. Upon closer investigation, the organization discovered that a different version of the survey was used at each facility and that the survey was viewed as a joke by most respondents. Clearly, you wouldn't want to waste your time on that data. Another example of data with a credibility issue comes from a utility company that identified "reduction in overtime" as a measure of better leadership. After consulting an HR analyst, the company discovered that its system didn't differentiate between regular overtime and overtime due to power outages caused by severe weather and other external events. If overtime decreased, could you legitimately claim that leader training played a role—or were there simply fewer bad storms? What if overtime increased? Bad training or bad weather? This is a classic case of intervening factors. While reduction in overtime was a fine metric in the map, the actual data could not provide a credible analysis. It is far better to know the data issues ahead of time. It saved the utility company the time and effort of pulling, organizing, and analyzing all that overtime data to generate meaningless results.

In practice, maps may identify dozens of metrics. Don't panic if you don't have usable, credible data on all of them. What's important is having enough metrics to present a credible trail of evidence. Many solid and credible impact studies have been done with only two or three good metrics.

SUMMARY

Every map will be different, from investment to investment and from organization to organization. And your mapping skills will get refined over time. The bottom line is to create a map that represents the expected and agreed-upon observable, measurable outcomes of the investments. By defining the alignment between the people investments and the business goals, you will know what to measure, and your stakeholders will know what to expect. Now the measurable outcomes become everyone's business.

Here are five key things to remember when you set out on your journey to create a Measurement Map:

1. *Involve the right people.* Part of aligning with the business means including the business operations people in these discussions. After all, they are the ones with the expectations of what employees will do as a result of your intervention. They will also have access to the business data you'll need for your impact analysis.

2. *Agree on the strategic goal.* The idea behind alignment implies that you have an explicit end point—the strategic goal. If you don't know where you want to go, a map won't help.

3. *Make all KPIs quantifiable.* This may not seem possible at first, but to measure it, you've got to be able to count it. Ask: "What is the evidence of that?" and push to make it quantitative. Dashboards from the functional business units offer a great source of what is already being measured, making your data collection that much easier.

4. *Treat it as an art, not a science.* No two maps will look alike. Remember, the point is to illustrate alignment, create a common

language around what to measure, and build a credible map. If it achieves that, it's good map!

5. *Enjoy the process.* Having an explicit and overt conversation about how your investments in people specifically align with the organization's strategies can be eye-opening for everyone. Not only are you building a map, but you are also building credible relationships with your key stakeholders.

Showing Learning's Alignment with the Business: VW Credit, Inc.

A new employee at VW Credit, Inc.'s (VCI's) new hire orientation asked, "How will you know if your training works?" Paige Barrie, the senior manager of VCI Academy, had the answer.

BACKGROUND

As the captive finance company to Volkswagen Group of America (VWGoA), VW Credit, Inc. (VCI) serves two important customer bases: buyers and lessees VW, Audi, Bentley, Lamborghini, and Bugatti products and a 990-dealer network in the US. In addition to providing training for dealership personnel, VCI Academy provides learning and professional development to employees across the company, from credit analysts and collection agents to the business development staff that calls on dealerships.

When she became the leader of VCI Academy, Barrie had a background in performance improvement. The Academy's diverse team responsible for developing and delivering training included many individuals who had little or no background in instructional design. For Barrie, everything the Academy delivered needed to improve performance in some observable way. "Training for training's sake is a waste of time and money," Barrie said. "We had too many people saying, 'Let's write a course and create some objectives and then let's cross our fingers.'" Barrie also saw a recurring problem between her team of designers and the managers asking for training. Stakeholders would say, "I'm not really sure what I want, but I'll know it when I see it." Keeping in mind the Academy motto of "Think, Learn, Achieve," she wanted her team to learn how to communicate clearly with stakeholders and design training geared toward an end business result.

THE APPROACH

Measurement Maps provide a proven way to show alignment between learning objectives and business goals. Barrie knew this was a tool that would help her team focus on outcomes and communicate to executives the logical connection between training and VCI's key performance indicators (KPIs). Alignment would not be a one-time thing at VCI Academy, done only on high-visibility courses. Barrie wanted to instill this process in her team so that every course would have a Measurement Map, developed as part of the initial design.

Barrie's goal for her team members was to change the way they consulted with managers asking for training courses. She asked Capital Analytics to conduct a workshop showing the team how to link training to business results. "[My team learned] that by starting with the business result you want to achieve, instead of the objectives of the training, you start with the end goal," Barrie said. The team started with the fundamentals of business impact measurement and key performance indicators, from leading indicators to business results. Importantly, they started expanding their thinking from learning objectives to actual on-the-job outcomes in observable, measurable terms and how these connected to VCI's business goals of increased revenue and improved financial performance.

Following the workshop, VCI added a measurement discussion to the start of every new project. Key questions to ask before designing any course included:

- What is the business result you're aiming for?
- How will you know when you've reached that goal?
- What will achieving the goal look like?
- What do people need to be able to do in order to achieve that goal?
- What do people need to learn (that they don't already know) in order to be able to achieve the goal?

This process of working backward from the end result to the learning needs gave the team the material they needed to write learning objectives. The workshop also included instruction in writing action-oriented and achievable learning objectives for courses.

BUILDING THE MAP

To learn how to build a Measurement Map from scratch, the team came to the workshop with a particular initiative in mind: a new course they were going to develop for collection agents. The team started by discussing VCI's business goals and the role of the collection agent in supporting those goals. The flip charts filled as the team brainstormed what success would look like for VCI, identifying KPIs such as increased collections and lower borrowing costs. The discussion then examined how you would know if an agent was contributing to those end goals. Here, leading indicators included number of contacts made and the percentage of payment arrangements made with delinquent customers. The team then put all the brainstormed KPIs on sticky notes and began to sequence them on the wall. Much debate ensued as the team deliberated about the causal chain of evidence that they were creating. Once the linkages were agreed to, team members took turns telling the story of causal alignment from strategic goals down to the learning objectives, and from the objectives up to the goals. The team members refined the Measurement Map as they became comfortable with how their training truly would contribute to VCI's business goals.

When asked to reflect on the workshop, Barrie said, "I was thrilled, and for my team it was a real aha moment." She's been particularly delighted by one team member who had struggled with course design. After the workshop, Barrie saw a significant improvement in his performance. "He just got it," she said. "He adopted that process and it just changed the way he did his job." Barrie created a Course Commitment form for her team members to use when they meet with a stakeholder. The form helps them gather the necessary information to create a Measurement Map and write course objectives, including:

- The desired business result(s)
- The indicators of success
- The skills or tasks learners need to be able to do
- How the manager will know the learner can do it

When Barrie reviews course objectives, she is able to tell if the designer has completed the Course Commitment form. "Sometimes I see the objectives and say, 'Hmm, where's your Commitment form?'" Barrie said. The inevitable response: "I didn't do one." In that case, she sends the designer back to the stakeholder. "That doesn't happen very often anymore," Barrie said. "When it does and they come back to me with that form, they say, 'That's so much easier when you do it that way,' or 'Wow, it just helps me focus so much better.'" Barrie has even used a similar process with vendors of off-the-shelf courses, questioning how courses will achieve their stated objectives. As a result, she's had vendors customize off-the-shelf courseware to VCI's needs or even change their course objectives.

At the end of the Measurement Map workshop, the team realized that their anticipated one day of collections training would be insufficient. The skills they outlined as necessary to deliver on the business goals would require more than a day of training to attain. The team went back to their stakeholders and walked them through the mapping process. "The managers realized that what we thought they wanted and what they actually wanted weren't the same," Barrie said. "So there was real value in sitting down and talking about it with the Commitment form and drawing out the Map. And the managers realized what they were asking for was actually way more than what they needed." The entire process resulted in the managers aligning on the business result they were looking for, as well as better alignment between the trainer, the stakeholder, and the final product. After the workshop, Barrie said everyone was able to speak the same language. One of her designers told her, "This just changes the way I work with managers now. There's no more assuming anything."

Barrie reports to VCI's director of human resources (HR), David Bruce. Bruce was thrilled with the capabilities of the VCI Academy team. "With new tools like Measurement Mapping, Paige and the VCI Academy team have literally transformed how we look at learning and development at our company," Bruce said. "While we used to focus on the types of training we provided and how much of it we did, we now talk in terms of how our programs can improve organizational performance. This is a bold approach to learning and development, but results are what get the attention of our stakeholders."

ALIGNING WITH THE BUSINESS

When Barrie encountered the questioning new hire in orientation, she was making a presentation about VCI's philosophy on training. "I was explaining how we weren't going to do training for training's sake, and if it didn't improve performance we weren't going to do it," Barrie said. "At the end I asked if anybody had questions. I was shocked when a new employee who had been with the company maybe a week said, 'Yes, I have a question. How will you know if your training works?'" After recovering from her initial surprise, Barrie went to the board and drew a Measurement Map (Figure 6.A), explaining how the Academy ensures that training is aligned with business goals. The inquiring employee and the rest of the new hires in the session completely understood the connections on the Measurement Map. They were also impressed with the Academy's outcomes-focused approach to learning. "She said, 'Wow, you really put a lot of thought into this,'" Barrie remembered. "I said, 'Yes, we do.'"

Collection Agents: Sample Measurement Map™

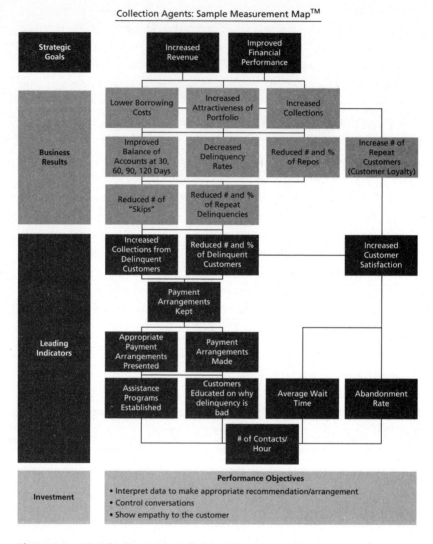

Figure 6.A VCI Collection Agent: Preliminary Measurement Map

VCI Academy has quickly established a high level of credibility with new hires, students, and executives by having a simple, yet powerful, way to demonstrate the logical connections between training and business outcomes. The company averages 23,000 hours of training per year for 1,000 employees, or about three full days of training per person each year. "If they're going to take the time to go to training, they want to know that it's valuable," Barrie said.

CHAPTER **7**

Improving on
the Basics

*You can have data without information, but
you cannot have information without data.*

—Daniel Keys Moran,
American computer programmer and science fiction writer

Companies spend millions of dollars on the launch of new products, from research and development to engineering, production, distribution, and marketing. It is then up to the sales force to sell the new product. It is no wonder that sales training is of great importance to these companies. A lot is riding on the quality of those learning interventions. So when a major U.S. auto company was launching its new and improved SUV, it invested in what the auto industry calls "ride and drive" experiential training. It was a traveling tour going to more than 30 cities over the course of a few months, providing some 8,000 sales consultants with the opportunity to drive the new product head-to-head against the competition on elaborate tracks or courses that simulated various driving conditions.

The learning objectives for the event were clear and the content was aligned, so when posttest results from the first session in the pilot city were less than stellar, a red flag went up. It seemed that sales consultants weren't grasping the SUV's new safety features. The initial thought was that the test's answer grid must be wrong, or maybe the questions were poorly written. Under closer examination, the training team discovered that the physical displays for the safety module—a core hands-on activity—had been incorrectly built, causing consultants to simply skip over key teaching points. Without a good posttest aligned with the learning objectives, the tour could have reached 8,000 consultants but would have failed to deliver the message of a key competitive advantage. On-site organizers redesigned the display overnight and alerted the tour manager of the issue so it could be permanently corrected. Much-improved day two posttest results confirmed that they had addressed the problem.

As evidenced in this story, Level 2 is not just about proving a learning gain. It is also about improving the quality of training. This chapter is all about the basics of learning evaluation—Level 1 and Level 2—and designing and deploying them to yield credible data and actionable insights. If they don't provide that, then why waste the students' time?

THE BASICS

Most learning organizations are collecting some sort of data on the effectiveness of their learning. According to a 2009 study conducted by ASTD Research, 92 percent of learning organizations are doing Level 1 satisfaction surveys while 81 percent are testing knowledge gain to evaluate learning.[1] Two of the reasons for the popularity of these measures are timeliness and ease of collecting data. After all, Levels 1 and 2 are typically within the control of the learning organization: designed, deployed, administered, tracked, and reported by the learning and development (L&D) team. But are these sources of insights and the data they collect really being used to their potential? Our experience says, "Not quite." The ASTD study confirms that, revealing that only 36 percent feel their Level 1 results provide high value and 55 percent feel their Level 2 results do so. While higher levels of evaluation (behavior change, impact, and isolation) may provide more meaningful results to the C-suite, does this mean we should abandon these lower levels? Absolutely not! What's needed are better-quality Level 1 and Level 2 strategies. When the early levels are done poorly, such evaluation becomes a waste of money as well as time and energy for students and the learning team. However, when done well, there can be tremendous value in these simpler levels in terms of helping the learning department improve the quality of its offerings—and the better the offering, the greater the likelihood that it will ultimately impact the business. If the course is poorly designed and students see no value, chances of it moving any needles are slim to none, so jumping right to Level 4 and expecting to see impact would be futile.

Too often, we see course evaluations relegated to the role of so-called "smile sheets," included as an afterthought, hastily designed, and tallied to prove how good the training was. In one incredible scenario, a learning leader, anxious to retain funding for his program, instructed the survey administrator to "pull out the bad ones" before tabulating results. The administrator, knowing the value of student feedback and the use of measurement to continuously improve, was in a bit of a political bind. She suggested to the learning leader that perhaps the survey could be compiled in two ways—one would include all results and be used to evaluate and improve the program. The second, she begrudgingly offered, could be used for his internal marketing purposes. Fortunately, the leader relented and used the results from the full data set, recognizing that publishing two sets of results could expose his manipulation (and likely jeopardize his future budget, if not his career).

While measurement results can certainly be used for marketing, the notion of manipulating the data for desired results takes us back to the measurement strategy and the fundamental question: Why are we measuring? We hope a big part of the answer is to gain insights to improve the quality of your offerings!

Most issues with the basics, though, are not around manipulation of data. Rather, the issues are around the quality of the instruments and the quality of the analysis. Hastily constructed instruments may lead to the "garbage in, garbage out" phenomenon that no amount of analysis can help. There are many resources available to learning professionals looking to develop better instruments. We highlight some of the fundamentals that we have found most useful for practitioners. We then delve into the analysis of Level 1 and Level 2 data—an area rich with potential that, to date, is largely untapped by most learning organizations.

IMPROVING LEVEL 1

Have you noticed how PowerPoint instantly made everyone an expert at creating presentations? Yet we've all sat through hideous PowerPoint presentations with too much text, too many bullets, and dizzying animations. Just having a tool does not make someone an expert at using it. The same goes for developing surveys. Everyone has taken them, so somehow that seems to make everyone proficient at designing them. Wrong! Just as with good presentations, there are guidelines for good surveys that have successfully guided our practice and the gathering of useful and actionable data.

Two key concepts drive the creation of good Level 1 surveys: the content and the design. We refer to content as the "what"—what things should we ask on our survey? Design, then, is the "how"—how should we ask those things? The following guidelines combine the research of Kirkpatrick and Kirkpatrick,[2] Kaufman and Keller,[3] Morrel-Samuels,[4] and Phillips[5] with real learnings from real clients.

Content

There is no single best survey. The point of the survey is to gain actionable insights that can verify and/or improve the quality of your training. Content considerations fall into eight categories. In all cases, be sure that each question can provide data that is actionable. Don't waste the students' time with questions whose results you will never use. (The following guidelines apply to all delivery methods, unless noted.)

1. *Instructor.* If you are conducting live training, you will want to know how students are receiving your instructors. You may want to ask about such things as:
   - Knowledge (are instructors credible?)
   - Level of preparedness (are they familiar with and ready to deliver the content?)
   - Delivery (do they deliver in a way that helps students learn?)

2. *Content.* You will want to know if the content is on target.
   - Relevancy (how relevant is the content to the student's job?)
   - Appropriateness/sufficiency of activities and exercises

3. *Course design*. The content may be great, but is it put together well?

- Logical
- Easy to follow
- Engaging

4. *Job application or impact*. Are students likely to do anything differently back on the job? This kind of question gets you a sneak peak at the likelihood of seeing Level 4 results down the road.

- Applicability (can it be immediately applied back on the job?)
- Impact (do students believe it will make a difference in job performance?)

5. *Recommendation*. Will students encourage others to attend the course or to avoid it?

- Would you recommend the course? (This is akin to Reichheld's "the ultimate question."[6])

6. *Custom questions*. A given course may have some unique elements that you want to ask about. Be sure your survey can accommodate custom questions that:

- Are specific to the course
- Address important and unique elements (i.e., a specific learning activity)

7. *Demographics*. From job position to tenure and ethnicity, we are often inclined to ask for this information so we can examine results from different perspectives. Before you ask, consider these points:

- What will you use it for?
- Can you get it from another source (learning management system [LMS] or HR system)?
- Will it affect responses?

8. *Manager involvement*. We rarely see this on a survey, yet it has been shown to be the most important factor when it comes to learning transfer.[7] Understanding the supervisor's involvement can quickly point out potential challenges students will face

when trying to put new skills to work back on the job. We are gaining tremendous insights by asking about:

- Support before training
- Expected support after training
- Being allowed to attend training without interruption

Design

Nailing down the right—and actionable—questions for your learner reaction survey is critical. So too is having a survey design that works well to gather those actionable insights. Practice and research suggest six key considerations in the design of a survey.

1. *Comparability*. Why does this matter? If you want to do comparisons between courses, conduct any analysis over time, or prepare summary reports across your curricula, you need standardization. Think ahead as to how you will want to compile, analyze, and view this data. Try mocking up your desired reports as part of the design of your survey. This can quickly point out what elements need to be comparable (as well as what data you really need to capture, such as instructor, course code, and date).

   - Develop standard survey sections (i.e., "Instructor," "Content," etc.), *but* use them for reporting purposes only. Do not use section heads in the survey. According to research, respondents tend to automatically respond similarly to items they think are related.[8]
   - Develop standard questions for use across all surveys.
   - Keep sequencing consistent across all surveys.
   - Pay attention to the placement of questions that may vary by delivery method (i.e., instructor-led vs. web-based training [WBT]) so summary reporting makes sense.
   - If you opt for custom questions, try to keep them grouped together so they can be easily separated for summary reporting.

2. *Scale*. We are often asked, "What is the best scale?" In the face of a proliferation of opinion on this, Morrel-Samuels's research published in the *Harvard Business Review* offers some guidelines.[9]

   ■ Use an odd number of responses in the scale (yes, it is possible that people are neutral regarding your training).

   ■ Select the number of response options. While some may argue for five, we recommend seven, and Morrel-Samuels recommends seven or 11. While 11 options may be helpful for customer satisfaction surveys, for training purposes we feel that 11 is simply too many. It looks onerous to the student and implies a degree of precision that likely isn't discernible. So why seven over five? Consider the typical scale of 1 to 5 (e.g., strongly disagree/strongly agree), where 3 is neutral. What does a 4 mean? Is it someone who is just north of neutral, or is it someone who never, ever gives a perfect rating? In other words, is it a 4-minus or a 4-plus? This does matter, as learning leaders could be very happy with an average score of 4. But what if it is really made up of 4-minuses? It may create a false sense of confidence in the quality of the course. The seven-point scale addresses this. Here 4 is neutral, and the 2, 3, 5, and 6 responses offer the needed discrimination. When using a seven-point scale, we recommend reporting a "top box percentage" in addition to simply reporting the average score. This is the percentage of respondents selecting 6 or 7. It captures those folks who never give perfect scores (as well as those who do) and includes them in this summary score. The other advantage of a seven-point scale is simply the greater variance you get from it versus a five-point scale. This wider variance makes is easier to identify changes in a course's performance over time or across instructors or audience demographics.

   ■ Put the small numbers at the left and larger number to the right (see Figure 7.1).

   ■ Include descriptors only at the anchors (e.g., strongly disagree/strongly agree), allowing the student to create the interval labels. Don't try to figure out the nuances between "slightly agree" and "somewhat agree." Use numbers instead. With good anchor words, students can figure out the continuum without further words. Be sure the anchor words are paired to avoid confusion (paired: strongly disagree/strongly agree; not paired: strongly disagree/very effective).

3. *Question design.* Well-constructed survey items make it easier and faster for respondents, plus they yield more reliable and comparable data.

   ▪ Avoid merging two topics into a single question. Instead of "The instructor was enthusiastic and knowledgeable about the content," try "The instructor was knowledgeable about the content."

   ▪ Write items that can be answered using your anchored continuum. This is easier when the item is written as a statement rather than as a question (see Figure 7.1).

   ▪ Design questions so they can use a consistent response scale throughout the survey. In other words, try to avoid shifting from strongly disagree/strongly agree to not effective/very effective. Revise the questions so they use the same response scale.

   ▪ Use open-ended questions only if you plan to use the answers. We love open-ended comments, but recommend a discerning approach to them. Do you have the capacity (time and resources) to process the answers? What will you do with the responses? Is there value in the verbatim comments for your reports? As with all measurement, it's best to know up front why you want the data and what you're going to do with it.

4. *Consistency.* Are respondents racing through the survey without really paying attention, marking 7 on everything just to get out of class? A couple of approaches can verify whether this consistency is intended or is just from racing to be done.

   ▪ Ask a qualitative question in parallel with a quantitative one. You'll be amazed at the simple richness of the qualitative responses (see Figure 7.1).

Scale (small numbers to the left; paired anchors)

The activities helped me understand the content.

| 1 | 2 | 3 | 4 | 5 | 6 | 7 |

Strongly
Disagree

Strongly
Agree

Question Design (statements are better than questions)

How effectively did the facilitator use the materials?

| 1 | 2 | 3 | 4 | 5 | 6 | 7 |

Not
Effectively

Very
Effectively

The facilitator used the materials effectively.

| 1 | 2 | 3 | 4 | 5 | 6 | 7 |

Strongly
Disagree

Strongly
Agree

Consistency (qualitative question helps consistency; adds richness)

In a word, how would you describe this session?

_____

Using a number, how would you describe this session?

| 1 | 2 | 3 | 4 | 5 | 6 | 7 |

No Value

High Value

Learner-Focused (make it about the student)

The instructor was respectful.

| 1 | 2 | 3 | 4 | 5 | 6 | 7 |

Strongly
Disagree

Strongly
Agree

The instructor treated me with respect.

| 1 | 2 | 3 | 4 | 5 | 6 | 7 |

Strongly
Disagree

Strongly
Agree

Survey Length

42. I wish this survey were over.

| 1 | 2 | 3 | 4 | 5 | 6 | 7 |

Strongly
Disagree

Strongly
Agree

Figure 7.1 Survey Design

- Change the wording in a couple of questions so that the desired answer is negative. Suddenly, the person giving all 7's has been busted. Be careful, though, as these questions are more difficult to automatically score and report.

- Keep all items of similar length or word count.

5. *Learner-focused.* Think of the learner with each question, and word it so it is about his or her experience. This tends to yield more honest responses.

   - Focus questions on the respondent (see Figure 7.1).

   - Don't bother with questions about the facility or food. The instructor can give you that feedback. You really aren't asking for students to tell you, one more time, that they would rather have steak than chicken.

   - Include open-ended questions only if you are going to use them (see item 3, question design). It is time-consuming for the students, and it sets an expectation that you will do something with their feedback.

6. *Survey length.* We are all familiar with survey fatigue. As a survey drags on, the thoughtfulness of the responses, and hence the quality of the data, tends to diminish.

   - Be very aware of any survey going over 20 questions (see Figure 7.1).

   - How many courses might a student take over the course of a year? Does each have a survey? In some sales training environments, we've seen as many as 20 short courses that all must be completed in 30 days. That's a lot of surveys! Remember the user when designing and requiring surveys.

IMPROVING LEVEL 2

One of the biggest problems with Level 2, or testing of knowledge or learning gain, is the poor quality of the tests themselves. How often do we find ourselves ready to launch a course, but suddenly scampering to come up with a posttest? Too often. And this generally leads to poorly constructed tests. Done well, tests can reinforce learning for the student, and give insights into the effectiveness of content and delivery to the instructional designer. Before rushing to put together your next test, think about three things:

1. Are the course objectives written as performance-based learning objectives?
2. Is the test aligned with the learning objectives?
3. Does the test follow the basic guidelines for good test writing?

The next sections address each of these at a high level. For the deep dive, Dr. Sharon Shrock and Dr. Bill Coscarelli are the authorities on creating great tests. Their book *Criterion-Referenced Test Development: Technical and Legal Guidelines for Corporate Training* is a must-have for anyone serious about test development for learning.[10]

Performance-Based Learning Objectives

Many learning objectives call for the recall of facts (e.g., "List the five advantages of our product over the competition") or for a vague sense of knowledge (e.g., "Understand how a consumer appreciates our advantages"). Learning guru Robert Mager[11] insisted that effective learning requires objectives that specify what the learner should be *able to do* (in observable terms) as a result of the training. This leads us to performance-based learning objectives. Throughout this book, we beat the drum for alignment. We'll beat it again here. Remember the Measurement Map? At one end are strategic goals; at the other are the performance-based learning objectives. Good objectives are derived from what the business needs its performers to do. Good training will fulfill those objectives and will be clearly aligned with the strategic goals.

There is a science to writing this kind of objective. Mastering it takes a bit of discipline, but the rewards are great:

- Clear definition for the designer and the student regarding the intended outcomes of the course
- Specificity regarding what mastery looks like (and hence what a test should include)
- Measurement criteria for performance back on the job

The science includes two main elements: the structure of the objective and the observable verb. First, let's examine the structure. A good performance-based learning objective consists of three parts. The following examples use the design of training for a hotel guest registration agent, who is responsible for explaining the location of the elevators and the guest's assigned room.

1. *Condition*. The circumstance under which the learner will perform (e.g., "At the conclusion of each guest registration . . .")

2. *Performance*. What the observable performance is (e.g., ". . . the agent will use the hotel map to explain the location of elevators and the guest's room . . .")

3. *Criteria*. How the performance will be measured, in terms of quality, quantity, and/or time (e.g., ". . . every time").

The second element gets at that observable verb. What is the type of learning that you are doing? And what do you want students to be able to do? Benjamin Bloom's research into mastery performance and higher levels of thinking led to the creation in 1956 of the taxonomy that bears his name: Bloom's Taxonomy.[12] This hierarchy has become a foundational element within the educational community, and others continue to refine it.[13] Consider Figure 7.2, and think back to our typical learning objectives: "List the five advantages of our product over the competition." "List" clearly falls into the "remember" level—Bloom's lowest in terms of levels of thinking. Is "list" really what we want our salespeople to do? Or do we want them to apply or analyze? Once you answer those questions, you are now much better positioned to write the right objective, and you know better what the instruction must include and what level of thinking you want to test. (See Appendix 7A for a helpful list of verbs for each tier in the hierarchy.)

Alignment of Tests with Learning Objectives

When we talk about alignment of tests, we are talking about how well the test aligns with the condition, performance, and criteria of the objective. If a sales training course focuses on how salespeople should analyze a customer's wants and needs, then the test should try to mimic that. A test that goes after memorization of facts would

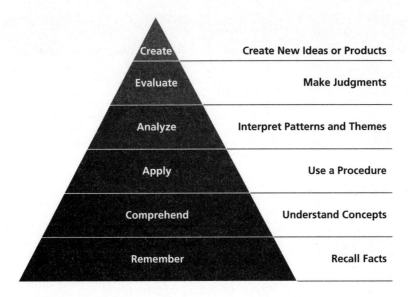

Figure 7.2 Bloom's Taxonomy (refined)

not be a good indicator of mastery of the course content, nor would it reinforce the learnings.

As you get to the higher levels of thinking, it becomes more challenging to test. Shrock and Coscarelli offer guidelines for determining what type of test question is most appropriate for each level (see Figure 7.3).[14]

Often, the business requirements for testing demand a standardized and automated approach to support ongoing data collection and reporting over time. While it might be nice for every student to take an essay test, the practicalities from a time, grading, administration, and usefulness perspective may preclude that. As can be seen in Figure 7.3, well-designed multiple choice questions can test as high as "analyze." According to Ken Phillips, a frequent measurement and evaluation presenter at the American Society for Training and Development (ASTD), "Multiple choice questions are easy to grade and when developed correctly—they neither contain obvious clues to the correct answer nor are overly difficult—are the most valid."[15] Further, most automated testing engines support multiple choice questions very well.

We now turn our attention to guidelines for crafting good questions.

Level of Learning Objective	Recommended Testing Types	
Create	Essay Demonstration	Oral Exam
Evaluate	Essay Demonstration	Oral Exam
Analyze	Essay Demonstration	Oral Exam Scenario Based Multiple Choice
Apply	Observation OJT	Scenario Based Multiple Choice
Comprehend	Matching Fill-in	True/False Multiple Choice
Remember	Matching Fill-in	True/False Multiple Choice

Figure 7.3 Determining the Type of Test

Guidelines for Multiple Choice Questions

In our years of working with clients on all levels of measurement, improving the quality of test questions is one of the easiest and lowest-hanging fruits. Based on our experience as well as the work of other experts noted in this chapter, we have compiled our top 10 guidelines for creating good multiple choice test questions. Even if you haven't fully adopted performance-based learning objectives and Bloom's Taxonomy, simply applying the following guidelines will improve the quality of your tests. Quality tests are aligned tests that are fair to the student and to the organization: well-written, comprehensible questions that reinforce learning and don't give away the answers. (See Appendix E for samples of each of the following.)

1. *Put the details in the stem.* In other words, keep the responses (the answer and the distractors) short and to the point.

2. *Use parallel format/structure for responses.* If three of the responses are similar in format and the fourth is not, it is likely that the fourth one is either obviously right or obviously wrong.

3. *Do not use double negatives.* This could confuse the student, and make test results misleading.

4. *Avoid "all of the above."* It is often the right answer, and is a lazy approach to writing a question. The same is true for "none of the above."

5. *Arrange responses in logical order.* It allows the student to focus on the heart of the question rather than on the arrangement of responses.

6. *Responses should be of similar length.* Believe it or not, research has shown that the longest response is usually the correct one. Make all responses similar in length so the student cannot simply guess the right answer.

7. *Watch out for grammar (tenses and plurals).* Use of some singular and some plural responses can give away the correct answer. Words like *an* are also giveaways that the correct answer starts with a vowel; *a(n)* would be better. Finally, bad grammar is just poor form and could confuse the question.

8. *No "gimmies"—make all responses plausible.* Responses that are obviously wrong improve the odds of someone guessing the right answer. Coming up with good distractors can be challenging. Matt Allen of the Human Resources Research Organization offers these suggestions: (1) use common misunderstandings or confusions about the program content; (2) use other familiar, but incorrect, phrases or concepts; (3) use common errors made with the program content; and (4) skip a step in a multistep process.[16]

9. *No trick questions.* These are unfair to the student and do not provide an accurate assessment of learning.

10. *Make sure it's useful.* "All our posttests must have 20 questions." Why? Don't waste the student's time with filler questions. Be sure all questions are in support of the learning objectives.

How do you know if you have a well-written test? Our favorite tool is an item analysis, which shows question by question how many people chose each of the responses. Do an item analysis as part of a pilot or after the first group of students completes the test. You can quickly identify bad questions or useless distractors. Perhaps everyone is getting a particular question wrong. It may be the question or the distractors or the answer that is the problem. If a distractor is being underselected, it's likely not a plausible response (see guideline 8). Or, as was the case in the "ride and drive" example at the start of this chapter, there was nothing wrong with the test—it was the content of the course that was the problem! Remember, tests do more than provide a measure of learning; they also provide actionable insights into the quality of the training.

IMPROVING THE ANALYSIS

The previous discussion was all about creating good instruments that can provide usable data for analysis and reporting. It's from this analysis that you'll get the real insights from your Level 1 and Level 2 efforts. Naturally, you need data before you can do meaningful analysis. We've seen the lack of organized data collection hinder many well-intended measurement initiatives, so a brief discussion of some of the fundamental considerations for collecting data is warranted. We will then present two simple yet powerful techniques for getting the most out of basic learning evaluation data. We call them "the denominator" and "segmentation."

Data Collection

Giving a survey to a class of 20 students is pretty straightforward. It can be easily administered by the instructor, then tallied and reported. However, if that same course gets taught dozens of times by multiple instructors, the tabulation becomes a bigger issue. And what if you have 10, 20, or 100 courses, each offered multiple times? And what about web courses? Determining how you will deploy the survey, collect completed surveys, compile the data, and report the results must be figured out. The same is true for Level 2 tests. Excel and an administrator can do only so much. There are wonderful commercially available automated survey and testing tools that can do much of the heavy lifting. This book is not intended as the "how to" around survey and test deployment and administration. Rather, we offer our experience regarding the key considerations of designing a manageable and repeatable Level 1 and Level 2 data collection process. Most important, think of how you want to use the data, the necessary level of granularity, and the various types of reports and analyses you want to do. As suggested earlier, mocking up desired reports at the outset really helps determine what data you will need to collect and how much detail you will need to store. This, along with the following considerations, will guide your data collection process.

- How will you administer/deploy surveys and tests?
  - How will it be different for live versus virtual versus web?
  - Do you have a survey/testing engine or platform?
  - Can surveys and tests launch from your learning management system (LMS)?

- How will the data be captured?
  - Will data capture be electronic? Will it be on paper? Will someone have to key in data, or can data be scanned?
  - Do you want to associate data with the student? Where will the student ID come from, and how is it verified?
  - Will you capture item-by-item detail or only final scores?

- Where will the captured data be stored and aggregated?
  - Will you have a single repository for all survey and test results?
  - How integrated should survey and test results be with your LMS?
  - Does your LMS support this?
  - What sort of information technology (IT) support may you need for handling data?

- What types of reports do you want?
  - Who are the users of the reports, and what will they want to know?
  - How frequently do you want reports? Can you standardize your reporting?
  - Have you mocked up reports to be sure you will have the data necessary to produce them?

- Will you want to export data to Excel or other analysis tools?
- What sort of IT support may you need for reports?

The best implementations that we have seen are with learning organizations that have a tight tie with an IT data analyst, or better yet, have someone with solid data analysis skills on staff within the learning department. Not only does this help with the design and deployment of the data collection, but it also provides great value in developing reports and conducting meaningful analyses.

The Denominator

The denominator concept, offered by Mary Lee of AAA of Northern California, Nevada, and Utah, is so simple that it always amazes us to see how infrequently it is applied. It primarily applies to Level 0 reporting—the proverbial "butts in seats" tallies—but has universal application. Consider the example in Figure 7.4 that shows training completions by department for a given course. The service department may be patting themselves on the back, as they have the highest number of completions.

Now, presume this is compliance training and everyone needs to get trained. Enter the denominator—in other words, "out of how many?" Is it 36 out of 40? Or, as in this example, 36 out of 94? Rather than butts in seats, we're talking about training penetration, or completion rates. Including the denominator always tells a more complete story. And as can be seen in Figure 7.5, the service department has some work to do!

Department	# Trained
Sales Dept.	29
Service Dept.	36
Production Dept.	31
Overall	96

Figure 7.4 Data Representation without the Denominator

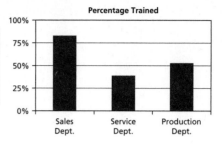

Department	Total Population	# Trained	% Trained
Sales Dept.	35	29	83%
Service Dept.	94	36	38%
Production Dept.	58	31	53%
Overall	187	96	51%

Figure 7.5 Data Representation Including the Denominator

How important is it to know your denominator? One of our multinational clients found out the hard way. The company had launched a major leadership development initiative targeting its 1,500 frontline supervisors. When seeking budget approval for year two, the learning and development team pulled a report by department to show the distribution of the 500 employees they had already reached. When asked for a similar distribution of the remaining frontline supervisors yet to be trained, they discovered that actually there were nearly 1,900 in that job category! The 1,500 number was a commonly held myth within the company, and no one had ever challenged it—or confirmed which position codes made up the "frontline supervisor" job category. This difference in denominator took the penetration rate from 33 percent down to 26 percent, and the number yet to be trained went from 1,000 to 1,400. Needless to say, budget talks were challenging.

The Power of Segmentation

When we talk about segmentation, we mean slicing and dicing the data by different individual and organizational demographics. It means moving beyond the overall average, be it a survey or test score or even sales volume and turnover, and looking at results by segment of the population. By example, a large international sales organization implemented Level 1 using online surveys for all its offerings. The company assigned a team of analysts to track results to uncover potential issues with courses, and to gauge student satisfaction. Every now and then, they would see a blip—a quick downward or upward trend—in satisfaction, but it quickly corrected itself the next week. As the blips didn't measurably affect the cumulative satisfaction score, they wrote them off as anomalies. As part of a larger measurement initiative, the learning organization provided this data to its measurement consultant. One of the consultant's standard practices was to segment data, and immediately started slicing and dicing the Level 1 results by various factors. What was found was eye-opening to the team of analysts who studied the data every day. Students in Eastern Europe didn't care very much for the training being offered. Students in China were its biggest fans. What was going on? The data didn't have the answers, but surely did pose the question.

With the facts before them, the learning department sought to uncover what was going on. It turned out that all training (WBT and live) was conducted in English. The Chinese students loved this, as they were known for seeking opportunities to improve their English skills. So, perhaps they didn't really care what the content was—they were just happy for the opportunity to learn English. The Eastern European students were quite the opposite, not passionate about learning English and a bit offended that all their training was offered only in that language. Their dissatisfaction likely had nothing to do with either the content or the instructional design. The learning department suddenly realized that the blips were actually real—real data trying to tell a story. And it was a story that could be told only by segmenting the data.

The example in Figure 7.6 demonstrates how simply looking at the overall Level 1 average can mask what is really going on. After all, 6.3 and 6.4 scores across the board look fine. But by segmenting the results by instructor, the data suggest a possible issue with instructor Hess. Similarly, segmenting by region provides more meaningful and actionable information. Using this cut of the data, the learning leader would likely want to investigate what's going on in the North, as well as discover what is working so well in the East.

Have you ever wondered how different populations of students are benefiting from your training? Are all students benefiting equally? Any demographic cut of the data is considered segmentation, and can shed perspective on your results. Tenure is one such demographic, if you can get the data (tenure either in a job position or with the company). Consider the example in Figure 7.7 of Level 2 results cut by tenure

Course: Marketing 101				Out of 7			
Instructor	# of Sessions	Total Evals	Avg # Evals/ Session	Instructor Score	Content Score	Recommend Score	Overall
Anderson	4	44	11.0	6.3	6.2	6.3	6.3
Brown	6	82	13.7	6.4	6.4	6.4	6.4
Franklin	7	102	14.6	6.6	6.7	6.6	6.6
Henry	5	61	12.2	6.5	6.6	6.5	6.5
Hess	5	58	11.6	4.9	6.0	5.8	5.6
Jones	7	92	13.1	6.5	6.5	6.5	6.5
Smith	5	65	13.0	6.7	6.6	6.7	6.7
Overall	39	504	12.9	6.3	6.4	6.4	6.4

Course: Marketing 101				Out of 7			
Region	# of Sessions	Total Evals	Avg # Evals/ Session	Instructor Score	Content Score	Recommend Score	Overall
North	8	127	15.9	5.2	6.2	6.0	5.8
South	7	101	14.4	6.4	6.1	6.4	6.3
East	11	131	11.9	6.9	6.9	6.8	6.9
West	13	145	11.2	6.5	6.5	6.5	6.5
Overall	39	504	12.9	6.3	6.4	6.4	6.4

Figure 7.6 Level 1 Segmentation

of the sales force. By looking at the learning gain of each segment, you can quickly obtain some valuable information. Once salespeople hit seven months on the job, the value of the Fundamentals of Sales course seems to diminish. In fact, it may be a waste of time for people with more than a year on the job to even take the class. Interestingly, it looks as if the more seasoned staff can benefit from training that

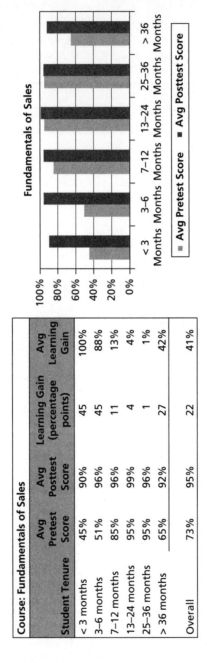

Course: Fundamentals of Sales

Student Tenure	Avg Pretest Score	Avg Posttest Score	Learning Gain (percentage points)	Avg Learning Gain
< 3 months	45%	90%	45	100%
3–6 months	51%	96%	45	88%
7–12 months	85%	96%	11	13%
13–24 months	95%	99%	4	4%
25–36 months	95%	96%	1	1%
> 36 months	65%	92%	27	42%
Overall	73%	95%	22	41%

Fundamentals of Sales

■ Avg Pretest Score   ■ Avg Posttest Score

Figure 7.7 Level 2 Results by Tenure

136

refreshes their basic selling skills. These results suggest that a deeper investigation into the needs of the seasoned workforce is warranted.

We end this discussion with two notes of caution. First, remember the garbage in, garbage out phenomenon. For any of the analyses to be of value, you first must have good data collection instruments—your surveys and tests. Second, a good analysis provides indicators of what is going on. It does not tell you why or what changes should be made. Don't jump right to solutions. The "ride and drive" team quickly discovered their first instinct (an incorrect answer grid) was not the problem, and deeper investigation was needed. Even with great data, it still takes the human element to uncover the root cause behind the numbers.

SUMMARY

While almost all learning organizations invest time and effort in the basic levels of measurement, most see limited value in the data. By developing high-quality surveys and tests, you can gather insightful and actionable data—data that can prove, and perhaps more importantly improve, the quality of your training. Many standard reports may only list tallies of course completions. By remembering the denominator, you can get a better picture of the throughput and reach of your training. Finally, take advantage of the power of segmentation. Once you have the data, looking at it through different lenses will help you pinpoint areas for improvement, whether it's helping a struggling instructor or changing your deployment strategy for new hires versus veterans. Improving the basics of learning evaluation enables you to increase the value of some of the easiest measurement data you can get.

NOTES

1. ASTD Research, "The Value of Evaluation: Making Training Evaluations More Effective," 2009.
2. D. Kirkpatrick and J. Kirkpatrick, "Evaluating Training Programs: The Four Levels," in *Evaluating Training Programs*, ed. D. Kirkpatrick and J. Kirkpatrick (San Francisco: Berrett-Koehler, 2009).
3. R. Kaufman and J. Keller, "Levels of Evaluation: Beyond Kirkpatrick," *Human Resource Quarterly* 5, no. 4 (1994): 371–380.
4. P. Morrel-Samuels, "Getting the Truth into Workplace Surveys," *Harvard Business Review*, February 2002, 111–118.

5. K. Phillips, "Eight Tips on Developing Level 1 Evaluation Forms," *Training Today*, Fall 2007, 1–6.

6. F. Reichheld, "One Number You Need to Grow," *Harvard Business Review*, December 2003.

7. M. Broad and J. Newstrom, *Transfer of Training* (Reading, MA: Addison-Wesley, 1992).

8. Morrel-Samuels, "Getting the Truth into Workplace Surveys," 113.

9. Ibid.

10. S. Shrock and W. Coscarelli, *Criterion-Referenced Test Development: Technical and Legal Guidelines for Corporate Training* (San Francisco: Pfeiffer, 2007).

11. R. Mager, *Preparing Instructional Objectives: A Critical Tool in the Development of Effective Instruction* (Atlanta, GA: Center for Effective Performance, 1997).

12. B. Bloom, *Taxonomy of Education Objectives* (Boston: Allyn & Bacon, 1956).

13. D. Krathwohl, "A Revision of Bloom's Taxonomy," *Theory into Practice* 41, no. 4 (Autumn 2002): 212–218.

14. Shrock and Coscarelli, *Criterion-Referenced Test Development*.

15. K. Phillips, "Developing Valid Level 2 Evaluations," *Training Today*, Fall 2009, 6–8.

16. In K. Phillips, "Developing Valid Level 2 Evaluations."

Leadership Program at a Fortune 500 Financial Company

C hapter 7 focuses on getting more value out of the basics of learning evaluation. One of the key points is how to improve that value by improving the quality of the data collection instruments themselves. The discussion of survey design (see the section "Improving Level 1") provides guidelines that are actually applicable to any type of survey. In fact, much Level 3 evaluation is often survey-based, gauging the learner's perspective on his or her behavior change. Frequently such surveys also include the learner's manager and peers to get a fuller understanding of the degree of change. The following case study demonstrates how a well-thought-out measurement strategy can use surveys, including those that already exist in an organization, to answer important business questions.

BACKGROUND

In the face of the market downturn in 2008 that led to rampant financial breakdowns and insecurities throughout the world, a Fortune

500 financial company hunkered down to ride out the storm. Senior leadership focused on keeping costs as low as possible. At the same time, human resources (HR) had a mandate to improve behaviors and develop human capital. In turn, HR focused on ensuring that everyone in a leadership position throughout the company adopted a uniform and comprehensive leadership philosophy.

Mayank Jain was the company's Vice President of Workforce Planning and Strategy. He looked at the company's leadership program and asked, "Is this really worth it? Are we optimizing our dollars spent?" Jain wanted his executive peers to be equipped for a fact-based discussion about whether to fund development programs and, if so, how much to fund. His colleague Nigel Harrison, Director of Human Capital Strategy and Analytics, led a team that collaborated with Jain to find the answers to these questions and provide the executive team with hard evidence.

THE INVESTMENT

The leadership development program Harrison's team analyzed was a company-wide initiative, with curriculum components for each level of employee—from individual contributor to senior leader. Most people completed the program when they were first hired, or when they were promoted to a leadership position. The curriculum included numerous courses for each level, and the learning objectives were wide-reaching and might be completed over a long period of time. They impacted a diverse array of skills and competencies, many of which were not easy to measure.

In collaboration with the learning team that created the leadership program, the analysts created the following list of metrics that the program should impact. Each of these metrics was already being measured by the company. The measurement model added the time frame in which it would be reasonable to expect a change in each metric.

- *First year:* Trainee engagement and retention
- *Second year:* Trainee's leadership abilities and leader's team's engagement, as measured by:
    - Trainee's leader effectiveness scores

- Trainee's leadership rating
- Team productivity and retention

- *Third year:* Trainee's promotion likelihood and promotion rate, as measured by:
  - Trainee's potential and readiness for promotion
  - Ready now successor rate
  - Average potential rating

THE BASIS FOR THE STUDY DESIGN

The executive aspect of the leadership development initiative was particularly expensive. Because of the serious investment of time and money, the company wanted to take the evaluation further for this element, to a cost-benefit analysis. Jain and Harrison built on an earlier analysis that Harrison had conducted for the company on strategy training for senior leaders, using it as a basis for their analysis of the leadership program. The strategy training had been conducted by a local university and taught strategic thinking to senior leaders. It included a sizable cost per attendee, and 30 senior leaders were sent each year.

Senior leaders completed surveys following their completion of the course; the survey asked if their work performance had improved as a result of the course. Approximately half of the attendees answered yes. From here, the analysis showed the cost in dollars and time to send the leaders to the program and put that number next to the figure of approximately 15 who thought they were improving. The question became one for the finance department: How much of an improvement would we need to see in those 15 people to get the desired benefit for the cost?

Harrison called this "framing the decision for them in rational terms. They could say maybe these people improve 1 percent as a result and therefore $X is a reasonable cost." What if the analysis said the 15 attendees would have to improve their performance by 10 percent to meet that cost? "Maybe the course can't do that and isn't worth the money," Harrison said. "The break-even approach is what we called it. We can't calculate the benefit of this course, but we're going to give a framework to help them think about whether it's worth it."

FINDING THE IMPACT OF LEADERSHIP DEVELOPMENT

With the metrics in hand, Harrison's team developed an approach for valuing engagement, retention, and promotion rate.

Valuing Engagement

Leaders who completed the training were compared to those who had not after the same time period in order to measure engagement differences between the trained and the untrained. The difference in the level of engagement (if present) was valued according to a simple model based on external studies that approximated fully engaged employees to be 25 percent *more* productive than average, and under-engaged employees to be 25 percent *less* productive than average. Disengaged employees were considered to be 50 percent less productive than average.

The team used the differences in leader effectiveness scores to lend weight to the argument that the higher engagement was caused by better leadership. It was not given a value in itself because the team supposed that better leadership leads to higher engagement, and to value both would be double counting.

Valuing Retention

The team also compared retention rates for the trained and the untrained. They calculated turnover costs based on the full cost to replace: recruiting and training costs plus productivity loss. If the detailed cost of turnover was unknown, the team used an approximation of 1× annual salary.

Valuing Promotion Rate

In order to find the return on increased promotion rate, the team used the observation that externally available talent generally requires a salary premium over the average for a given role, while an internal promotion from a lower salary grade will generally command a lower salary than average for that level. The net present value of this difference over the expected life of the hire yielded the value of each additional promotion.

The team included other benefits of internal hiring, such as the lower turnover of internal hires, improved engagement of the organization from internal development, and the effect of subsequent promotions that can occur when an individual is moved up.

By showing the financial value of these metrics against the three-year goals listed earlier, the team was able to provide senior leaders with a big picture of how the leadership development program impacted the company over time.

PRELIMINARY RESULTS

At press time, the team had processed results on the leadership program's impact on retention and engagement. "We did see that people who were engaged with the program had better retention rates and definitely had better engagement," Harrison said. The team had identified an engagement-by-tenure curve in which a new employee with the company starts off very engaged, and then drops rapidly in engagement over the first six months. The employee bottoms out after about two years with greatest decline in the first year. People who have been with the company longer than two years generally have higher engagement—after the steep decline of the first two years, engagement starts to go up.

For leaders who completed the program, the engagement-by-tenure curve was still present, but it didn't dip as low and started turning upward sooner. "The drop in engagement was not as deep and protracted for people engaged in the program," Harrison said. Because the team was able to monetize engagement, they could show a return on investment using these numbers.

CHAPTER **8**

Hard Evidence Using Advanced Analytics

Information is the oil of the 21st century, and analytics is the combustion engine.

—Peter Sondergaard, senior VP at Gartner

I n this book, we've given you a progressive set of a tools to help you understand the impact your training programs are having, as well as the ways those programs contribute to business outcomes. In the past, learning and development (L&D) professionals have struggled to demonstrate the business impact of training programs, because the existing evaluation models are typically based on survey data. The traditional learning measures—Kirkpatrick's four levels (i.e., satisfaction, learning gain, behavior change, and results) and Phillips's return on investment (ROI)—provide incredibly useful data for the professionals who design and deploy training. As one CLO discussed in a recent presentation, they are learning's early warning system (i.e., the canary in a coal mine). However, survey-based impact results don't necessarily resonate with the C-suite. What is missing from L&D's traditional measurements is the operational data that creates direct alignment of learning to business outcomes and provides a real quantitative demonstration of business impact. We're talking about analyzing the operational business data behind those "leading indicators" and "business results" on the Measurement Map.

THE QUEST FOR ISOLATED IMPACT

Showing the value of learning programs is important work and one of the goals of just about any measurement strategy. The ability to show the return on investment (ROI) of training has historically enabled countless learning departments to show the value of their work to their organizations and secure continued funding for important initiatives. But the oft-asked (and often frustrating) question remains: How much of the change in the business outcome can actually be attributed to training versus something else? This question is really asking for the *isolated* effect of training. Isolation allows you to explain, with confidence, what impact can be attributed to the training and not other factors such as a new products, marketing campaigns, adjusted commission structure, new technology adoption, or economic conditions (to name a few things often seeking credit for good results). Isolation also allows you to calculate training's contribution that is based on actual business metrics—a calculated impact that will pass muster in the CFO's office.

But the real value of calculating an isolated business impact is in understanding where the investment is working (and not working) in your organization. With this knowledge, you have quantitative evidence to fine-tune the learning, thereby optimizing the investment. We know of no other way to optimize your learning in a complex environment without first isolating the effects of the investment. Optimization was once the foray of only the most sophisticated L&D departments. Today, driven by the ever-changing global marketplace and made possible by the constantly improving access to data and analytical tools, optimization will soon be a fundamental technique for evaluating all forms of human capital investments. Chapter 9 will get deeper into the power of optimization. First we must conquer isolation: the gateway to advanced analytics.

When we talk about isolation, we are referencing a scientific design concept that combines logic and statistics to clear away the other variables impacting performance. This concept, called an observational study, is commonly used in clinical drug trials to determine the effects of a drug versus other lifestyle factors that may impact an individual's health or the course of a disease. In human performance, it's easy to think of dozens—if not hundreds—of things in the workplace that may influence performance: everything from team makeup, engagement, and tenure to rewards and incentives and to the success and reputation of the company in the marketplace. And what about the relative moodiness of one's boss on a given day? The comfort of one's workstation? Proximity to the windows and average daily exposure to sunlight? The mind reels when you begin to consider the complex web of factors that determine how an individual employee performs at work on a given day.

Thus you begin to understand one of the shortcomings of the typical application of the Kirkpatrick methodology. Survey-based measurement is simply incapable of credibly isolating the impact of any one factor. In reality, almost every learning leader we talk to wishes they could get to isolation, but most shy away from even talking about it. It may be that they feel isolation is unnecessary. More likely it is because they do not understand it, do not know how to do it, or don't believe they can get the data. In other words, the sentiment is often that isolating impact is just too difficult to do, so they fall back to surveys, saying surveys are "good enough."

As marketplace evangelists who have been pushing the training industry to see the benefits of applying the advanced analytics that are practiced in almost every other corporate discipline, we register our disagreement. Survey insights are *not* good enough for L&D to keep pace with the changing workforce and successfully compete in today's marketplace. Traditional learning evaluation methods arose during a time when hard assets were the primary generators of revenue in the vast majority of organizations, and employees were groomed for 20- to 30-year careers with the same company. As we detailed in Chapter 1, the acquisition and development of talent now represents a fundamental driver of business success. Organizations that are managing constant, rapid change in their workforces cannot afford for their L&D departments to ignore the competitive advantage of human capital analytics.

All of this is not to say that isolation is easy to accomplish. If you look at Figure 8.1 (the analytics continuum we introduced in Chapter 2), you'll see a steep cliff between correlations and causation. Establishing causation (i.e., isolating the impact) is no small feat. It requires special skill sets, access to data not typically found within L&D, and the collaboration of high-level stakeholders. You may have had a statistics course at some point in your academic journey, but rarely do learning professionals use this type of math regularly, if at all. Now is the time to start thinking about collaborating with a statistician to complete this work.

As you'll see in Chapter 9, the benefits of isolation can easily outweigh its cost on major human capital investments. Isolating the impact of an investment is the only way to begin to optimize the investment. Optimization is a prescriptive analysis that examines results already achieved to identify where future investments are most needed. By statistically controlling business variables (the logic and the math that allow you to isolate impact), you can understand where an investment

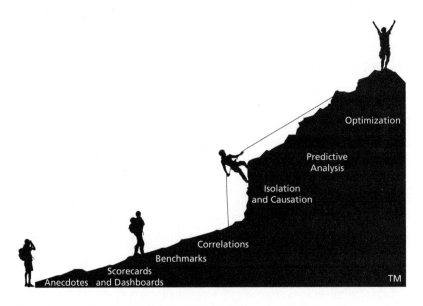

Figure 8.1 Continuum of Human Capital Analytics

is most effective, and less effective, in order to make targeted adjustments that improve impact over time. It allows you to intelligently invest in people, using the same science that analysts use to ensure store shelves are stocked with just the right amount of product or create financial models that safeguard the growth of a 401(k) plan.

CAUSATION: WHAT REALLY DRIVES PERFORMANCE?

In order to isolate an investment's impact on the business, we must establish causation. When two variables change together in some consistent way (e.g., training and improved performance), they appear to be related and are said to be correlated. Survey-based methodologies for evaluating investments are able to establish a correlation between the investment and the recipient's performance. Phillips's ROI methodology uses this correlation to associate a financial gain with the investment. Many of you have heard the expression that "correlation does not equal causation." When two things appear to be related, it's important to investigate whether other factors may be involved.

For example, there is a similar trend for ice cream consumption and murder rates—as more ice cream is consumed in the United States, more people are murdered. Is it fair to say that eating ice cream increases the likelihood that one's life will be violently cut short? Let's look at additional data: Both ice cream consumption and murder rates also correlate with drowning. How can the consumption of ice cream, murder rates, and drowning be related? These events are clearly correlated, but it is a fourth factor, high temperature, that is the cause. In hot weather, more people congregate outdoors, increasing the likelihood of conflicts leading to murders. Hot weather, in rather obvious ways, also leads people to indulge in ice cream and water sports to cool off, and more people being in or on the water increases the likelihood of drownings. These links are all correlations and thus do not say much about actual causes. To assert that ice cream sales have a causal effect is not only silly, but irresponsible. But in business, causality may be less obvious, leading even the wise man to misinterpret a strong correlation as causation.

As we seek to establish causation, we are trying to identify the connection between an investment and a business effect, or determine which metric drives another. Ideally, we can identify the investments that positively impact our business metrics. Authors Wayne Cascio and John Boudreau present the following three criteria for causation.[1] To support the conclusion that x causes y:

1. The cause must precede the effect. In other words, y did not occur until after x.

2. There must be a correlation between the cause and the effect. A correlation analysis must show that x and y are related.

3. Other explanations of the relationship between x and y can be eliminated as plausible rival hypotheses.

This third requirement is the most difficult, and is dependent on having a solid research design. Cascio and Boudreau caution that "ruling out all other factors" is far easier said than done. It's perhaps the biggest barrier to isolation and also what makes isolated business impact studies so useful. We offer an approach that blends statistics with the best-articulated case the chain of evidence provides. In addition to a deep dive into as much data as we can access, we look for anecdotal evidence, success stories, and any other supporting evidence that tells the same story as the math and logic. Ultimately, proof is a combination of mathematics and old-fashioned reasoning.

ISOLATING THE IMPACT: IMPROVING LEVELS 4 AND 5

In our first book, *Human Capital Analytics: How to Harness the Potential of Your Organization's Greatest Asset*, we gave an in-depth explanation of the methodology and statistical processes involved to isolate impact. Following is an overview of two of the key concepts involved in isolation work: test and control groups and prior performance. For more information, see Chapter 6 of *Human Capital Analytics*.

Test and Control Groups

One of the first things we look for when evaluating an investment is the ability to identify test and control groups of learners, defined as participants and nonparticipants. We think in terms of some group participating in x (the test group) and some other group not participating in x (the control group), and we look for performance differences between those two groups.

There is one key difference between establishing test and control groups in a clinical drug trial and doing so to isolate the impact of a human capital investment: The groups in the drug trial are contrived for the purposes of testing the drug, while the test and control groups for a human capital measurement study are naturally occurring based on the way the investment is deployed within the organization. In a clinical setting, selection of participants and timing of treatments is very intentional and controlled. In the human capital studies, we need to conduct an observational study, following participation as events naturally unfold. The majority of human capital investments are rolled out over time. Even if an investment is applied to an entire company, it is unusual for everyone in the company to receive the investment at the same time. A staggered rollout allows people who have *not yet received* the investment to be treated as the control group, or nonparticipants.

Test and control groups are crucial to isolating impact, because they allow you to rule out many of the other factors affecting performance. The idea is that both groups are equally affected by the factors outside of the training: the economy, performance incentives, changes in leadership, the weather, and so on. When establishing the groups, you'll want to identify the factors that are likely to influence performance and ensure that they are present for both groups. For example, everyone will be affected by the economy and the company's reputation in the marketplace. However, perhaps only a certain region received a performance incentive during the test period. You wouldn't want to use that region as your control group (unless it also comprises your test group).

Prior Performance

A crucial component in establishing causation is the inclusion of prior performance. Without knowing the learners' performance before attending training, you really can't quantify how their performance has changed. For example, consider the following statement: "All call center representatives who attended training have low call handling times." This is a perfect example of a correlation between training and call handle times. You have no way of knowing whether the reps' call handling times were already low even before training or are low because they attended training, or they are low because top performers who would be most receptive to training were selected to attend.

What you are really after is the *change* in performance, and the only way to get that is to include data on prior performance in your study design. As you consider prior performance, ask yourself, "What was the change in performance from *before* to *after* the training program?" Once you've identified the performance change for the test group, you will need to establish a comparable period of time to observe the performance of the control group.

Including prior performance is an invaluable way to mitigate selection bias (either intentional or unintentional). Sometimes people are put into a training program as a reward; other times it's the last step to rehabilitate an underperforming employee. It's easy to say that the trainees improved after training because they were predisposed to do so—they were already the high performers who were extra motivated to attend training. By incorporating their prior performance, we can evaluate them based on their change in performance over time and consider how their improvements (or declines) compare to their similar colleagues who did not attend the training.

By establishing comparable test and control groups and including prior performance in your analysis, you will have addressed two of the critical components of a good observational study design.

A GENTLE GUIDE TO THE STATISTICS OF CAUSATION

There are two statistical concepts that are fundamental to establishing causation: certainty and impact. Certainty is the likelihood that something did not occur by chance. Suppose a friend flips a coin and it lands heads up. He tells you it's a magic coin, much more likely to land on heads than tails, and offers to sell you the coin. You are extremely skeptical. After all, it might be a perfectly normal coin, he might have just changed his story slightly had the coin landed on tails. Suppose he flips the coin again, and it lands on heads again. You are still unimpressed; after all, if you flipped a coin twice, you have a 25 percent chance of ending up with heads both times. But what if he flips it three times, and they are all heads? Four? You might begin to pay attention. Would 19 heads out of 20 make you take notice? What about 40 out of 50? At some point, you will increasingly acknowledge that this coin may in fact be something out of the ordinary. But what *is* that point?

This is exactly the sort of question we struggle with every day, although the questions are much more complicated. What if 15 out of 20 trainees improved their performance, and only 11 out of 20 in the control group did so? Or what if performance of the test group improved 7 percent while the control group improved 3 percent? How much more certain could we be if those numbers were doubled? Statistics has various methods for answering these sorts of questions, such as establishing the strength of the relationship between training and performance, determining the magnitude of a change in performance, and verifying if the change is real (i.e., statistically significant and not random chance).

A couple of different kinds of factors can go into these tests of statistical significance. The results are statistical models. Most of our models can be expressed like this:

Outcome variable (or dependent variable) = Function of one or more input variables (or independent variables)

Thus, a training example might be expressed as:

Change in performance = Function of whether person participated in training

In other words, does the fact that the person received training help us predict whether his or her performance will improve? Of course, any number of factors might go into our assessment of whether the person might be expected to improve. Perhaps we are talking about sales performance, and we know that those with higher salary bases are already peak performers, so we should account for that factor. Perhaps there are four regions of the country, so we need to take location into account. Note that there is always a single outcome variable, or business outcome, on the left side of the equation, and there may be any number of factors on the right. Some of these factors might fall into categories (such as training status or gender), and some are

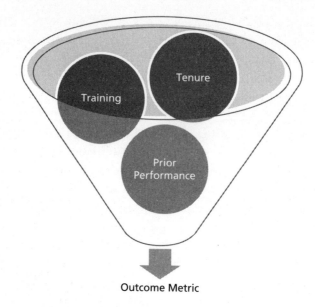

Outcome Metric

Figure 8.2 Sample Function—One Metric

continuous numbers that might vary over a range (such as salary or tenure within the organization).

Figure 8.2 shows an example of what we mean by a function. Several items can go in, but only one number comes out.

STATISTICAL MODELING AND SIGNIFICANCE

Regression modeling is a popular technique that can be used to quantify the relationship between two or more variables. When applied to human capital, it can look at historical data that measure an investment and determine whether outcomes measured at a later point in time are the result of that investment. For example, consider an investment in training for salespeople. To determine whether the investment was worthwhile, we could compare the sales for a six-month period before and after the training. If we see an increase in sales (while controlling for other changes), we could determine that for every dollar spent on training, there was an increase of $1.50 in sales. Then a simplified depiction of the regression model would be: Sales = 1.50 × Training dollars.

There are many other methodologies similar to regressions that are even more powerful. For example, you might want to factor in categorical variables like the geographic region or the season; general linear models (GLMs) allow you to combine categorical variables and continuous ones in the same model. Structural equation modeling is much like regression, but it allows models where variables have complex interdependencies, or hierarchies. In human capital analytics, the analysis can become very complex.

When evaluating a model, we look for the overall fit of the model, as well as its statistical significance. Depending on the type of model, there are statistical measures that tell us how well the model explains the relationship we are measuring. One simple measure is R^2 (R-squared). It tells us what percentage of the variation in the data is explained by the model. Suppose in our regression model measuring the relationship between sales training and increased sales, we find that our R^2 is 0.60. This means that 60 percent of the increase in sales can be directly linked to the increase in our training investment.

Another aspect of our analysis is the certainty of the results. Certainty is determined by the level of statistical significance or confidence. The main drivers are the quantity and variability of the data. In business, 95 percent is a standard and acceptable level of confidence. So, for our example, this means that there is only a 5 percent chance (100 – 95 percent) that the relationship between training and sales happened by chance. To tie this together, we can say that "We are 95 percent confident that 60 percent (R^2) of the increase in sales is a direct result of the training investment."

ISOLATION AND THE ANALYTICS CONTINUUM

There are two points that are important to note as we consider isolation in the context of the larger continuum of analytics presented in this book. First, you don't have to use all of the techniques presented in the earlier chapters in order to isolate an investment. You do, however, need to align the investment to business outcomes and create the Measurement Map with your stakeholders (see Chapter 6 for details on building a Measurement Map). You won't be able to design the study without understanding the business metrics the training is trying to impact, nor will you know which metrics to consider in your analysis.

Second is the time frame in which you are attempting to isolate impact. Ideally, alignment is part of the program design, but if you've already deployed an investment, it's not too late to gather stakeholders, create the Measurement Map, and design an isolation study. As we'll show in the next chapter, the benefits of isolation—optimization—can still be realized well into the rollout of a major investment. It may take time for changes in performance to show up in your metrics. You will want to account for this in your study design to ensure that sufficient time has passed for post training performance data to capture those changes. The "time to impact" can vary and is dependent on the nature of the investment. Call center training, for example, will typically show its impact as soon as the representatives are back on the phones. Leadership development will take significantly longer to show up in a measureable way. Using the Measurement Map, your stakeholders can help you determine a reasonable time period in which to expect the changes to appear in the identified metrics.

SUMMARY

Survey-based evaluation models can give you an early indication of your investment's potential to impact business metrics. With so much riding on the performance of an ever- changing workforce, investments in human capital demand direct alignment to business outcomes and a quantitative demonstration of business impact. By isolating training's impact from other variables, you can answer the oft-asked (and often frustrating) question: How much of the change in the business outcome can actually be attributed to training versus something else? Isolation allows you to explain, with confidence, what impact can be attributed to the training and not to other factors. Isolation also allows you to calculate training's contribution based on actual business metrics—giving you an ROI that will pass muster in the CFO's office.

The real value of calculating an isolated business impact is to be able to understand where the investment is working (and not working) in your organization. With this knowledge, you have quantitative evidence to fine-tune the learning, thereby optimizing the investment.

When we talk about isolation, we are referencing a scientific design process that combines logic and statistics to clear away the other variables impacting performance. Isolating the impact of an investment is the only way to optimize the investment.

In order to isolate an investment's impact on the business, we must establish causation. As we seek to establish causation, we are trying to identify the connection between an investment and a business effect, or determine which metric drives another. There are two key concepts to designing a study that establishes causation: Test and control groups allow you to show a difference between the trained and untrained employees. Prior performance considers the change in performance over time, mitigating any possible selection bias in the training program.

As you approach the isolation stage of your analytics journey, you will need to include a statistician on your team. The two statistical concepts most important to establishing causation are certainty and impact. Among the statistician's tools, regression modeling and general linear models are the most relevant here. Another important note on your journey: You do not need to tackle the concepts in this book in order, but you do need to align to business outcomes before attempting to isolate impact. You also need to consider time frame. Some investments will impact business metrics immediately, while others will take time to appear in a measurable way.

NOTE

1. W. Cascio and J. Boudreau, *Investing in People: Financial Impact of Human Resource Initiatives* (Upper Saddle River, NJ: Pearson Education, 2011).

Achieving Business Impact at a Major Utility Company

CHALLENGE AND LEARNING INVESTMENT

A multinational electricity and gas company has the goal of being the foremost international electricity and gas company by being an innovative leader in energy management. In order to live up to the vision and meet the organization's ambitious goals, this electricity and gas company recognized the need to engage leaders at all levels to help drive change throughout the organization. The cornerstone of this effort is a three-tier leadership development strategy for senior, middle, and first-level leaders.

In 2009, they launched a leadership development program to their largest audience of leaders—the nearly 3,000 first-level leaders who were charged with driving change from the front line. The program had the overall goal of developing capable and effective leaders who could impact business results. The program's six-unit curriculum was delivered over 12 to 15 months, with two to 10 weeks back on the job between each unit.

To further support the learning, the program had a component for managers of the leaders attending the training that included a one-day Manager's Support Workshop. The workshop informed managers about the leadership development program and provided them with best practices for supporting their leaders back on the job.

The leadership development program had the following key learning objectives:

1. Reinforce leadership qualities that were identified through the organization's performance management process.

2. Demonstrate the global principles of effective leadership development.

3. Set a foundation for first-level leaders to develop their leadership qualities, to build a greater understanding of what it takes to be effective in their organization's culture, to deepen business acumen, and to develop an expanded network of peers within the broader organization.

Leaders attending the program developed the skills to help them create high-performance teams. Through role playing and other activities, leaders further developed their competencies in support of the organization's leadership framework, which consisted of four leadership qualities: create the future, consistently deliver great performance, build relationships, and develop self and others.

WAS IT WORKING?

Two years into a five-year deployment, the electric and gas company sought an assessment of the business impact of the leadership development program. At a high level, this organization wanted to answer the following questions:

1. Was the program impacting the business?

2. How important was support from the Line Manager in realizing the program's impact?

3. Could the program be refined to improve results of future learners?

Answers to these questions would direct future investment in this leadership development initiative.

THE EVALUATION

To answer these questions, this organization's L&D partnered with Capital Analytics (now Vestrics) to conduct an impact study, which included a statistical analysis of the leadership development program's impact on key business metrics, an online learning transfer survey to gather participant feedback, and a series of participant interviews to gain a qualitative evaluation of impact.

Because the program is based primarily on soft skills, its learning objectives proved difficult to quantify using traditional methods of training evaluation. To show stakeholders a return on the investment in the program and to understand how the program's deployment could be improved, the study used a statistical causal model of human capital analysis. The study considered the organization's performance review system as a baseline to track changes in performance over time. Other metrics included changes in merit pay, bonuses, retention, and turnover during and after training.

A key objective of the program is to build leadership competencies. These competencies are reflected in the organization's performance management process and are included in their review system. Under this particular review system, employees were reviewed on two factors:

1. **The WHAT**: performance objectives

2. **The HOW**: demonstration of leadership qualities

By adding the HOW to the performance appraisal, this organization sent the clear signal that behaviors and outcomes matter. The leadership development program intentionally addressed the HOW by focusing on the four leadership qualities. As such, the HOW score became a key metric in the intervention's evaluation. The WHAT score was a secondary metric, showing performance-related effects of the leadership qualities in action.

To evaluate the impact of the initiative, the program graduates were compared to a control group of similar leaders who had not yet attended training. By comparing prior performance to post performance for both groups, the study was able to uncover the effects of the program. The study also looked at interactions between multiple variables to isolate the program's business impact from other factors (such as geography, leadership changes, and the work environment). Findings were segmented by employee demographic groups to show the organization precisely where—and with whom—the program showed varying degrees of impact.

THE IMPACT

The leadership development program's impacts were wide-ranging throughout the organization, including *better performance ratings, reduction in leader turnover, and improved merit increases in the United States.*

Performance Ratings

Based on the review scores, managers were generally selecting program participants from those front-line leaders who could benefit most from leadership training. In comparing 2009 to 2010 review results, program participants showed significantly more improvement than their untrained colleagues. Trainees' HOW scores, which represent the leadership qualities that are the focus of the program, improved in both the United Kingdom and the United States. In the United Kingdom, the average HOW scores rose 11.8 percent for participants and only 2.2 percent for the untrained. In the United States, the average HOW scores rose 12.4 percent for participants and only 5.9 percent for the untrained.

Turnover

Turnover among trainees was lower than the baseline rates for the untrained in both the United Kingdom and the United States. Untrained employees represented a whopping 97 percent of turnover.

Merit Pay

In addition to being a reward for positive behaviors on the job, merit pay was also used in this study as an indicator that participants were demonstrating the skills and behaviors taught in the program. The influence of the program on merit pay differed by country.

Reflecting global economic conditions, merit pay decreased overall during the study period. In the United States, those who enrolled in training were earning less in merit pay before training started than those who did not enroll. By the time training was complete, trainees were receiving higher levels of merit pay than the untrained. The same did not occur in the United Kingdom, where training was not a predictor of merit increases.

OPTIMIZING THE INVESTMENT

The timing of the study (approximately halfway through the deployment of the leadership development program) allowed the organization to use the findings to optimize the program's impact going forward. They used the findings from their Levels 1 and 2 analyses to make content and design changes to the program, and the advanced analysis led to additional improvements.

As you've learned in this book, applying a scientific methodology can isolate the impact of learning investments from other variables in the work environment. By then segmenting results by demographic group, an analysis can identify where—and with whom—an initiative is working best. This electric and gas company's analysis leveraged this optimization technique to determine the varying degrees of the program's impact across their target audience.

For example, reducing turnover was not among the original goals of the program. The organization has historically been a very low turnover organization. However, the study found an impressive return on investment in turnover alone. In particular, the organization's Band D leaders in the United Kingdom had the highest turnover rate (6.1 percent) of all leaders covered by the program. Band D leaders were first-level leaders with more seniority, representing a difficult talent loss for the electric and gas company. *L&D gained targeted intelligence to use the program as a retention tool with its hard-to-replace leaders.* Further, the organization knew that some leaders who had left the union to take on the leadership role were struggling. In fact, many were leaving their leadership roles and returning to the union (staying within the company but changing roles). By understanding how the program helped with retention, L&D began to message internally that the program could help improve the success rate of leaders who had come from the union.

Because the data was segmented by demographic groups, the organization also learned that the impact on performance ratings peaked in two areas:

- **WHAT** scores showed the greatest increase for leaders with 20 years or more of tenure
- **HOW** scores showed the greatest increase for leaders with five or fewer years of tenure

This finding helped the organization select program participants with the highest potential for improvement. It also identified a need to explore other interventions to help increase WHAT and HOW scores for other groups.

Manager involvement was a third optimization opportunity. The study found that *leaders showed the greatest improvement if their managers attended the Manager Support Workshop.* Manager involvement also included supporting the participant before and after training, engaging in discussions of the program's content and helping participants find ways to apply it. In fact, participants with a nonsupportive manager actually showed a modest decline in performance. L&D began requiring the supervisor's attendance in the Manager Support Workshop before their first-level leaders could attend the program, referencing the study as proof that manager support is crucial to leaders' success in the training.

Hard Evidence Using Advanced Analytics: Valuing Training at Defense Acquisition University

BACKGROUND

Defense Acquisition University (DAU) supports the Defense Acquisition Workforce of the U.S. Department of Defense (DoD) by providing training to more than 150,000 civilian and military employees in the fields of acquisition, technology, and logistics. As the stewards of a $216.7 million budget, the leaders of DAU wanted to ensure they were accountable for those tax dollars by maximizing the effectiveness of their learning investments.

In the past, DAU had commissioned a number of studies employing survey and qualitative data to examine the impact of its training investments. These prior studies had indicated a positive impact on acquisition outcomes. The leaders of DAU were ready to take the next step in their measurement journey and find quantitative proof of training's impact. They partnered with Capital Analytics (now Vestrics) to design a quantitative impact measurement model as a proof of concept (PoC).

The proof of concept would serve as a model for future impact measurement. Specifically, the proof of concept measured the effectiveness of DAU's learning programs in terms of job impact, acquisition outcomes, and contributions to the Better Buying Power (BBP) initiative. BBP is the DoD's mandate to "do more without more." It includes "the implementation of best practices to strengthen the Defense Department's buying power, improve industry productivity, and provide an affordable, value-added military capability to the Warfighter."[1]

DESIGNING THE STUDY

Early in the design process, Capital Analytics began an assessment of the available data for analyzing training outcomes. In the past, DAU leaders had seen data availability as the biggest barrier to calculating a quantitative return on investment (ROI) of DAU training. Not only were program outcome data limited, but the data that were available had limited integrity and were often inaccessible. The Under Secretary of Defense for Acquisition, Technology, and Logistics had established a strategic initiative in 2013 to identify key data gaps and to begin collecting the necessary data for future analysis.

The initial study design included a quantitative assessment of links between Mission Assistance consulting services (one of DAU's flagship initiatives) and acquisition outcomes. As the Capital Analytics team began to dig into the data from DAU, they discovered that the data simply weren't available for such an analysis. DAU was committed to a quantitative analysis, so the Capital Analytics team looked at the available data to see the potential for analysis. The study was revised to analyze relationships between DAU training consumption and changes in acquisition outcome measures (i.e., cost, schedule, and performance).

The acquisition outcome measure selected was SAR-to-SAR recurring unit cost growth. Each Major Defense Acquisition Program (MDAP) is required by law to submit a Selected Acquisition Report (SAR) to Congress. The SAR outlines the budget for the MDAP and

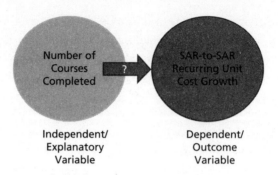

Figure 8.A Study Hypothesis

summarizes actual costs, schedules, and technical performance measures. The SARs reflect outcomes of MDAPs, making year-over-year SAR-to-SAR recurring unit cost growth an important acquisition measure. Based on the available data from the SARs, the team developed the following business question as the hypothesis for the study: What is the relationship between the number of courses taken and the acquisition outcome of SAR-to-SAR recurring unit cost growth? Is there a cost growth reduction (or increase) because of the relationship? (See Figure 8.A.)

Based on this business question, DAU pulled data on the SAR-to-SAR recurring unit cost growth, acquisition employee demographic data, and acquisition employee training data. The data included 67 employees who had collectively completed 205 DAU courses. After the course completions, these employees were assigned to one or more of 59 MDAPs. Capital Analytics used linear regression to analyze the collective data sets and look for relationships among the variables.

THE FINDINGS

The analysis found a statistically significant relationship between course completions and recurring unit cost growth. The fact that the relationship is statistically significant means the reduction in costs is not occurring by chance alone. In fact, the more courses an acquisition employee completed, the less that employee's MDAP costs grew. For

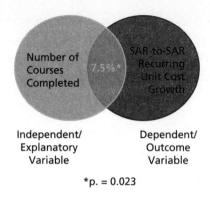

Figure 8.B Shared Relationship

the cumulative MDAP programs that the PoC learners were assigned, there was a total cost growth reduction of $7,425,560 that is correlated with training.

While the study did not isolate the impact of training, it did find that approximately 7.5 percent of the cost variance could be accounted for by the number of courses completed. The remaining 92.5 percent was attributed to other factors, such as employee tenure, age, or level of education (all factors outside of the proof-of-concept model). Since 7.5 percent of the variance in cost growth was found to be due to training, $556,913 of the cost growth reduction can be directly attributed to training. (See Figure 8.B.)

The most important takeaway for DAU leaders from the proof-of-concept study was that they were, in fact, having a measurable impact on reducing cost growth. Further, they had the numbers to show their impact.

CONTINUING THE JOURNEY

The proof-of-concept study showed DAU that it can, in fact, provide a quantitative valuation of training. Like many training organizations in the early stages of a rigorous measurement journey, DAU started small, gained an early win, and has a strong foundation to grow its measurement strategy.

Taken together, the findings from the primary hypothesis and the ancillary business question show that there is a meaningful correlation between DAU's courses and strategic acquisition outcomes as defined by subsequent program cost growth reductions. In the end, DAU's training investment has proven to yield value strategically and financially.

This study was the first real quantitative training valuation proof-of-concept initiative undertaken by a neutral third party. As a proof-of-concept study, relatively small data sets were employed, time and budget were restricted, and a subset of DAU program variables was examined. These encouraging findings and the success of this study indicate that with an expanded data set and enhanced time and budget, more DAU program variables should be explored to achieve DAU's mission to establish a quantitative valuation and financial ROI.

NOTE

1. Department of Defense, Better Buying Power website, http://bbp.dau.mil, 2014.

CHAPTER 9

Optimization through Predictive Analytics

Many learning leaders will read this book with the aim of finding a return on investment (ROI) for their programs, allowing them to show their organizations just how important training is to business success. It's a worthy goal and one we're happy to support. ROI is sometimes criticized, not entirely fairly, for being a historical marker. It is not uncommon to find people who look at ROI only in a backward fashion—they want to clarify the value of what they have done, rather than prepare for the next year's work. It's useful to know the outcome of past work so as not to repeat the same mistakes. By calculating an isolated ROI, you will be armed with powerful justification at budget time.

Stopping with ROI fails to capitalize on the ultimate benefit of strategic measurement, and this is a point we can't stress enough. If you want to rise to the challenges presented by the changing workforce, you must embrace predictive analytics. This powerful data science will radically change the way you plan and deploy learning programs.

A blanket approach to learning programs will not equip your workforce to compete in today's marketplace. Talent is the most important asset and competitive edge of the majority of contemporary organizations, which emphasizes the ever-growing importance of being able to develop that talent. This especially resonates for learning and development (L&D), but also for all departments in the organization, as talent development is increasingly being recognized as everyone's responsibility. As you saw with VW Credit in Chapters 5 and 6, engaging stakeholders and getting aligned with the business enabled the VCI Academy to better engage learners with training finely tuned to meet their needs. In this chapter's case study, you will see how VF Corporation leveraged analytics to quantify the role of managers in employee engagement. The benefits of increased engagement have been extolled by almost every human resources (HR) thought leader. *Forbes* cited a Hay Group study that found that "companies with highly engaged workers grew revenues two and a half times as much as those with low engagement levels."[1] As VF Corporation knows, when you have engaged employees you are able to do more with less—a challenge that almost every corporate learning leader has taken on since the economy began to sour in 2008.

PREDICTIVE ANALYTICS

Have you ever deployed a learning program knowing that some portion of the participants would get absolutely no benefit from taking it? Most learning leaders have, so don't feel shy about answering yes. This happens every day in leading organizations all over the world: both large and small, for-profit and nonprofit, public and private. It's the status quo because it does manage to produce results—if a certain percentage of the people do get a benefit from the program, you're still able to show a net benefit to the organization. It has also persisted because most organizations can't pinpoint which individuals will benefit.

Corporations spend an estimated $145 billion annually[2] on training initiatives, but more than half of those dollars fail to result in tangle returns, with performance gains from learning investments estimated at less than 10 percent.[3] You've probably heard of predictive analytics. It's certainly a hot topic in HR circles, and predictive analytics has been used in a wide variety of other disciplines. It's likely that you have colleagues in other departments throughout your organization who use predictive analytics every day: finance, supply chain, and marketing, to name a few. Thomas H. Davenport in *big data@work* has multiple examples of the use of predictive analytics in multiple industries and many different job functions. In simple terms, predictive analytics means using quantitative methods to derive insights from data, and then drawing on those insights to shape business decisions, to forecast, and, ultimately, to improve business performance. Predictive analytics is emerging as a game changer. The current business environment has created the perfect storm for predictive analytics to finally take hold. With access to disparate organizational data, advanced technology, and the power of software, L&D is now positioned to make sophisticated, data-driven business decisions and to demonstrate the business impact of learning investments.

You can apply predictive analytics to learning initiatives using the performance of a program's initial pilot learners or first cohort to improve the impact of the program going forward. You can learn which types of learners stand to benefit from the learning program, as well as those who will receive little or no benefit. By understanding who has the potential to benefit, you'll be able to achieve three things:

1. Dramatically increase the impact of a learning program by filling the learner audience with people who have the potential to benefit from it.

2. Tweak the program or identify other investments for learners who have a low probability of benefiting from the program.

3. Save money by only choosing participants who are most likely to make an impact after completing the program.

This is what we call optimization. As we explained in Chapter 8, optimization is a prescriptive analysis that examines results already achieved to identify where future investments are most needed.

HOW TO OPTIMIZE INVESTMENTS

If you've been following the advice in this book, you are ready to optimize your investments. Isolation is the most difficult part of our analytics journey, both from a mathematical perspective and in terms of logistics. It requires you to pull data that you may not typically access—the data that describes your learners' performance back on the job. Once you have isolated an investment's impact on the business, your next step is to begin segmenting the data by different organizational and individual characteristics. In Chapter 7, we discussed how segmentation can provide deeper insights into your Level 1 and Level 2 data. When we shift our focus now to segmenting isolated business impact data, we begin to see the predictive power of the data.

To do this segmentation, you will need access to demographic data. In most organizations, this data is relatively easy to access. Your learning management system (LMS) may contain some of it, and the rest should be available through the human resources information system (HRIS). As noted in Chapter 7, demographics are made up of two classes of information: individual demographics and organizational demographics. Examples of each are shown in Figure 9.1; you should collaborate with your stakeholders to create a list of demographics that are relevant to your organization. Note, as seen in the figure, that we use the term *demographics* in a liberal sense, referring to any characteristic of the workforce. Importantly, the term extends beyond the definition of demographics of the Equal Employment Opportunity Commission (EEOC) to incorporate things like job grade and region.

Individual Demographics	Organizational Demographics
Age/gender/ethnicity	Employee engagement scores
Tenure	Number of new accounts opened
Position/job grade	Number of complaints
Education	Revenue/FTE
High potential status	Voluntary turnover
Prior performance	Occupancy rates
Number of accounts	Workers comp costs

Figure 9.1 Types of Demographics

Now it's time to go back to your business results. Say you attributed a 5 percent net increase in sales to a recent training event. That 5 percent gives you your isolated ROI. However, it's highly unlikely that the 5 percent increase can be evenly attributed to every salesperson who attended the training. There were probably some salespeople whose sales increased by 10 percent and some who didn't change at all (or perhaps even saw a decline in performance). In order to optimize the investment, you must determine the characteristics of those who improved the most, as well as the characteristics of those who improved the least (or not at all, or even declined). We call this demographic segmentation of the business impact. Segmentation equips you to deploy learning to those who will benefit most. It also triggers you to alter performance improvement plans for those who are not benefiting.

Remember when we talked about change in performance over time in Chapter 8? You can see here why it's important to look at differences between pre- and post-training performance as opposed to overall performance. You're not trying to uncover, say, the top salesperson. The head of sales can already see who that is simply by looking at gross sales by rep. You're trying to see who improved because of the training. It may be that the top sales reps don't benefit at all from training because they are already performing at their peaks. It may also be that bottom reps also don't stand to benefit from the training because the training is too advanced for them and they lack the fundamentals. Demographic segmentation can't tell you the reasons behind these variations in impact. To uncover this, a qualitative root cause analysis is typically required. However, segmentation will tell you how to deploy the investment in the future.

We often use examples from sales training to explain the principles of isolation and segmentation. It typically represents a significant investment in most organizations, and it's also a fairly straightforward way to illustrate results (increases in performance are typically expressed in dollars or units). In our optimization work, we most commonly evaluate learning programs, but change management initiatives can also be evaluated and optimized. This chapter's case study gives an example of optimization in action with investments that are not as readily linked to the bottom line as sales training initiatives. The VF case study provides an example of how to optimize a performance management process.

GETTING THE DATA FOR OPTIMIZATION

This work requires acquiring data at the individual level, both performance data and demographic data. Of utmost importance in this kind of analysis is protecting the anonymity of the individual. Any statistical evaluation requires populations of people, and is not concerned with any single individual. It is imperative that any data acquisition make every attempt to mask the identity of individuals. After all, analysis and reporting will all be done at an aggregate level. You aren't looking at the performance of a specific person, but the performance of types of individuals. The demographics should allow you to create an archetype of the best candidate for a training program: for example, sales reps in the Northwest market who have between two and five years of tenure with the organization and are between the ages of 22 and 35. From here you can create a list of representatives who will most likely benefit from the sales training program.

In some organizations, performance data aren't available at the individual level. A good example is in banking, where many key performance indicators (KPIs) may be at the branch level. If this is the case in your analysis, consider how the metrics are reported. For example, if performance data are available by branch office, your analysis will be based on the business unit performance (in this case, the branch) and segmented on its characteristics rather than on characteristics of the individuals.

On occasion, we encounter objections to pulling demographic data, ranging from privacy to political concerns. We share two commonly expressed concerns, then present strategies to help obtain this valuable data. First, the concerns:

1. We don't want sensitive individual information leaving the department.
2. Demographic segmentation sounds like it will encourage discrimination.

Regarding number one, when requesting information, be sure you instruct the data analyst pulling the data that you do not want any information that can identify an individual. The data analyst can set up an alternate key that still allows you to tie demographics to performance data while masking the identity of the actual individual. Objection number two can be an alarming argument. First, not all demographic information is EEOC-type data. Data such as job grade, department, region, or tenure are not really protected classes of information. Yes, sometimes age, ethnicity, and gender could provide keen insights. If these are considered important characteristics for analysis, then stick to your guns. When done correctly, optimization will absolutely not be discriminatory. It's not about promoting or preventing the advancement of any one individual's career. It's about ensuring that employees receive the development they need to maximize their performance, and it's about ensuring employees aren't wasting their time with training programs that don't stand to benefit them.

PREDICTIVE ANALYTICS—A LEARNING GAME CHANGER

Investing in people is nothing new. Historically, we've had anecdotal evidence that programs such as onboarding, skills training, and leadership development made a difference, but we couldn't pinpoint where and how they were actually having an impact on the business. Applying predictive analytics to learning investments benefits both the organization and the employee. The organization stands to gain increased profits, reduced expenses, and positive improvements to other business metrics. Employees benefit because the learning and development (L&D) department can offer programs that will help employees to do their jobs better and not waste time on training they don't need. The longer-term effects of better learning include increased engagement, retention, and a stronger talent pipeline.

The idea of combining data from disparate systems is a relatively new one for most HR organizations. Some HR departments are already building internal analytics departments, reflecting an evolution from outside consultants doing the work to internal "people insights" departments. These departments are compiling HR data warehouses that pull together data from engagement surveys, the LMS, HRIS, recruiting systems, performance management, and more. HR data warehouses will go a long way toward easing the work required to apply predictive analytics to people investments because they amass and normalize a large portion of the data required for an analysis. But even with an

HR data warehouse, analysts still need to go outside of HR is acquire operational and business performance data. We're a long way from integrated data warehouses as a corporate standard, but that is the direction in which the industry is moving.

An HR data warehouse is by no means a requirement to start optimizing your investments. Even if your HR group is creating one, we urge you not to wait for its completion to put predictive analytics into action in your learning department.

PIONEERS OF PREDICTIVE ANALYTICS IN HUMAN RESOURCES

While our work has traditionally focused on optimizing specific investments, forward-thinking HR departments are optimizing nearly every aspect of their people management. We would be remiss not to mention Google as a trailblazer in applying predictive analytics to people management. The company approaches "HR with the same empirical discipline [it applies] to its business operations."[4] As one of the most valuable companies in the world, Google's approach to people management is distinctive when compared to much older companies with long-recognized brands or significant acquisition strategies. Dr. John Sullivan cites Google's "extraordinary people management practices" as its "path to corporate greatness":

> "New path" firms dominate by producing continuous innovation. And executives are beginning to learn that continuous innovation cannot occur until a firm makes a strategic shift toward a focus on great people management. A strategic focus on people management is necessary because innovations come from people, and you simply can't maximize innovations unless you are capable of recruiting and retaining innovators. And even then, you must provide them with great managers and an environment that supports innovation.[5]

Google is rich with examples of how it applies data to its people practices. One of the most famous is its retention algorithm, which predicts when an employee will think about leaving the company and allows Google's People Operations group to act before the employee is lost. Another initiative uses predictive modeling to anticipate staffing needs, thereby mitigating management problems and enabling highly effective workforce planning.[6]

Most companies have barely scratched the surface of insights available by applying predictive analytics to human capital. Beginning to optimize your learning investments is a great way to start familiarizing yourself with your company's data and its possibilities. By aligning even one learning investment with business outcomes and then optimizing that investment, you will begin to see a shift in the way your organization plans, designs, and deploys learning programs. Further, you'll lead an L&D group that can prove—and improve—its impact on the business.

CONCLUSION

Measurement of learning and development programs serves two primary purposes: to prove and to improve. Many learning leaders may begin their measurement journey seeking to find the ROI of their programs, allowing them to validate training and secure future funding. If you are able to calculate an isolated ROI, you will be armed with powerful justification at budget time. However, going beyond ROI is where the richness of measurement really kicks in—when you start using measurement to improve, and not just to prove. This strategic shift means moving into the world of optimization through predictive analytics. This is where you will find the deep insights that will prepare you to rise to the performance and development challenges presented by the changing workforce. This powerful data science will radically change the way you plan and deploy learning programs.

The current business environment, coupled with technological advances in data aggregation and analytics software, has created the perfect storm for predictive analytics to finally take hold. By embracing this evolving science, learning and development departments will be able to improve their value to their organizations by:

1. Dramatically increasing the impact of a learning program by filling the learner audience with people who have the potential to benefit from it.

2. Tweaking the program or identify other investments for learners who have a low probability of benefiting from the program.

3. Saving money by only choosing participants who are most likely to make an impact after completing the program.

This form of analysis, or optimization, examines results already achieved to identify where future investments are most needed. First, you isolate the investment's impact on the business, then begin to segment the data by organizational and individual characteristics. These characteristics—or demographics—give insights into who is receiving the most (and the least) benefit from a program. These insights lead to a profile of the best candidates for the program. In other words, you can target your deployment for greatest impact.

This work requires you to combine data from disparate systems across the company. This means going beyond human resources and learning management systems into the world of operational business data. New technologies such as data warehouses are beginning to facilitate this organizational view of human performance and analysis.

This level of analysis, and especially the integration of cross-functional data, is new to most companies. As more and more organizations are pushing for evidence-based decisions, the value of this kind of analysis is undeniable. Get started. Even if you don't have the integration into other data sets yet, begin by simply segmenting your training data; you may be surprised by what you find. Revisit your measurement map to understand what business data will be needed to do a more robust analysis down the road. Then select an investment that has an engaged stakeholder and take the next step to collect the data to isolate and optimize the impact. With evidence in hand, you will sense a shift about how you look at measurement. By aligning and mapping your learning investments to business outcomes, and by measuring the impact and identifying opportunities for optimization, you will change how you think about planning, designing and deploying those investments. You will be well on your way to not only proving—but to improving—the impact of learning on the business.

NOTES

1. Bain Insights, "How to Bring Fickle Shoppers Back to Your Brand," *Forbes*, June 8, 2012, www.forbes.com/sites/baininsights/2012/06/08/how-to-bring-fickle-shoppers-back-to-your-brand/

2. American Society for Training and Development, "2013 State of the Industry," 2013.

3. Corporate Executive Board (CEB), CEB Acquires KnowledgeAdvisors, 2014.

4. David A. Garvin, "How Google Sold Its Engineers on Management," *Harvard Business Review*, December 2013.

5. John Sullivan, "How Google Is Using People Analytics to Completely Reinvent HR," TLNT, February 26, 2013, www.tlnt.com/2013/02/26/how-google-is-using-people-analytics-to-completely-reinvent-hr/

6. Ibid.

Optimizing Performance Management: VF Corporation

Although this book has focused on learning and development investments, as we discussed in our first book, *Human Capital Analytics*, this work can also be applied to process improvement investments. This case study shows how the methods described in this book are applied to understand and improve the launch of a performance management process at VF Corporation.

BACKGROUND

VF Corporation is the $7 billion global apparel company that owns such brands as The North Face, Wrangler, Vans, Lee, 7 for All Mankind, Nautica, Majestic, Rustler, JanSport, and many others. While many of these brands are VF's legacy brands, the company has grown largely through acquisition in recent years. Today's portfolio represents diverse markets and cultures. VF's leaders recognized the need to unify the brands and drive a high-performance culture across the disparate divisions, locations, and brands.

In 2010, VF launched Maximizing Performance, a company-wide performance management process, to support its goal of building a culture of performance and to improve business results. A key component in VF's development of a high-performance culture was getting all associates aligned with corporate goals. With unique cultures across its many brands, VF wanted associates to understand how their individual job roles and departments contributed to their brand and how their brand contributed to the company as a whole.

VF determined that a key indicator of progress toward a high-performance culture was the annual engagement survey. VF believed that the activities and behaviors encouraged by the Maximizing Performance process would be linked to improved individual performance and engagement, and that these would be linked to profitability. VF partnered with Capital Analytics to explore the connections between employee participation in Maximizing Performance, employee performance, and engagement during the rollout of Maximizing Performance. One goal of the study was to help VF understand, during deployment, how to make adjustments to continually improve the new process.

THE STUDY

VF's stakeholders selected two brands to include in this business impact study: Brand A is a recently acquired, young, trendy brand, whereas Brand B is a legacy brand with a long and rich history. Each represents a different workforce and culture with younger versus older workforces and contemporary versus traditional products. VF's stakeholders agreed that these brands were different enough from each other to provide a representative view of participation, engagement, and ultimately the business impact of the new performance management process across the full portfolio of brands. The study focused on U.S.-based, salaried associates of Brand A and Brand B and considered Maximizing Performance activities from January 2010 through June 2011. The evaluation was designed in three phases, mirroring VF's rollout process for Maximizing Performance. (See Figure 9.A.)

PHASE ONE

Phase One focused on the development of performance plans, analyzing compliance (presence of a plan), and the quality of the plans

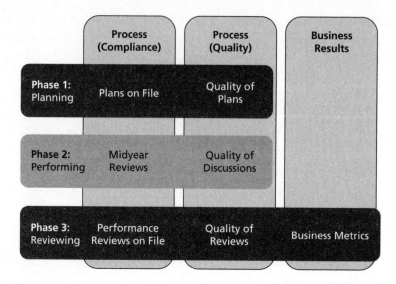

Figure 9.A   Three Phrases of Maximizing Performance

themselves. The performance plans included objectives, competencies, and individual development plans. The stakeholders hypothesized that having a plan, and especially a high-quality performance plan, would be an indicator of employee commitment, showing that they understood how they connect and contribute to the organization. Capital Analytics' researchers evaluated the quality of plans using a weighted rubric. Having a plan, and especially a good-quality plan, would be the first step toward building a high-performance culture.

Phase One began by running a descriptive analysis to determine levels of compliance. In other words, were employees adopting the new Maximizing Performance process? Early analysis showed that women and minorities were the least likely to have plans on file. VF wondered what was going on. When analysts ran a multivariate analysis that included gender, ethnicity, *and* job role, the lack of compliance had nothing to do with women or ethnicity. Job role was the culprit. The noncompliance was really among the administrative individual contributors. These jobs were filled primarily by women and minorities. Appreciating that a high-performance culture needs to be inclusive of all employees, this finding led VF to explore underlying causes. They discovered that managers simply did not know how to create good goals and development plans for their administrative individual contributors. In response, VF increased efforts to support managers in engaging administrative individual contributors in the process. This is a great example of the value of segmenting data and taking corrective action to optimize future investments in Maximizing Performance.

Early in the Maximizing Performance process, VF also discovered that associates were confused over the differences between job descriptions, goals, objectives, and development plans. The evaluation of plan quality quantified this confusion. As clear and measurable goals are key to Maximizing Performance, VF recognized the need for further training and communication to clarify these important concepts. As evidence of the value of having clear and measurable goals, managers of employees who had good plans (and the employees themselves) acknowledged that feedback and reviews were easier, less confrontational, and more productive due to these clearly spelled out goals.

PHASE TWO

Phase Two consisted of tracking ongoing progress against performance plans and providing developmental feedback to improve performance. From the outset, the manager's explicit role in the Maximizing Performance process was to assist with plan development and revisions and to provide interim reviews, coaching, and feedback. It was hypothesized that regular discussions around performance would improve goal attainment as well as engagement

Overall, with both brands, the prominent driver of compliance and quality of plans was the presence of a manager who participated fully in the Maximizing Performance process. In light of this finding, VF focused on manager participation, believing that the act of a manager supporting an associate in the development of his or her plan would help the associate feel more connected to the business and result in improved individual performance and increased engagement scores. The data supported this belief. Both brands showed a high associate compliance rate of over 90 percent when the manager had a performance plan on file. Furthermore, manager involvement was also linked to higher-quality performance plans.

PHASE THREE

Phase Three focused on the annual performance appraisal process. Here stakeholders hypothesized that associates with higher-quality plans (better aligned with the business) would earn better performance reviews and report higher levels of engagement. Performance reviews, turnover data, promotion and salary records, and the annual engagement survey provided data for the analysis.

A comparison of results from the company's employee engagement survey, conducted before launching Maximizing Performance and a year later, revealed a relationship between changes in "Engagement with Manager" and the quality of the employee's plan. In other words, employees who had better plans reported that their level of engagement with their manager had improved. (See Figure 9.B.)

Phase Three results suggested that, as hypothesized, having a plan and an involved manager were connected to higher employee engagement. However, the analysis did not reveal links between Maximizing Performance and the other business metrics evaluated. VF believes that the leading indicators of success are present (those seen in Phase

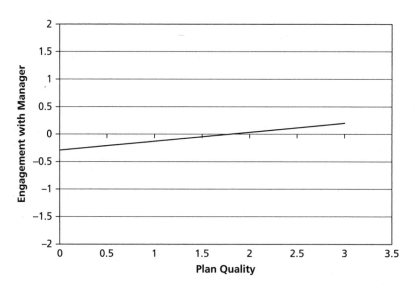

Figure 9.B Improved Plan Quality Improves Engagement with Manager

One and Phase Two), and it will take more time for impact to appear in the other metrics.

Importantly, VF discovered that they had further work to do in program implementation before they could expect to see a broader measurable business impact. They acknowledged the need to provide further support to managers in developing plans and providing feedback. By knowing where (and why) the process was not being adopted, VF has taken steps to optimize further investments in Maximizing Performance. After implementing the identified improvements, and allowing sufficient time for adoption of the changes, a follow-up study may reveal deeper insights into the relationship between Maximizing Performance and performance reviews, turnover, promotion and salary trends, and employee engagement.

CONCLUSION

VF continues to deploy Maximizing Performance with the knowledge that engaged managers are critical to the development of a high-performance culture. Engaged managers encourage their associates to participate in their own professional development process. Explicitly showing employees how they contribute to the company's goals is improving engagement at VF and fostering a high-performance culture.

CHAPTER **10**

In Conclusion—
Get Started

The best and most successful companies have always been those that are able to innovate continually. Without responding to global market forces, even the top companies are doomed to shutter their doors. The era of big data has ushered in an entirely new realm of possibilities for attracting and retaining customers, increasing profits, and decreasing costs. Thomas H. Davenport, a leading thought leader on analytics and business process innovation, wrote in *Harvard Business Review* in 2006, "Organizations are competing on analytics not just because they can—business today is awash in data and data crunchers—but also because they should. At a time when firms in many industries offer similar products and use comparable technologies, business processes are among the last remaining points of differentiation."[1]

Examples abound of companies that attribute their success to analytics. Caesars Entertainment, for example, led its industry in optimizing the placement of gambling machines and offering incentives to customers to keep them playing. Like other forward-thinking organizations, Caesars has taken that analytical expertise and applied it to its human capital management. Says Eric Schmidt, chairman at Google, "Innovation and data are at the core of who we are at Google and we apply those same principles to HR."

Throughout this book, we've shared a number of case studies about companies that have aligned their learning investments to business outcomes, conducted basic analyses to improve their offerings, measured impact against outcomes, and optimized investments using predictive analytics. As these case studies show, a rigorous measurement strategy employing a range of evaluation tools and analytical methodologies has tremendous power to transform the way the learning and development (L&D) function interacts with the business. The learning leaders in our case studies have been able to deploy learning programs that meet learners at the point of need and help to increase engagement and retention. Furthermore, the ability to offer hard proof of an investment's impact on the business is invaluable in a world of tightening budgets and having to do more with less. Using isolated business impact to optimize learning investments is about to become the standard in L&D. It will no longer be acceptable to deploy a program without knowing that the attendees will perform their jobs better after taking it.

Bersin by Deloitte's 2013 research revealed that 86 percent of organizations focus primarily on reporting and looking retrospectively at their investments in people, and only 4 percent are employing predictive analytics to forecast future outcomes or to assess the business impact of their programs. Interestingly, in 2011 Bersin by Deloitte research revealed that 72 percent of survey respondents stated that they *should* measure business impact, but only 10 percent actually do. Why the discrepancy? If it is important and critical, why don't we go after it?

Predictive analytics requires real data science, and many organizations are not prepared for it. One reason predictive analytics is missing from many L&D agendas is that cause-and-effect relationships are perceived as difficult or impossible to establish when it comes to human performance. As we've shown you in this book, rigorous analysis is eminently possible with stakeholder buy-in, the right skill sets, an aligned vision of the connection to outcomes, and a commitment to measure and improve. Exploration of causal relationships between human resources (HR) factors (e.g., hiring sources, training days, tenure, employee engagement, etc.) and business metrics (e.g., gross profit, reduced costs, customer retention, customer churn rate, etc.) is possible, viable, and crucial in the face of the changing workforce.

Here is the most important takeaway from this book: It's not too late to start, regardless of how much (or how little) measurement is part of your current practices. For some, a measurement strategy or a measurement map is the best first step. For others, improving on the basics to uncover deeper insights can provide quick wins and build momentum for more sophisticated measurement. Still others will identify one or two high-profile investments to optimize, which is a good way to become familiar with your available data and resources. The most important part of any analytics journey is making the commitment to begin. Measurement is a fluid process—even the most robust strategy will adapt over time to changing business needs. What we've found in our work is that measurement tends to beget more measurement. Chip and Dan Heath, authors of *Made to Stick* and *Switch*, described it well, pointing out that "Once we know something, we find it hard to imagine what it was like not to know it." Once your stakeholders and clients see the benefits of your initial efforts, they'll demand more.

NOTE

1. Thomas H. Davenport, "Competing on Analytics," *Harvard Business Review*, January 2006.

Talent Development Reporting Principles (TDRp)

Managing Learning Like a Business to Deliver Greater Impact, Effectiveness, and Efficiency

Dave Vance, Executive Director
Peggy Parskey, Assistant Director
Center for Talent Reporting

Talent Development Reporting principles (TDRp) is an industry-led initiative to better manage learning and development in particular and all key talent processes in general. Application of TDRp will enable you to improve the bottom-line results of your company more effectively and efficiently. In particular, TDRp will help you and your organization:

- Identify your key company goals.
- Align learning to these key company goals and establish the expected impact of your initiatives on business outcomes.

- Identify, report, and manage the most important effectiveness and efficiency measures for your key initiatives.
- Manage key initiatives through the year to deliver planned results.

In brief, TDRp will enable you to run learning like a business. This means identifying the right learning and development programs, carefully planning those programs, collaboratively establishing goals with program sponsors and stakeholders, and executing with discipline throughout the year to ensure that the planned, agreed-upon results are delivered as effectively and efficiently as possible. This approach will allow you to deliver the greatest impact for your budget and will help you be viewed as a valued, strategic partner.

WHAT DOES TDRp PROVIDE?

TDRp began in 2010 when Kent Barnett, CEO of KnowledgeAdvisors, and Tamar Elkeles, VP of Learning for Qualcomm, engaged a group of industry thought leaders to develop standards for learning and development (L&D), much like accountants have in generally accepted accounting principles (GAAP) in the United States or International Financial Reporting Standards (IFRS) elsewhere. The effort resulted in a framework for reporting and managing that provides a chief learning officer (CLO) with all the necessary tools to run learning like a business, including:

- Guiding principles
- Standard outcome, effectiveness, and efficiency measures
- Three standard statements employing these measures:
  1. Outcome statement
  2. Effectiveness statement
  3. Efficiency statement
- Three recommended executive reports employing key measures from the three statements:
  1. Summary report for the CLO, CFO, and CEO
  2. Program reports for the CLO, directors, and program managers
  3. Operations report for the CLO and directors

- Detailed implementation guidance:
  - How to conduct discussions with the CEO to establish priorities and goals
  - How to conduct impact discussions with the sponsors
  - How to create the TDRp statements and reports

More than a set of measures or reports, TDRp is designed to answer the most common questions facing learning leaders:

- What should we measure, and how should it be defined?
- How should these measures be reported?
- What do CLOs need to manage their function?
- What information do CEOs need to assess the value of L&D to the business?
- How should CLOs and their staff use TDRp reports to manage the function?
- How can we show the value of our work?

TDRp was developed for L&D in 2011 and expanded to other talent processes (like talent acquisition and performance management) in 2012. Hundreds of organizations are now implementing TDRp.

The Home of TDRp

The Center for Talent Reporting, a nonprofit 501(c)(6) organization, was established in 2012 to improve the measurement, reporting, and management of human capital. The board of directors is composed of industry leaders. The Center is supported by income from members, sponsors, workshops, and an annual conference.

ASSUMPTIONS

There are several important assumptions underlying the framework and recommendations contained in this report. Stating these up front may help eliminate or reduce potential misunderstandings and will provide context for the recommendations.

The learning and development function is broadly defined to include all the programs and initiatives designed to increase human capital to enable greater organizational and personal capacity, effectiveness, and efficiency. With this understanding L&D would include formal and informal learning, performance support, leadership, new employee orientation, and tuition assistance. Some L&D functions will have all these responsibilities whereas others have fewer or more.

The primary purpose of learning and development is to build organizational capability that enables the organization to achieve its goals or achieve its goals more quickly or at lower cost.

Whenever possible, learning will be aligned strategically to the goals of the organization. Learning leaders will meet proactively with sponsors to discuss and agree on the role of learning in meeting the organization's goals and will set appropriate goals for the learning program or initiative.

The recommended reports and the underlying data will be used appropriately by competent, experienced learning leaders to manage the function to meet agreed-upon goals and to continuously improve.

THE FRAMEWORK

Figure A.1 illustrates the framework for our approach where data sources and measures serve as the foundation for the three statements and three executive reports.

- *Guiding principles* provide direction for the entire executive reporting process.
- *Data sources.* Multiple data sources will typically be required to support executive reporting. In most organizations these would include financial data (like the income statement for the enterprise and for the L&D function), the learning management system (LMS), and other learning-related systems for data on participants, courses, and perhaps Levels 1 and 2; evaluation systems for data on Levels 1 to 4; and a variety of other data sources like a human resources information system (HRIS), enterprise resource planning (ERP), talent management, and customer relationship management (CRM).

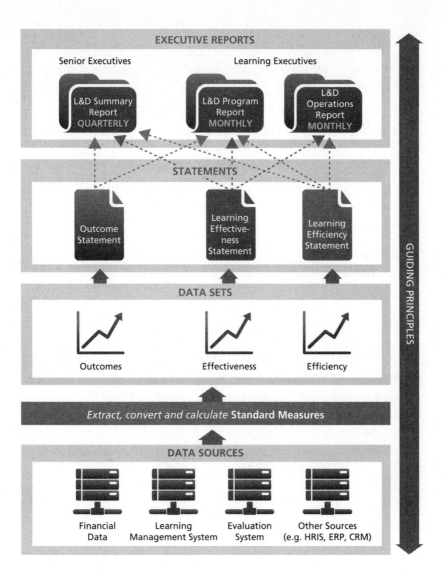

Figure A.1 Executive Reporting Process

■ *Standard measures.* The selected standard measures would then be extracted or calculated from these data sources and managed in one or more data sets. An example of a calculated measure would be L&D expenditure per employee, which would draw the L&D expenditure from financial data and divide it by the employee count from an HR source.

■ *Data set(s).* The standard measures reside in the data set(s) or warehouse, which includes all the detailed data required for the statements as well as drill downs to answer specific questions. (For example, which class or instructor is pulling down the overall Level 1 rating?)

■ *Statements.* The three standard statements will be constructed from the measures contained in the data sets, and in turn will be the basis for the executive reports.

■ *Executive reports.* Three executive reports will be constructed from the statements for business executives and for learning executives.

We start our more detailed discussion with the guiding principles, followed by an elaboration on standard measures, statements, and executive reports.

GUIDING PRINCIPLES

These principles provide direction for the L&D standards, statements, and reports just as GAAP provides direction for accounting concepts, statements, and reports. The principles also provide direction for the management of the L&D function and the use of the measures, standards, and reports.

There are eight guiding and generally accepted reporting principles for executive-level L&D reporting.

1. Executive reporting should employ concise and balanced measures that are reported in a consistent and clearly defined format.
2. Executive reports should be produced and communicated with frequency and thoroughness to enable appropriate management of the function.
3. Executive reporting should include actionable recommendations.
4. Data integrity and completeness should be maintained.
5. Appropriate analytical methods should be employed.
6. The impact and value or benefit of programs and initiatives should be provided whenever appropriate.

7. The full costs of L&D should be captured and reported.

8. Executive reporting and the underlying databases should support continuous improvement.

The first principle about employing the right measures is especially important, so the following detailed guidance is provided:

1. Key effectiveness, efficiency, and outcome measures should be reported and tracked on a regular basis. These include organizational goals and the contribution of L&D to those goals; key volume, cost, and utilization measures; and Levels 1 to 5 measures.

2. Goals should be set for key outcome, effectiveness, and efficiency measures. Performance to goals should be tracked and reported.

3. Executive reports should include, at a minimum, results for last year, current year plan or goal, current year-to-date (YTD) results, and a forecast for the current year. Detailed reports typically include just the results, which may be daily, weekly, monthly, quarterly, or yearly.

This guidance not only influences the format of the reports, but, in combination with the assumptions of strategic alignment and proactive sponsor discussion, it offers critical management principles for all learning leaders to follow in terms of setting goals, tracking YTD progress, and forecasting how the year is expected to end.

STANDARD MEASURES

Every organization should employ three types of measures using industry-standard definitions, although the choice of measures will depend on the goals of the organization and L&D function as well as the challenges they face for the coming year. The three types of measures are outcomes, effectiveness, and efficiency.

1. *Outcome measures* capture the impact L&D is expected to have on the organization's most important goals. For example, a sales training initiative might be expected to contribute 20 percent toward the company goal of increasing sales by 10 percent.

2. *Effectiveness measures* are indicators of how well learning contributes to organizational outcomes. In short, they are about quality. For L&D the effectiveness measures are simply the Kirkpatrick/ Phillips Levels 1 to 5. An organization need not report all five measures.

3. *Efficiency measures* are indicators of an organization's activity and investment in learning. Examples include the numbers of learners, number of courses, cycle times, utilization rates, costs, and percentage of employees reached by training.

An organization just starting its measurement journey may have only five of each type to start, whereas a more mature organization may have 10 to 20 for each. (Many organizations strive to collect hundreds of measures. This is a mistake. The goal is to have just the right number—the select few that their managers will use on a monthly basis to run learning like a business.)

THREE STANDARD STATEMENTS

The standard statements organize the standard measures, just as the three primary financial statements (income statement, balance sheet, and cash flow statement) organize financial data. The three reporting statements are constructed from the standard measures contained in the data set or warehouse and include the following:

1. Outcome statement showing the outcome measures.
2. Effectiveness statement showing the effectiveness measures.
3. Efficiency statement showing the efficiency measures.

At a minimum, it is recommended that each high-level statement include last year's results (where applicable), current-year goal or plan, and year-to-date results. Detailed statements might include just actual results and greater frequency (monthly versus quarterly data for example). Historical data may also be displayed graphically to help discern trends.

For executive reporting, key measures from each statement should be included to provide a complete picture on how well L&D is performing and impacting business objectives. It is also important to note that compiling and managing these comprehensive data sets is vital in addressing questions that arise from executive-level discussions.

Let's look at each in greater detail.

The Outcome Statement

The outcome statement brings together the key goals or desired outcomes (results) of the organization along with the impact or contribution L&D is expected to have on achieving those outcomes. The report should include the primary goals of the organization (e.g., a 10 percent increase in sales) for the year (whether supported by learning or not), any other goals that will be supported by learning, and the expected impact or importance of learning on achieving those goals.

Goals might include revenue, market share, cost, profit, operating efficiencies, productivity, cycle time, quality, safety, customer satisfaction, leadership, employee engagement, retention, and risk mitigation. The goals should be shown in descending order of priority and should be stated in specific, measurable terms.

The impact of learning on the organizational goal may be expressed in terms of a Level 4 measure (quantitatively or qualitatively) or, if that is not possible, the application rate (Level 3) may serve as a proxy or indicator for the impact of learning.

Let's start with cases where the expected impact of learning (Level 4) on business outcome has been discussed with the sponsor prior to the program's initiation and a goal has been agreed upon. For example, it is agreed that the program, properly designed, developed, delivered, and reinforced, should make a 70 percent contribution toward the goal of a 20 percent reduction in injuries. In other words, training is expected to account for a 14 percent reduction in injuries. Progress toward this goal can be reported assuming the 70 percent contribution as long as the sponsor remains comfortable with it. A follow-up study may be done after the program is completed to confirm the 70 percent contribution (isolation factor) but often is not necessary. For some programs, a qualitative assessment (isolation) of learning's contribution (Level 4) may be used for both goal setting and reporting using adjectives such as *high, medium, low,* or *essential.*

There are cases where it is not possible, feasible, or desirable to set goals and report in terms of Level 4 impact (quantitatively or qualitatively). For these programs or initiatives a Level 3 measure may serve as a proxy or an indicator for having an impact on the desired business outcome. For example, the sponsor and learning leader may have agreed that learning will make an important contribution to achieving the goal of a 20 percent increase in sales if 80 percent of the participants apply the three key concepts they have learned. Here, the application rate of 80 percent becomes the goal for learning, and progress can be reported through the year. It is understood that an application rate considerably less than 80 percent will put the 20 percent increase in sales at significant risk.

In other cases, the expected impact of learning may be agreed upon in advance with the sponsor but not necessarily in the same terms as the goal. For example, suppose the organizational goal is to improve leadership scores on the employee opinion survey (EOS) by five points, and the sponsor believes more coaching by senior leaders is key to getting the improved score. A goal is set for leaders to spend one hour per week coaching their direct reports (This would be a proxy for impacting the EOS goal.) Assume further that a needs analysis showed that leaders were willing and able to spend the time but were not doing so solely because they lacked the necessary coaching skills. The Level 4 impact would be the actual coaching time. (No effort is made here to isolate the impact of more coaching on the five-point increase in score.)

Occasionally, the measure of learning impact may include Level 5 where year-to-date results will typically represent an estimate made by the sponsor and learning program manager based on data from the effectiveness statement.

Clearly, there are many different ways to relate the impact or contribution of learning to the business outcomes. Typically, a combination of the foregoing methods would be used reflecting not only the different types of initiatives (some are more amenable to quantification and isolation than others), but also the comfort levels of the sponsors in setting quantitative goals for learning. The key is to identify all the relevant corporate goals, meet with the sponsors, discuss the role of learning (if any), and then agree on the expected impact or contribution that learning may have on achieving the goal. Typically, there will be some high-priority goals for which no learning is planned.

Figure A.2 provides an example of a high-level outcome statement for the private sector. Key business outcomes such as revenue, leadership, and safety are shown in priority order. The statement also illustrates a variety of impact measures for learning.

- Priorities 1 (Revenue) and 3 (Safety) employ the quantitative isolated impact of learning.
- Priorities 2 (Engagement) and 4 (Costs) employ the qualitative isolated impact of learning.
- Priority 5 (Retention) indicates there is no training planned for this business priority.
- Priority 6 (Call Center Satisfaction) employs the application rate as a proxy for the impact of learning.

To reiterate, the plan values for the outcome measures come from a discussion with each sponsor.

The Effectiveness Statement

The effectiveness statement focuses on how effectively or how well the organizational outcomes are achieved. An effective organization is one that delivers the intended results, and the effectiveness statement focuses on the components or intermediate steps necessary to achieve the intended result. Effectiveness measures largely come from survey data, and the scores enable L&D to ensure that learning content and delivery meet the following criteria:

- Acceptable quality
- Application to the job
- Impact
- Creation of value

Moreover, effectiveness measures enable the L&D organization to continually improve performance.

Since there are multiple, important measures of effectiveness, the learning leader needs to view all measures holistically and use the entire suite of measures to manage and gauge success effectively. In practice, it will typically be necessary to make trade-offs since it may be impossible

Learning & Development
Sample High-level Business Outcome Statement for the Private Sector
with Mixed Impacts and Proxies
Results through June

Priority	Business Outcomes and Impact of Learning and Development Initiatives		2011 Actual	For 2012		
				Plan	Jun YTD	% of Plan
1	Revenue: Increase Sales by 20%					
	Corporate Goal or Actual	%	10%	20%	17%	85%
	Impact of L&D Initiatives: 25% contribution to goal	%	1%	5%	4%	80%
2	Engagement: Increase Engagement Score by 3 Points to 69.4%					
	Corporate Goal or Actual	Points	1 pt	3 pts	1.9 pts	63%
	Impact of L&D Initiatives: Low Impact on Goal	H/M/L	Low	Low	Low	
3	Safety: Reduce Injuries by 20%					
	Corporate Goal or Actual	%	10%	20%	15%	75%
	Impact of L&D Initiatives: 70% Contribution to Goal	%	5%	14%	11%	75%
4	Costs: Reduce Operating Expenses by 15%					
	Corporate Goal or Actual	%	5%	15%	10%	67%
	Impact of L&D Initiatives: Medium Impact on Goal	H/M/L	Low	Medium	Medium	

No.	Outcome / Measure	Unit				
5	Retention: Improve Retention of Top Performers by 5 Points to 90%					
	Corporate Goal or Actual	Points	-3 pts	5 pts	2 pts	40%
	Impact of L&D Initiatives	None planned				
6	Call Center Satisfaction: Improved Satisfaction Score by 4 points to 80%					
	Corporate Goal or Actual	Points	1.6 pts	4 pts	2.9 pts	73%
	Application of Key Behaviors	%	84%	95%	91%	96%
	Number Trained	Number	40	40	24	60%
Other Important Business Outcomes and Impacts						
A	Company with New Regulations					
	Corporate Goal or Actual	% In compliance	100%	100%	100%	100%
	Impact of L&D Initiatives: Essential	Essential	Essential	Essential	Essential	
B	Onboarding of Service Reps					
	Impact of L&D Initiatives: Reduce Time to Competency by 20%	%	NA	20%	17%	85%
	Number Onboarded	Number	25	50	21	42%
C	Become an Employer of Choice					
	Impact of L&D Initiatives: Medium Impact on Goal	H/M/L	Low	Medium	On Plan	
	Increase Reach to 95%	%	73%	95%	53%	79%
	Number of Unique Participants	Number	14,321	21,500	16,500	77%

Figure A.2 High-Level Business Outcome Statement for the Private Sector

or undesirable to maximize achievement of all measures given that not all measures are of equal importance. The measures may also be used to manage and mitigate the risk faced by the learning manager.

Recommended effectiveness measures for consideration include the following:

Level 1: Quality of content, instructor, environment, alignment to organizational goals, and relevance

Level 2: Learning or knowledge and/or skills gained

Level 3: Application to the job (may include measurement of reinforcement)

Level 4: Impact

Level 5: Value

Since Levels 3 (in some cases), 4, and 5 represent the ultimate effectiveness of the learning program, they appear in both the outcome and effectiveness statements. Some organizations, especially early in the measurement journey, may not include any Level 4 or Level 5 measures.

A well-designed learning survey completed at the end of the course or shortly thereafter should have several Level 1 questions and at least one question for each of the other four levels. Although the respondent has not had time yet to apply the learning, he or she can provide intent to apply, an opinion about alignment, and likely impact and value. Answers to these questions tend to be excellent indicators or predictors of actual Levels 3 to 5 results.

In addition to the data from the learning survey just described, many courses will contain a Level 2 test of knowledge either embedded in the course or to be taken at completion. Likewise, more substantive Levels 3 to 5 data may come from a survey administered several months after the course to all participants or to a sample. Alternatively, Levels 3 to 5 data may also be gathered from a focus group or one-on-one interviews with a sample of participants.

It is also possible to combine results from all five levels into a single measure of learning effectiveness.

There will be multiple levels of the effectiveness statement. Just as business unit income statements roll up into a consolidated income statement for the enterprise, effectiveness statements by program, college, or unit would roll up into a consolidated effectiveness statement for enterprise L&D.

Figure A.3 provides an example of a high-level effectiveness statement.

Learning & Development **Sample High-Level Effectiveness Statement** **Results through June**					
			For 2012		
		2011 **Actual**	**Plan**	**Jun** **YTD**	**% of** **Plan**
Level 1: Employee	% top two boxes	75.6%	80.0%	78.9%	98.6%
(All programs and	% top two boxes	80.0%	85.0%	85.6%	100.6%
Initiatives)	% top two boxes	81.9%	85.0%	88.2%	103.8%
Quality of Content	% top two boxes	74.6%	85.0%	83.2%	97.9%
Quality of Instructor	Average of	78.0%	83.8%	84.0%	100.2%
Relevance	measures				
Alignment to Goals					
Total for Level 1					
Level 1: Sponsor	%top two boxes	75.0%	80.0%	77.0%	96.3%
(Select programs)					
Level 2: (Select	Score	78.0%	85.0%	83.0%	97.6%
programs)					
Level 3: (Select	% top two boxes	80.9%	85.0%	86.5%	101.8%
programs)	% who applied it	61.0%	75.0%	78.0%	104.0%
Intent to Apply (From survey at course completion)					
Actual Application (After three months)					
Level 4: (Select	Contribution	19.5%	30.0%	32.4%	108.0%
programs)	to goal	NA	25.0%	26.2%	104.8%
Estimate by Participants (End of course)	Contribution				
Estimate by Participants (After three months)	to goal				
Level 5: (Select	Thousands $	$546	$800	$345	43.1%
programs)	%	29%	35%	32%	91.4%
Net Benefits					
ROI					

Figure A.3 High-Level Effectiveness Statement

The Efficiency Statement

The efficiency statement brings together all the activity and cost elements necessary to judge how efficiently the outcomes were achieved. An efficient organization is one that executes at least cost. Efficiency measures will come primarily from the learning management system (LMS) or other learning-related system, other back-office systems, and the income statement or department expense report. These measures are used to ensure that the function is well managed and reaching the desired audience.

Like the effectiveness measures, the recommended efficiency measures should be viewed holistically. The learning manager should use the entire suite of measures to manage efficiently and to gauge success, realizing that some measures are more important or more relevant than others.

Recommended efficiency measures include cost, volume, utilization, program and vendor management, and reach measures, as well as the following indicators:

- Budget and opportunity costs
- Cost reduction
- L&D expenditure per employee, L&D staff per employee
- Average costs, average class size
- Total and unique participants by type of learning and by program or initiative
- Hours by type of learning and by program or initiative
- Courses by type of learning and by program or initiative
- Utilization by course, hours, type of learning, staff, participants
- Program management of courses
- Cycle times
- Vendor management
- Reach

Figure A.4 provides an example of a high-level efficiency statement (first page only).

The Definition of Terms and Measures document provides 70 common L&D terms. Find it at www.centerfortalentreporting.org under Resources > Learning & Development.

Learning & Development Sample High-Level Efficiency Statement Results through June					
			For 2012		
		2011 Actual	Plan	Jun YTD	% of Plan
Total Participants	Number	109.618	147,500	67,357	46%
Total Unique Participants	Number	40.729	45,313	36,998	82%
Courses Taken by Type of Learning					
ILT Only	% of total	56%	43%	46%	107%
MLT Only	% of total	3%	9%	8%	87%
E-Learning Only	% of total	35%	40%	40%	98%
Blended	% of total	6%	8%	7%	91%
Total Courses	% of total	100%	100%	100%	100%
Utilization					
E-Learning Courses	Number	60	74	70	95%
Available	Number	50	72	64	89%
Taken by More than 20	%	83%	97%	91%	94%
% Taken by More than 20					
Reach					
% of Employee Reached by L&D	%	85%	88%	72%	88%
% of Employee with Development Plans	%	92%	98%	95%	96%
Program Management					
Courses					
Total Developed	Number	22	36	24	67%
Number Meeting Deadline	Number	16	33	21	64%
% Meeting Deadline	%	73%	92%	88%	95%
Total Delivered	Number	143	178	167	94%
Number Meeting Deadline	Number	89	160	139	87%
% Meeting Deadline	%	62%	90%	83%	85%
Cycle Time					
Performance Consulting	Days	39	30	33	67%
Design and Development for ILT	Days	56	45	44	109%
Design and Development for WBT	Days	48	40	39	113%
Investment					
L&D Expenditures	Million $	15.8	20.2	9.9	49%
Cost Reduction	Thousand $	63	295	168	57%

Figure A.4 High-Level Efficiency Statement

The Three Statements

All three statements are necessary for a complete and balanced picture of the L&D organization, just as all three financial statements are needed to know the complete financial status of a company.

To achieve the desired outcome in an effective and efficient manner, a learning program or initiative must:

- Be strategically aligned to the goals of the organization—in other words, be the right learning (prelude to the creation of the outcome statement and also measured in the effectiveness statement).

- Employ the form of learning best suited to achieving the goals (evidenced by high scores on the effectiveness statement).

- Be well received, facilitate the desired learning, be applied, and have the intended impact on the organizational goal (evidenced by high scores on the effectiveness statement and high contribution on the outcome statement).

- Be executed at least cost to accomplish the outcome (evidenced by appropriate cost, volume, ratio measures, and utilization rates on the efficiency statement).

THE THREE REPORTS

The three executive or high-level reports are constructed from the three statements, just as management reports in an organization are constructed from underlying financial and activity reports. The three executive reports include one targeted for use with senior executives (CEO, SVP, etc.) and two targeted for use with executives who are learning managers with responsibility for programs, budget, and people. Each report, along with its purpose, target audience, and frequency, is depicted in Table A.1.

The summary report is intended to serve as a stand-alone report for the senior executive while the learning executive is expected to use the other two reports to manage the function. Typically, though, the learning executive would share the summary report with learning leaders and staff so they know what is being reported to senior management.

Table A.1 The Reports

Report	Purpose	Target Audience	Frequency
1. L&D Summary	Convey progress against high-level goals	Business and Learning Executives	Quarterly
2. L&D Program Report	Manage programs and initiatives to deliver planned results	Learning Executives, Directors, and Managers	Monthly
3. L&D Operations Report	Manage L&D operations efficiently	Learning Executives and Directors	Monthly

These three high-level reports are intended to focus on the most important measures at an aggregate level. Where greater detail is required to answer questions that are triggered by the reports, the statements or underlying database will provide the data to answer those questions. The three executive reports combined with the three statements and underlying data set should provide comprehensive reporting on the effectiveness, efficiency, and organizational impact of the learning programs.

All three high-level reports should include the following for each measure:

- Last year's results
- Current-year plan
- Year-to-date results
- Year-to-date results compared to plan
- Forecast for the current year

This constitutes the minimum recommended for executive reporting with the understanding that organizations will add measures of relevance where applicable. (Comparison of current-year plan to last year's results, current YTD results to last year's YTD results, and forecast to plan are optional.) Just as with the statements, detailed reports may focus just on actual results (no forecasts or comparison to plan) and provide higher-frequency data. In addition, some may choose to display some of the data visually in a dashboard and provide analytical commentary. It is recommended that a quarterly Learning and Development (L&D) Summary Report be generated with data, visuals, and analysis to enforce a discipline similar to financial reporting.

Of course, the key to successful management of the learning function lies not just in the reports themselves but in the analysis and actionable recommendations that flow from the reports. Consequently, the guiding principles include recommendations on reporting, and further work is planned to provide guidance on using the reports.

The L&D Summary Report

The L&D Summary Report should contain the most significant measures from the outcome, effectiveness, and efficiency statements aggregated at the highest level. The report should be concise and limited to one or two pages with support material available as appropriate. The report should be interpreted for the audience either in a face-to-face presentation or in writing with a focus on summary conclusions and actionable recommendations.

Since the summary report contains multiple, important measures from all three underlying statements, the report must be read holistically to obtain an accurate picture of progress against goals. In practice, it will often be impossible to achieve all the stated goals as the year progresses requiring that trade-offs be made among goals. Moreover, changes in the external environment (economy, market, competition) or internal environment (company goals and priorities, or learning department resources) may impact the achievement of planned goals.

A sample L&D Summary Report is provided in Figure A.5. This particular report is organized into four sections: impact, effectiveness, efficiency, and L&D investment.

Notice that plan and actual are shown for each key corporate goal along with the expected impact of training on achieving that goal. The number in parentheses reflects the expectation of the sponsor. If this expectation changes during the year, then the YTD results and forecast would be adjusted accordingly.

Results of pilot studies and results of completed programs are also shown in the YTD column.

The report's format and choice of measures should reflect what is most important to the leaders of the organization and the L&D function.

The Program (or Initiative) Report

The L&D Program Report should include the measures necessary for senior leaders and staff in the L&D function to manage program and initiative results on a monthly basis. These typically would include the following for key learning programs and initiatives:

- Corporate goal supported by the learning program or initiative
- Impact of the learning program or initiative on the corporate goal
- Number of participants
- Number of courses
- Completion date
- Level 1 for employees and sponsor
- Level 2
- Level 3
- Sample size for Levels 1 to 3 (for example, $n = 1,872$)

A sample program report is provided in Figure A.6.

The rows focus on the courses or initiatives in support of a particular goal. Goals appear in the top half of the report with year-to-date results and the forecast in the bottom half. There are many ways to construct this type of report, but two rules should be observed:

1. Show the corporate goal and results on the *same* page as the L&D program goal and results. This is critical to remind the learning managers and staff why the learning program is being undertaken. Don't break the connection between the two!

2. Bring the goals and results for the elements of the L&D program together on the same page. Don't show results without referring to the goals!

Since the report is organized around a particular organizational goal, the format should work regardless of how the L&D function is

Learning & Development
Sample Executive Summary Report for the Private Sector
Results through June

			For 2012		
	2011 Actual	Plan	Jun YTD	% of Plan	Forecast
Impact of Learning and Development Initiatives					
Revenue: Increase Sales by 20%					
Corporate Goal or Actual — %	10%	20%	17%	85%	20%
Impact of L&D Initiatives: 25% Contribution to Goal — %	1%	5%	4%	80%	5%
Engagement: Increase Engagement Score by 3 Points to 69.4%					
Corporate Goal or Actual — Points	1 pt	3 pts	1.9 pts	63%	3 pts
Impact of L&D Initiatives: Low Impact on Goal — H/M/L	Low	Low	Low		Low
Safety: Reduce Injuries by 20%					
Corporate Goal or Actual — %	10%	20%	15%	75%	20%
Impact of L&D Initiatives: 70% Contribution to Goal — %	5%	14%	11%	75%	14%
Costs: Reduce Operating Expenses by 15%					
Corporate Goal or Actual — %	5%	15%	10%	67%	18%
Impact of L&D Initiatives: Medium Impact on Goal — H/M/L	Low	Medium	Medium		Medium
Retention: Improve Retention of Top Performers by 5 Points to 90%					
Corporate Goal or Actual — Points	–3 pts	5 pts	2 pts	40%	5 pts
Impact of L&D Initiatives — None planned					

Call Center Satisfaction: Improve Satisfaction Score by 4 Points to 80%						
Corporate Goal or Actual	Points	1.6 pts	4 pts	2.9 pts	73%	4 pts
Application of Key Behaviors	%	84%	95%	91%	96%	95%
Number Trained	Number	40	40	24	60%	40
Effectiveness						
Participant Feedback	% Favorable	78%	84%	84%	100%	85%
Sponsor Feedback	% Favorable	75%	80%	77%	96%	78%
Learning	Score	78%	85%	83%	98%	84%
Application Rate	% Who Applied it	61%	75%	78%	104%	79%
Efficiency						
% of Employees Reached by L&D	%	85%	88%	72%	82%	88%
% of Employees with Development Plan	%	92%	98%	95%	97%	96%
% of Courses Developed on Time	%	73%	92%	88%	95%	90%
% of Courses Delivered on Time	%	62%	90%	83%	85%	87%
L&D Investment						
L&D Expenditure	Million $	$15.8	$20.2	$9.9	49%	$20.2
Opportunity Cost	Million $	$3.4	$2.9	$1.3	45%	$2.9
Cost Reduction (Internal to L&D)	Thousand $	$63	$295	$168	57%	$325

Figure A.5 Executive Summary Report for the Private Sector

Learning & Development
Sample Executive Program Report—Medium Complexity
For a Safety Initiative

Enterprise Goal: Reduce injuries by 30% in 2022

Expected Impact of Learning: 18% reduction in injuries due to training (60% contribution toward the goal of reducing injuries by 30%)

Sponsor: Swathe, VP of Manufacturing

		Program Goals			
		Level 1			
Metric	**Value**	**Employee**	**Sponsor**	**Level 2**	**Level 3**
Deliver Phase 1 Courses for Factory A					
Unique Participants	3,000	80%	90%	90%	65%
Total Participants	6,000				
Complete by 5/30	3				
Develop Phase 2 Courses for Factory B			90%		
Deliver Phase 2 Courses					
Unique Participants	1,000	80%	90%	90%	70%
Total Participants	3,000				
Complete by 9/30	4				
Deliver Phase 3 Courses for Factory A			90%		
Deliver Phase 3 Courses					
Unique Participants	500	80%	90%	90%	70%
Total Participants	2,000				
Develop Phase 4 Courses					
70% Complete by 12/31	2		90%		
	------	------	------	------	------
Total		80%	90%	90%	68%
Courses Developed	Number	9			
Unique Participants	Number	4,000			
Total Participants	Number	11,000			
Cost (including opportunity cost)	Thousand $	$700			
Gross Benefit @ $1,000 per injury	Thousand $	$900			
Net Benefit	Thousand $	$200			

June Year-to-Date Results

| Enterprise Goal:
Impact of Learning: | Injuries reduced by 20% from first six months of last year 12% reduction in injuries
due to training (based on the expected 60% of training on reducing injuries) | | | | | | Current Forecast
30% reduction
18% reduction (60%) | |

		Year-to-Date Results		Level 1				Current Forecast	
	Metric	Value	% of Plan	Employee	Sponsor	Level 2	Level 3	Value	% of Plan
Deliver Phase 1 Courses	Unique Participants	2,800	93%	85%	88%	95%	62%	3,200	107%
	Total Participants	5,542	92%	n=1872		n=5542	n=270	630	105%
Develop Phase 2 Courses	Complete by 5/30	3	100%		90%			3	100%
Deliver Phase 2 Courses	Unique Participants	100	10%	80%	90%	92%	61%	1,100	110%
	Total Participants	234	9%	n=39		n=98	n=7	3,200	107%
Develop Phase 3 Courses	Complete by 9/30	1	25%					4	100%
Deliver Phase 3 Courses	Unique Participants	0	0%					450	90%
	Total Participants	0	0%					1,800	90%
Develop Phase 4 Courses	70% Complete by 12/31	0	0%		60%			1	50%
		-----	-----					-----	-----
Total				83%	82%	94%	62%		
Courses Developed	Number	4	44%					8	89%
Unique Participants	Number	2,900	73%					4,300	108%
Total Participants	Number	5,826	53%					11,300	103%
Cost (including opportunity cost)	Thousand $	$350	50%					$690	99%
Gross Benefit @$1,000 per injury	Thousand $	$477	53%					$925	103%
Net Benefit	Thousand $	$127	63%					$235	117%

Figure A.6 Executive Program Report

215

organized. If the L&D function is organized by a college or program structure, then one dean or director will be responsible for all the elements and courses listed. Alternatively, if L&D is organized by function with one director responsible for performance consulting, another for design and development, and another for delivery or implementation, then multiple directors will be responsible for success of the programs in support of a single organizational goal. The recommended elements are included with the understanding that each organization will add other relevant elements.

Since this report is used to manage individual programs and initiatives in the L&D function, it contains a much greater level of detail than the CEO report. It also contains learning jargon since all its users will be learning professionals. Like the CEO report, however, it continues to highlight the connection between the learning program or initiative and the organizational goal as well as the impact that learning is having on the goal.

A separate program report would be generated for each business outcome containing the programs aligned to that particular outcome.

The L&D Operations Report

The L&D Operations Report pulls key measures from the effectiveness and efficiency statements and adds a column for Forecast since it is now an executive report. ILT stands for instructional-led design and WBT stands for web-based training. Figure A.7 shows such a report.

The Three Reports

These three reports should provide all the measures and information necessary to manage the learning function at a high level. More detailed reports are always available to answer specific questions.

CONCLUSION

In conclusion, TDRp is designed to help you run learning like a business. TDRp provides industry-standard definitions for measures, three standard statements, and three customizable management reports.

Learning & Development Sample Executive Operations Report Results through June						
			For 2012			
		2011 Actual	**Plan**	**Jun YTD**	**% of Plan**	**Forecast**
Effectiveness Measures						
Level 1: Participant Feedback (All programs)	% favorable	78%	84%	84%	100%	99%
Level 1: Sponsor Feedback (Select programs)	% favorable	75%	80%	77%	96%	78%
Level 2: Learning (Select programs)	Score	78%	85%	83%	98%	84%
Level 3: Application Rate (Select programs)	% who applied it	61%	75%	78%	104%	79%
Level 4: (Select programs)	Contribution to goal	NA	25%	26%	105%	25%
Level 5: (Select programs)						
Net Benefits	Thousands $	$546	$800	$345	43%	$800
ROI	%	29%	35%	32%	91%	33%
Efficiency Measures						
Course Management	Number	22	36	24	67%	35
Total Developed	Number	16	33	21	64%	33
Number Meeting Deadline	%	73%	92%	88%	95%	94%
% Meeting Deadline	Number	143	178	167	94%	178
Total Delivered	Number	89	160	138	87%	155
Number Meeting Deadline	%	62%	90%	83%	85%	87%
% Meeting Deadline						
Cycle Time						
Performance Consulting	Days	39	30	33	67%	32
Design and Development for LT	Days	56	45	44	109%	45
Design and Development for WBT	Days	48	40	39	113%	39

(continued)

Reach						
% of Employees Reached by L&D	%	85%	88%	72%	82%	88%
% of Employees with Development Plans	%	82%	98%	95%	96%	96%
Investment						
L&D Expenditure	Million $	$15.8	$20.2	$9.9	49%	$20.2
Cost Reduction (Internal to L&D)	Thousand $	$63	$295	$168	57%	$325
Opportunity Cost	Million $	$3.4	$2.9	$1.3	45%	$2.9
Total Participants	Number	109,618	147,500	67,357	46%	145,000
Total Unique Participants	Number	40,729	45,313	36,998	82%	43,000

Figure A.7 Executive Operations Report

Moreover, TDRp also provides the underlying management principles and guidance necessary to align learning to your organization's objectives, get agreement with the sponsors on expected impact, and manage with discipline on a monthly basis to deliver planned results. It is a simple and consistent yet flexible framework to help you become a valued, strategic business partner.

More information is available from the Center for Talent Reporting at www.centerfortalentreporting.org, including:

- Introduction to TDRp white paper focusing on all six HR processes (20 pages)
- Full TDRp white paper going into much greater detail on TDRp for L&D (50 pages)
- PowerPoint presentations on TDRp
- Definitions of terms and measures document for L&D
- Detailed implementation guidance
- Measures library
- Sample statements and reports

Also, feel free to contact Dave Vance at DVance@Centerfor TalentReporting.org.

APPENDIX **B**

What It Takes

What It Takes	What We Have	What We Need
Alignment: Curriculum Alignment		
Skills/Capabilities ■ Learning champion with political connections ■ Engaged stakeholders ■ Instructional designer/performance improvement analyst		
Technology/Infrastructure ■ None		
Data ■ Performance data to identify high performers		
Alignment: Initiative Alignment		
Skills/Capabilities ■ Learning champion with political connections ■ Engaged stakeholders ■ Instructional designer/performance improvement analyst		
Technology/Infrastructure ■ None		
Data ■ None		

*Recommended if LMS does not provide desired data/reports—OR—if organization is pursing more advanced analysis.

What It Takes	What We Have	What We Need
Engagement: Utilization		
Skills/Capabilities		
▤ Measurement project owner		
▤ Reporting/business analyst		
▤ Data analyst/programmer*		
Technology/Infrastructure		
▤ LMS or other tracking system		
▤ Reporting tool		
Data		
▤ Course file		
▤ Course offerings		
▤ Course completions		
▤ Student file		
▤ Student demographics (from LMS or HR)*		
▤ Instructor file*		
Engagement: Reaction		
Skills/Capabilities		
▤ Measurement project owner		
▤ Reporting/business analyst		
▤ Survey designer		
▤ Data analyst/programmer*		
Technology/Infrastructure		
▤ LMS or other tracking system		
▤ Survey development and deployment tool		
▤ Data capture and storage method		
▤ Reporting tool		
Data		
▤ Course file		
▤ Survey questions		
▤ Survey responses		
▤ Student file		
▤ Student demographics (from LMS or HR)*		
▤ Instructor file*		

*Recommended if LMS does not provide desired data/reports—OR—if organization is pursing more advanced analysis.

What It Takes	What We Have	What We Need
Learning: Learning Gain		
Skills/Capabilities		
▦ Measurement project owner		
▦ Reporting analyst		
▦ Assessment developer		
▦ Data analyst/programmer*		
Technology/Infrastructure		
▦ LMS or other tracking system		
▦ Test development and deployment engine		
▦ Data capture and storage method—final score		
▦ Data capture and storage method—item responses and initial scores*		
▦ Reporting tool		
Data		
▦ Course file		
▦ Question bank and answer grid		
▦ Item responses*		
▦ Initial score*		
▦ Final score		
▦ Student file		
▦ Student demographics (from LMS or HR)*		
▦ Instructor file*		
Transfer: Behavior Change		
Skills/Capabilities		
▦ Measurement project owner		
▦ Manager engagement		
▦ Reporting analyst		
▦ Survey designer		
▦ Observers		

*Recommended if LMS does not provide desired data/reports—OR—if organization is pursing more advanced analysis.

What It Takes	What We Have	What We Need
Technology/Infrastructure		
▦ LMS or other tracking system		
▦ Survey development and deployment tool		
▦ 360 Survey methodology		
▦ Observation Checklist tracking tools		
▦ Data capture and storage method		
▦ Reporting tool		
Data		
▦ Course file		
▦ Questions/items		
▦ Responses		
▦ Student file		
▦ Student demographics (from LMS or HR)*		
▦ Instructor file*		
Impact: Business Results, ROI, Isolation, and Optimization		
Skills/Capabilities		
▦ Learning champion with political connections		
▦ Engaged stakeholders		
▦ Measurement project owner		
▦ Reporting/business analyst		
▦ Data analyst/programmer (for each system: HR, operations, learning)		
▦ Statistician		
Technology/Infrastructure/Data		
▦ LMS		
▦ HR system		
▦ Business operations data		
▦ Statistical software		
▦ Reporting tool		

*Recommended if LMS does not provide desired data/reports—OR—if organization is pursing more advanced analysis.

What It Takes	What We Have	What We Need
Data		
▪ Course file		
▪ Student file		
▪ Completion data		
▪ HR data, including demographics		
▪ Employee history		
▪ Business operations data (multiple years)		

*Recommended if LMS does not provide desired data/reports—OR—if organization is pursing more advanced analysis.

Measurement Plan: Blueprints for Measurement

Utilization Blueprint: Level 0 (Engagement Phase)

Purpose	Data Sources
To ensure that solution is being used as intended and to monitor training participation against target	▪ Student master file ▪ LMS attendance records ▪ Instructor feedback ▪ Line manager and/or learner feedback
Questions to Be Answered	**Method**
▪ Does participation match forecast? If not, why not? ▪ Are learners attending/using the solution as it was designed? If not, why not? ▪ Have enough learners completed the training to justify higher levels of evaluation?	Use LMS to capture and report participation rates ▪ Entry of roster into LMS (Live) ▪ Completions posted in LMS (WBT) "Spot" phone calls to identify early issues ▪ Check-in with instructors ▪ Check-in with learner/manager
Timing	
▪ Following launch and continuously monitored throughout lifecycle	

(continued)

Utilization Blueprint: Level 0 (Engagement Phase) (*continued*)

Stakeholders	Use Info To . . .
■ Design/development team ■ Learning management team ■ Business sponsors	■ Revise content, if utilization problems ■ Assess deployment progress against targets ■ Reinforce employee interest in and importance of training
Reporting Requirements	
■ Monthly ■ On-demand track ■ Completions ■ In progress ■ No show	■ By curriculum/course ■ By instructor ■ By delivery type ■ By region/district ■ By time frame
Implementation Considerations	
■ Do we have the necessary technology in place ■ Do we have sufficient in-house expertise ■ Do we have resources to administer, maintain, and monitor	

Reaction Blueprint: Level 1 (Engagement Phase)

Purpose	Data Sources
To ensure that learning is perceived by learners as relevant to their job, and worth the time to participate	■ Learners ■ Line managers
Questions to Be Answered	**Method**
■ Do learners value the learning solution? ■ Is it relevant and applicable to their jobs? ■ What parts of the learning are working best/worst? ■ Can it be applied back on the job? ■ Do different demographics groups perceive the value differently? ■ Do learners and managers feel it was a good investment of their time?	Learner survey ■ Administered onsite and scored in LMS (Live) ■ At end of WBT ■ Use standard questions/standard scale ■ Add custom questions ■ Include open-ended Manager perspective ■ "Spot" phone call/survey to manager

Timing
▪ Following launch
▪ Continuous throughout course lifecycle (Live)
▪ Continue until results stabilize (WBT)
▪ Redeploy if audience, content, environment changes

Stakeholders	Use Info To . . .
▪ Design/development team	▪ Revise content, if activities/instruction problems
▪ Instructor/delivery team	▪ Revise delivery
▪ Learning management team	▪ Ensure that solution is positively received by audience, and viewed as relevant ▪ Compare courses ▪ Monitor improvements to courses ▪ Address instructor problems
▪ Business sponsors	▪ Build confidence in learning solution ▪ Assess continuation of investment

Reporting Requirements	
▪ Monthly ▪ On-demand	▪ By curriculum/course/instructor/delivery type/org. unit/audience demographics ▪ By time frame ▪ Report "top box" to management

Implementation Considerations
▪ Do we have the necessary technology in place?
▪ Do we have sufficient in-house expertise?
▪ Do we have resources to administer, maintain, and monitor?

Learning Gain Blueprint: Level 2 (Learning Phase)

Purpose	Data Sources
To ensure that participants have mastery of the knowledge and skills conveyed in the learning solution	■ Learners

Questions to Be Answered	Method
■ Do learners have mastery over the course objectives? ■ Is this part of a certification program? (This impacts validation requirements.) ■ Are learners struggling with specific content areas? ■ Are some trainers struggling with specific content areas? ■ Do different demographic groups perform differently?	Posttraining assessment (examples) ■ Criterion-referenced pre-/posttest ■ Learning checklist ■ Performance test Administered/scored ■ In class ■ On LMS How remediated?

Timing
■ Following launch and continuous throughout course lifecycle

Stakeholders	Use Info To . . .
■ Design/development team	■ Determine if test or content is the problem, if poor test performance ■ Revise accordingly
■ Instructor/delivery team	■ Revise delivery
■ Learning management team	■ Ensure that solution achieving learning goals ■ Monitor improvements to courses ■ Address instructor problems
■ Business sponsors	■ Build confidence in learning solution ■ Assess continuation of investment

Reporting Requirements	
▪ Monthly ▪ On-demand	▪ By curriculum/course/instructor/delivery type/organizational unit/audience demographics ▪ By time frame ▪ Report post-test and learning gain

Implementation Considerations
▪ Do we have the necessary technology in place? ▪ Do we have sufficient in-house expertise? ▪ Do we have resources to administer, maintain, and monitor? ▪ Is this for certification (what validation is required)? ▪ How will we set a "passing" score? ▪ How will we handle remediation?

Behavior Change Blueprint: Level 3 (Transfer Phase)

Purpose	Data Sources
To ensure that newly acquired knowledge and skills are being implemented back on the job	▪ Learners ▪ Line managers
Questions to Be Answered	**Method**
▪ Are learners able to apply their learnings on the job? What percent? ▪ What enablers/obstacles are they encountering? ▪ What are they applying? ▪ To what extent are managers providing support to integrate newly acquired capabilities? ▪ Do learners and/or managers see a performance change? What is the evidence?	Survey of learners and managers ▪ What is being applied? ▪ What performance gains are being experienced? Interviews of learners and managers (representative sample) ▪ In class ▪ On LMS Observation checklists (representative sample), mystery shoppers

(continued)

Behavior Change Blueprint: Level 3 (Transfer Phase) (*continued*)

Timing
■ After sufficient time for learners to have applied new knowledge and skills (typically within one month of training)
■ Conduct once shortly after launch and after content is stable
■ Possible additional assessments (especially if content changes)

Stakeholders	Use Info To . . .
■ Learning management team	■ Ensure that solution can be applied on the job ■ Identify obstacles implementation ■ Troubleshoot resolutions with line managers and sponsors
■ Line managers ■ Business sponsors	■ Work with learning team to build on success and/or to overcome obstacles, such as: 　■ Tools, systems, processes 　■ Feedback and reward systems 　■ Job dynamics (workload, priorities)

Reporting Requirements	
■ At conclusion of assessment	■ Quantitative results from survey ■ Qualitative from interviews ■ Looking for "evidence" and "obstacles" and "enablers"

Implementation Considerations
■ Do we have the necessary technology in place (if applicable)?
■ Do we have sufficient in-house expertise?
■ Do we have resources to conduct?

Business Results Blueprint: Levels 4–6 (Impact Phase)

Purpose	Data Sources
To determine the impact of the learning solution, and to calculate ROI	<ul><li>LMS (training records)</li><li>HRIS (personnel data)</li><li>Operations/business systems data (metrics from measurement map)</li><li>New sources?</li><li>Line manager/employee testimonials</li><li>Training department expense data</li></ul>
Questions to Be Answered	**Method**
<ul><li>What aligned business metrics are showing movement (correlated with training)? By how much?</li><li>Do different demographic groups perform differently?</li><li>What are the total costs associated with the learning solution (design/ develop/deploy/opportunity cost)?</li><li>What stories support the data?</li></ul>	Basic <ul><li>Use operational metrics data to compare before/after training for trained and untrained</li><li>Develop "impact case" stories from interviews</li><li>Calculate conceptual ROI</li></ul>Advanced <ul><li>Conduct statistical analysis on training and operational data to determine statistically significant relationships and to isolate impact</li><li>Use quasi experimental design model</li><li>Use demographic data and predictive analytics to determine optimization opportunities</li><li>Calculate isolated ROI</li></ul>

Timing
<ul><li>After sufficient time for learners to have applied new knowledge and skills; results to begin appearing in operational data (typically within one to six months after training)</li><li>Findings may drive changes to learning solution; re-evaluate after changes have had a chance to make an impact</li></ul>

(continued)

Business Results Blueprint: Levels 4–6 (Impact Phase) (*continued*)

Stakeholders	Use Info To . . .
■ Learning management team ■ Line managers ■ Business sponsors	Basic ■ Assess relationship between training and business results, and gauge a conceptual ROI Advanced ■ Isolate the role of training in changes in business results ■ Determine an isolated ROI to establish worth of investment ■ Prioritize deployment for greatest impact ■ Adjust solution where limited impact was found ■ Support accelerated deployment for greatest impact ■ Build general support for learning ■ Identify holes in data systems
Reporting Requirements	
■ At conclusion of assessment	Basic ■ Customized ■ Quantitative results from data analysis ■ Qualitative from interviews Advanced ■ Highly customized and graphical ■ Focus on statistically significant findings ■ Include qualitative to help tell the story of the data

Implementation Considerations

■ Do we collect all the necessary data?

■ Do we have access to all the necessary data?

■ Do we have sufficient in-house expertise?

■ Do we have resources to conduct?

■ How will results be shared across the organization?

■ What if the results suggest no impact?

Using Bloom's Taxonomy

The following are the six categories of the cognitive domain as defined by Benjamin Bloom[1] and refined by David Krathwohl.[2] The verbs in each group indicate the type of thinking skill needed to complete an assignment within that category. The verbs denote what a student is to do.

6. Create Builds a structure or pattern from diverse elements. Puts parts together to form a whole, with emphasis on creating a new meaning or structure.				
arrange	create	invent	pretend	set up
assemble	design	manage	produce	suggest
change	find an	organize	propose	suppose
collect	unusual way	originate	rearrange	synthesize
combine	formulate	plan	reconstruct	visualize
compose	generate	predict	reorganize	write
construct	hypothesize	prepare	revise	
	infer			

5. Evaluate Makes judgments about the value of ideas or materials based on given criteria.				
appraise argue assess attack choose	compare conclude criticize decide defend	dispute estimate evaluate give your opinion interpret	judge justify predict prioritize rank	rate select support value
4. Analyze Separates or breaks down material or concepts into component parts so that its organizational structure may be understood. Distinguishes between facts and inferences.				
analyze appraise calculate categorize classify	compare contrast criticize debate deduct	determine the factors diagnose diagram differentiate discriminate	dissect distinguish examine experiment infer	interpret inventory question specify test
3. Apply Uses a concept in a new situation or unprompted use of an abstraction. Applies what was learned in the classroom into novel situations in the workplace.				

apply
choose
compute
conclude
construct
	demonstrate
	determine
	draw
	employ
	find out
		give an
		  example
		illustrate
		interpret
		make
			operate
			practice
			prepare
			show
				sketch
				solve
				state a rule or
				  principle
				use

2. Comprehend Understands the meaning, translation, interpolation, and interpretation of instructions and problems. States a problem in one's own words.				
classify describe discuss explain express	identify indicate interpret locate paraphrase	put in order recognize report restate retell in your own words	review rewrite select sort	summarize tell trace translate

1. Remember Recalls data.				
arrange define duplicate fill in the blank identify	label list locate match	memorize name order recall	recognize relate repeat reproduce	spell out state tell underline

NOTES

1. B. Bloom, *Taxonomy of Education Objectives* (Boston: Allyn & Bacon, 1956).
2. D. Krathwohl, "A Revision of Bloom's Taxonomy," *Theory into Practice* 41, no. 4 (Autumn 2002): 212–218.

Guidelines for Creating Multiple Choice Questions

The following appendix introduces guidelines for creating multiple choice questions. The questions written in the gray boxes need some work. The questions written in the white boxes are revised to be more effective. The asterisks indicate the correct answer.

Rule 1: Put the Details in the Stem

Why is the placement of pruning cuts important?

A. Cuts closer to the main stem are less resistant to disease, because the cut will heal more slowly.
B. Removal of the terminal bud results in renewed growth near the pruning cut, because of the loss of auxin.*
C. If more than 20% of the branches are removed, the plant's health will suffer because of the loss of woody tissue.
D. All cuts should always be made the same distance from the main stem, to promote a more uniform shape.

(REVISED) Where is the best place to make a rejuvenating pruning cut?

A. Anywhere.
B. Near the main stem.
C. At or near ground level.*
D. ¼″ above an existing bud or shoot.

Rule 2: Use Parallel Format

Which of the following is a phase of plant growth?

A. Flower growth
B. Seed growth
C. Vegetative growth*
D. Photosynthesis

(REVISED) Which of the following is a phase of plant growth?

A. Flower growth
B. Seed growth
C. Vegetative growth*
D. Terminal growth

Rule 3: Do *Not* Use Double Negatives

Lack of adequate sunlight to plants does not cause:

A. Diminished stem growth
B. Decreased flower production
C. Dark green stems and leaves*
D. A leggy, leafless look

(REVISED) Which of the following is an effect of inadequate sunlight?

A. Greater stem growth
B. Increased flower production
C. Yellow stems and leaves*
D. Dense, compact growth

Rule 4: Avoid "All of the Above"

What nutrient is essential to proper plant growth?

A. Nitrogen
B. Phosphorous
C. Potassium
D. All of the above*

(REVISED) What plant nutrient promotes flower production?

A. Nitrogen
B. Phosphorous*
C. Potassium
D. Magnesium

Rule 5: Arrange Responses in Logical Order

The season for greatest root growth in cool season grasses is:

A. Fall*
B. Spring
C. Winter
D. Summer

(REVISED) The season for greatest root growth in cool season grasses is:

A. Winter
B. Spring
C. Summer
D. Fall*

Rule 6: Responses Should Be of Similar Length

At what angle should tree and shrub branches be pruned?

A. 30 degrees
B. 45 degrees*
C. 90 degrees
D. Whatever angle will prohibit standing water on the end of the branch

(REVISED) At what angle should tree and shrub branches be pruned?

A. 30 degrees
B. 45 degrees*
C. 90 degrees
D. Any angle

Rule 7: Grammar (Tenses and Plurals)

What are the characteristics of biennial plants?

A. An intact woody main stem
B. Green stems
C. Large storage roots*
D. Drought-resistant seeds

(REVISED) Which of these is a characteristic of biennial plants?

A. Intact woody stems
B. Green stems
C. Large storage roots*
D. Drought-resistant seeds

Rule 8: No "Gimmies" (Make All Responses Plausible)

Which of the following is found in most plant fertilizers?

A. Salt
B. Nitrogen*
C. Sugar
D. Grass seed

(REVISED) Which of the following is found in most plant fertilizers?

A. Calcium
B. Nitrogen*
C. Magnesium
D. Pre-emergents

Rule 9: No Trick Questions

I'm thinking of firing all the yes-men, naysayers, and equivocators. Do you agree?

This is a trick question, and unfair to the student.

Rule 10: Make Sure It's Useful

The Practitioner's Guide to Nursing can best be described as:

A. First published in 1957
B. In print in 35 languages
C. Thick as an encyclopedia
D. Written by three nuns

(REVISED) This question is just filler. Don't waste students' time.

Getting Your Feet Wet in Data: Preparing and Cleaning the Data Set*

The purpose of this book is to provide a road map for pursuing and executing an analytic approach to human capital investment. It is written at the 10,000-foot level so as to cover a broad range of scenarios. However, if you are looking for practical tips and specific techniques for analyzing the data, this appendix is for you.

You will never be able to find out whether your intervention is having the desired effect if your data isn't fully cleaned and prepped prior to statistical analysis. Depending on the complexity of your data and your project, this can be one of the more time- and resource-consuming aspects of the project. Engaging the data analyst who will be working on your project when the study is designed can be a big

---

*This section was originally published in Gene Pease, Boyce Byerly, and Jac Fitz-enz, *Human Capital Analytics: How to Harness the Potential of Your Organization's Greatest Asset* (Hoboken, NJ: John Wiley & Sons, 2012). Copyright © 2012 Gene Pease, Boyce Byerly, and Jac Fitz-enz.

time saver. He or she can help you work with your data owners to develop the data requirements for the project, ensuring that all needed columns are included and determining the most efficient format for the exported data. Having to go back to a data owner to ask for additional data can have a huge impact on the project time line.

DATA PRIVACY AND ENCRYPTION

Data privacy is increasingly becoming an important concern for many organizations. With more connectivity and electronic access, it is critical to protect personal information. One very useful technique is the removal of personally identifying information. This involves stripping the employee records down to a record ID or employee number and allows you to remove the proper name, the address, and so on. If further privacy is desired, some algorithm can be used to mask the identifier by changing into a different form in a way that allows it to be executed across several different databases. "Hashing techniques" map information to a simple code or number in a unique, repeatable way; your IT staff can help you with these. Even if the original data could be recovered eventually, it at least adds an extra layer of protection from prying eyes.

Discuss with your IT professional or systems administrator what security mechanisms are protecting your data and whether more are needed. Strong passwords, encryption, and ensuring the physical safety of the computer holding the data are all concepts you should discuss. If the data leaves the building, take appropriate precautions (your IT colleague can help you identify these). Sending data in unencrypted e-mail (or encrypting the data and sending the password along with it in plain text, which is somewhat baffling) is a bad idea. Remember, the data sets you will be developing offer powerful insights into your company's performance, and the information is all the more important to protect.

GETTING YOUR FEET WET IN THE DATA

Once you have secured data for your project, you should begin working with it as soon as possible. Learn as much as you can early on.

As explained in the discussion in Chapter 3 on analytics personnel, a data analyst is a key position in a measurement project and is the first point of entry for the data into your analytics team. The format of the data you request should be somewhat determined by the skill sets of the staff you have available. For example, spreadsheets are the most common, but more complex databases can be useful if you have the skill sets to take advantage of such formats. The most general, widely readable format is the comma-separated variable (CSV) text file that can be imported into almost any tool.

What Tools to Use

Unless you are working with very large datasets, a lot of the data preparation can be done in Microsoft Excel or Open Office Calc. However, larger projects—those with a greater number of rows or columns of data or having many different sources of data—often require the use of more advanced tools such as relational databases like Microsoft SQL Server, MySQL, or Oracle.

Statistical analysis is typically best suited to statistical packages such as SAS, SPSS, or R (a free, open-source tool), but Excel can be used for descriptive statistics and some basic statistical analyses. Caution should be taken, however, in equating the ability to run a statistical function in Excel with the statistical knowledge needed to correctly craft the question and interpret the output.

The Data Log

We strongly suggest that you keep a project log, with file names, locations, date received, person who provided the data, and a very brief description of the contents. Include the key fields that can be used to match the files together. Keys are simple unique identifiers that run throughout a data set and match to a field in another data set. Make careful notes about what you have and have not received.

You should always maintain an original data folder so that if problems occur, you can back up to a known accurate and correct version. Change the file status to "read only" on those files so that they are not accidentally edited.

VERIFYING COMPLETENESS

It is critical to review the data for completeness. Here are some suggestions for a typical human capital project:

- Make sure that you have all of the files that you were expecting in the data set and that they contain the information required to proceed with the project plan. If you have stakeholder agreement on the period of time to be covered in your measurement project, check to make sure that the files cover that time span. Don't just check the end points—check whether any data in the middle of the range is missing.

- Confirm that all groups in the study population are included (for example, both trained and control groups, or terminated and retained employees, and so on). Check for coverage of any important geographic or business grouping classifications.

- Check to see whether the amount of data matches up to your knowledge about the organization (for example, is the number of records about the same as the number of employees?). On the flip side, make sure that the data does not include things you were not looking for—out-of-range dates, people from outside the participant groups, and so forth.

- Identify columns of data that were not requested but that are included, to see whether they might be useful to the study.

CONFIRMING YOUR DATA QUALITY

Before data cleaning and processing start, it is important to confirm that the data received are of an acceptable level of quality and completeness. The following is a suggested list of data quality checks:

1. Is the list of columns complete?

2. Is the number of rows as expected? Does the last row of data look complete? (A bad file transfer can cut the end off a file, as is sometimes evidenced by an incomplete final record.)

3. Review lists of values for coded fields. Are they clear and in line with expectations? For example, if the specifications state that

in the Gender column, Female=1 and Male=2, are there any values in the data set other than 1 and 2?

4. Verify the range of values in each appropriate column of data. Do any of the columns have values that do not seem to be appropriately distributed or have extreme outliers? For instance, do most of the sales reps have average sales of $50,000, while Susan's average is $800,000? Look at the date fields to ensure that the time frame of data matches the data requirements established when designing the study. (Don't just look at the endpoints; check that the months/quarters/years in the middle are there as well.)

5. Do any required fields have missing values?

6. Are there any duplicate records? You may have to confirm with the data owner whether these are true duplicates or whether some excluded column of data would distinguish them (such that they ought to be retained for the study).

CLEANING UP THE DATA

The degree to which the data will need to be changed from the source will depend on the individual file. The data analyst should consult with the statistician to determine the best format for the files to be analyzed. Different statistical packages have different requirements as to format, column headings, and so on. A mix of lower- and upper-case in column values, such having "M," "m," "F," and "f" as codes for "Male" and "Female," may be read as two different values by some systems and as four by others.

If you are cleaning the data in Excel, specifying the data types of the columns can help uncover inconsistencies in the values received. Turning on filtering is a quick way to look at the list of unique values present in a column of data (and help you find unexpected values or misspellings/miscodings).

If you must recode any of your columns for the statistician (for instance, if a categorical variable needs to be represented as a number for the analysis), it is a good idea to add a column with the recoded values, rather than replacing the original data. Otherwise, it can be hard to detect an error (and may require starting over from a source data file to correct it).

Dates

Dates can be a major problem area because different systems have different conventions: separating numbers with a slash versus a dash, whether or not leading zeros appear before single-digit values, and whether years are shown with two digits or four. Similarly, different countries format dates differently, with American companies favoring a mm/dd/yy structure, and European countries tending to use dd/mm/yy.

When data is transferred between systems, these different formats sometimes lead to an obvious error; other times, the data may appear to load correctly but may actually contain errors. In a past project, one system represented a date as "mm/yy." The next system read those values as "dd/mm" and assumed that the date was for the current year. It was detected only when a sharp-eyed analyst noticed that there was never any data for November or December (the data set ended in 2010, so the last two digits were at most "10").

Graphing the number of data points that occur in each time period (say, month, quarter, or year) can help you discover places where you might be missing data.

Dealing with Outliers

Sometimes, the values of a particular metric are all very similar; in other cases, they may vary dramatically. The decision of whether to include all data points or exclude some as outliers can be a difficult choice that can have an impact on the results of the analysis.

COMBINING MULTIPLE DATA SOURCES

It is common to receive project data from multiple sources—for instance, human resources (HR) (the usual source for demographic and employment information) often uses a different database than the training department or sales. Combining multiple data sources can be a tricky business. Before you start, it is important to ensure that the data received from the different sources is complete and compatible.

1. Verify keys
   a. Are they unique where expected?
   b. Are they consistent across data sources?
   c. In cases of a compound key (e.g., identifying an employee requires knowing both an employee ID and a company code), are all of the necessary columns present in each file?
2. Verify match levels—do records match up as expected? For example, do all of the employees have employment history records?
3. Compare lists of values for fields that are drawn from multiple data sources. Do they match? For example, does each data source use the same specifications for region? If not, you will need a conversion key from your contacts for each data source.

You might manually line up columns in Excel or use some of its built-in functions, such as vlookup() and hlookup(), when dealing with smaller data sets, but more typically, you will be using some statistical language or database tool.

Once you have combined your files as appropriate, it is a good idea to choose a subset of your data (perhaps a dozen rows) and manually compare the data in your combined file with the source data to ensure that the merge occurred accurately. Whether you are doing this "by hand" or via code you have written, it is easy to make an error that would not be detected without a manual check.

LOOKING FOR PROBLEMS, AND SUGGESTIONS FOR DEALING WITH COMMON ONES

The following are some practical tips on working with data that will smooth the process of conducting a measurement project.

The Sniff Test

The overall point of the exploration of the data is to ensure that it passes the sniff test. Does the data make sense? Is it reasonable and complete? Some discipline in approaching this problem is essential. With 100 data points, you might look at a dozen in detail, and problems would likely become apparent. With thousands of points, most people feel overwhelmed and don't look at any data, even when looking at that same dozen would have alerted them to problems in the data set.

Naming Conventions for the Data

It is important in projects of even moderate complexity to develop a standard naming convention for data. Identifying the version of the data, with appropriate filters, inclusions, and exclusions, and being able to identify the columns of the data, will make the project go much smoother. The exact conventions are not particularly important, but having them set up from the beginning will help facilitate the project.

Dealing with Missing Data

Few projects proceed smoothly from start to finish. Even with the vast amounts of data organizations collect today, it is not uncommon to find that the data you need does not exist. Or, if it does exist, it is not in the form you need it. Some hypotheses will turn out to be untenable, and some need to be modified. Here are some of the bumps in the road that might occur. There is no master theory that can enumerate the possible problems and solutions (at least, not yet), but here are some common problems that occur in human capital projects.

The Data Exists But Is at the Wrong Level of Granularity

Suppose you are keen to measure the impact of a new tool that improves the performance of auto mechanics working at service centers. The tool is designed to reduce service times. The first and most central hypothesis is that mechanics who were using the new tool would record quicker service. When the data collection effort begins, a major snag appears: Service times are only tracked on the service center level, and it is not possible to say much about the performance of the individual mechanic. Or is it?

We have done projects like this, and salvaging the project is a matter of redefining the participant. The new hypothesis is: Service centers that provided at least one of the new tools to mechanics will show lower service times.

The data is somewhat less precise and focused but can still provide a very good answer to the ultimate question of evaluating the new tools. Note that this question could be tweaked in several ways—you might ask about "service centers that gave every mechanic the new tool" or "service centers that gave at least half the mechanics a new tool."

Operational Data Couldn't Be Obtained from Certain Sources

One common way around a lack of operational data is to make up for it with survey data. We prefer operational data, of course, but it is better to have some data for decision making than none at all. Don't give up too easily on operational data, because it is closest to the lifeblood of the company! Consider whether there are some alternatives to the data you are looking for that might work. If you don't have data directly on operations, might it be tracked in other ways? For example, is there a purchase order system or credit card receipts? Is there some sort of compensation based on performance that might mirror the information you need? In one project, we were unable to track the performance of pharmaceutical reps, but we were able to get even more useful data from their customers (physicians).

Data Couldn't Be Matched Up between Sources

Sometimes data is recorded by employee ID; sometimes by e-mail address; sometimes by proper name. Do your different data sources all use the same primary key? If so, that's great; you can proceed with the project. If not, consider whether there may be a data set that links together the data you need. Figure F.1 shows an example that links operations data and LMS data with human resources data, which has a map for the linkage.

A very common problem when merging databases is that a common field has a slightly different name (e.g., "EmpID" vs. "EID" vs. "Employee ID"). Another problem that occurs frequently is minor variation in the keys that link up sources, such as a hyphen as a

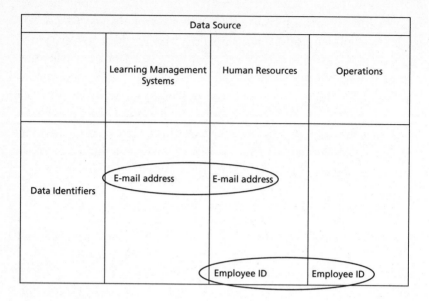

Figure F.1 Data Sources

separator in one data set where there is a space in the other, or a different prefix or suffix, or some other minor and easily fixed issue. A good data analyst has techniques for cleaning these fields. There are software solutions that merge multiple databases together based on "fuzzy matches" that involve multiple fields of data. Yet these are, as of this writing, complex and expensive solutions that are appropriate for databases that manage mailing lists but are not likely feasible for analytics projects.

TRANSFORMING ONE VARIABLE INTO ANOTHER

Alchemy (n): A form of chemistry and speculative philosophy practiced in the Middle Ages and the Renaissance and concerned principally with discovering methods for transmuting baser metals into gold.

Suppose you wanted to measure sales or perhaps evaluate whether a sales training program worked. Sales revenue is one metric, right? Not at all—there are many specific metrics involved, not one. Usually, a number of different views or transformations of the data can be more sensitive indicators, can eliminate bias or selection patterns, or can help get you better or, at least, different views of your organization. Taking the example of sales measurement, here are some of the specific measurements that can be used.

- The raw amount of a sale in dollars
- The number of items sold
- The number of customers to whom sales were made
- The average size of a sale
- Weekly sales
- Monthly sales
- The profit margin on a sale
- Repeat sales
- Sales of the base item in units
- Sales of accessories in dollars
- Percentage of improvement from the same period last year

For almost any variable, you can create variants based on units, financial values, and percentage increases. We go into detail on some of these next.

Difference Variables

A very useful variation of a metric is what we call a *difference variable*, which is created by comparing the value of a participant's data before and after a given date or occurrence. In effect, it measures the change over a given period of time. An example might be to subtract average monthly customer satisfaction ratings taken before a training program from those taken after the program. The main advantage of using the difference score is that it helps control for selection bias for the test and control groups. Another advantage is that it helps reduce the impact of wide variation among participants. A third advantage is that difference variables may be the simplest and most intuitive way to express what is going on with your business processes. For participants in the control group, who do not receive the investment, the before and after dividing point is the median date on which the test group received the investment. Creating a difference variable is a great way to simplify your analysis and control for selection bias. The impact of the investment is calculated by subtracting the difference score for the control group from the difference score for the test group. The only downside of a difference variable is that it can be difficult to quickly get the technique across to an audience.

Percentage Scaled Variables

There are occasions on which it is useful to compare multiple sets of data. For example, if training in your call center decreases average call-handling time by 20 seconds, increases sales by 1.2 units per person per month, and increases retention by one extra employee retained per month, what are the relative improvements there? Where is the greatest impact achieved? A solution is to express each of these values as a percentage change from the status quo. When percentage changes are used, improvements can be easily compared. Of course, speaking in the language of the stakeholders is important, so you may wish to socialize preliminary results with them to make sure you are not confusing anyone with a different measurement scale.

Hint: Most people find it most natural to see an improvement as an increase. It is also difficult to mix positive improvements with negative improvements conceptually. For example, sales revenue is supposed to go up, which is a positive improvement, but call-handling time should go down, a negative improvement. When presenting your results, try to use positive improvements, and try to avoid mixing positive and negative improvements. Transformations can be helpful on this. For example, if you wish to change "Average handling time" to "Seconds saved per call," you have turned a negative impact into a positive impact. Please note that we are not suggesting sugarcoating your results in any way, just advising you of ways to provide cognitive shortcuts to help your busy audience understand the results quicker.

Currency Value Variables

One of the ultimate goals of a measurement and evaluation project is to measure the financial impact on the organization. Why not turn your widgets into dollars before beginning the statistical analysis? This can be a better way to communicate with your stakeholders. If several metrics are competing for the attention of the stakeholders, it is good to get a feel for what is important to them. For example, one good way to express the results might be to turn them into currency. (If the analysis includes more than a single country, you may need to convert everything into a single common currency for clarity.) Other stakeholders think almost exclusively in terms of other units, such as failure rate on an assembly line or new vehicles sold.

How Many Participants Do You Need in a Study?*

The number of participants required to achieve a statistically significant answer is a hard value to estimate definitively, but there are ways to calculate decent approximations, if you know (or can assume) some things about the data. We like statistical significance at a fairly high level—preferably 99 percent—so that determines our preference. Statistical significance is the product of three factors:

1. *The effect size*. The effect size is a statistical way of saying how big of a difference is seen between the test and control groups. Not surprisingly, a 50 percent improvement is a lot easier to spot than a 1 percent difference.

2. *Variation*. There are several statistical terms for this, such as *variance* or *standard deviation*. Those are mathematical ways of

---

*This section originally published in Gene Pease, Boyce Byerly, and Jac Fitz-enz, *Human Capital Analytics: How to Harness the Potential of Your Organization's Greatest Asset* (Hoboken, NJ: John Wiley & Sons, 2012). Copyright © 2012 Gene Pease, Boyce Byerly, and Jac Fitz-enz.

measuring just how consistent results are. Human beings typically have a lot of variation in their performance, but it is a question of just how much. For example, the amount of variance in public schools is usually higher than that in private schools.

3. *Population size.* The more people in a study, the more certain you can be that the effects are real. If only two people are in the test group, an improvement might well be a lucky shot. If 100 are in the group, much more certainty can happen.

There are equations and techniques in statistics where, if you know the level of statistical certainty desired and can estimate or guess about two of the above three values, you can solve for a third. For example, if you know you want 95 percent certainty about your conclusions, you guess that your test groups might show an improvement of about 5 percent, and you have some initial baseline data to calculate the variance, you can estimate how big a population might be needed. Admittedly, this is guesswork, but it can give pretty good estimates, and the math is not difficult, although someone with a statistics background should be doing it.

We have conducted studies on as few as 45 participants and as many as 60,000. Having more participants naturally allows you more demographic variation, but sometimes investments are deployed only to a few hundred people. There are times when we are required to make an estimate, and it is not possible to get even this level of information. In experimental designs, scientists talk about "cells"—observations that fit a particular set of conditions. For example, if your variables were gender and race, a cell might be white males. In such a case, we find that when the data is subdivided, roughly 10 people in each cell are required to have some sense of what is going on and may result in statistical significance. What is a group? We might classify people into test and control groups, but what if we believe the training program has different effects for men and women? In that case, we would have four groups: untrained men, untrained women, and so forth. The rule of tens does not mean that there can be an average of 10 in each group, either; if there are four groups, having one group with 30 in it and 10 more participants spread among the remaining three groups does not yield significant results. The smallest group in an analysis is the limiting factor. The limits on statistical significance are usually set by the smallest group, so even if you have a cell with 100 people in it, it does not make up for the one cell with only five. Deciding what variables you want to use or combining cells are different ways of making sure these conditions are met.

Glossary*

ANOVA

A statistical technique that helps in making an inference for whether three or more samples might come from populations having the same mean; specifically, whether the differences among the samples might be caused by chance variation. ANOVA (short for analysis of variance) is used in situations where a single factor is believed to account for differences in the data, and that factor allows us to lump the observations into a small number of discrete categories.

business metric

A continuous variable of interest in a data set. A business metric may be used as a dependent or an independent variable.

business outcome

The dependent variable you select in a statistical question. You select a single business outcome from the set of business metrics.

categorical variable

A variable whose values are a finite, restricted set of enumerated values. Examples might include *gender* (male or female) or *job title* (e.g., engineer, salesperson, manager).

coefficient of determination

See *R-squared* (R^2).

cohort

A group of people who have a feature in common, particularly being of the same generation or entering a school or a company at the same time.

---

*This section originally published in Gene Pease, Boyce Byerly, and Jac Fitz-enz, *Human Capital Analytics: How to Harness the Potential of Your Organization's Greatest Asset* (Hoboken, NJ: John Wiley & Sons, 2012). Copyright © 2012 Gene Pease, Boyce Byerly, and Jac Fitz-enz.

continuous variable

A variable whose values can vary across a broad range. Continuous variables may be either real numbers or integers, or they may fall into a restricted range (such as 0 to 100). Compare with *categorical variable*.

correlation

A mutual relationship of two or more things. The degree to which two or more attributes or measurements on the same group of elements tend to vary together.

cost-to-benefit ratio

The cost of an intervention divided by the dollar benefit estimated to accrue to the participants.

data point

An observation recorded about some aspect of the company's performance at a particular point in time. A data point usually combines information from the participant, intervention, and metric worksheets. An example might be "Joe Smith, East Region, $30,200, 10/2001," which means Joe Smith of the East Region sold $30,200 in October 2001.

dependent variable

In a statistical question, the value of interest as an outcome. A single dependent variable is said to depend on one or more independent variables.

effect size

The amount of change in a dependent variable contributed by a particular change in an independent variable.

factor

A variable that can have different values that you believe affect a business outcome. In statistics, factors are referred to as *independent variables*. Factors might be an intervention, such as training, or any relevant piece of information, such as the region a salesperson operates in, the type of equipment a factory worker uses, or the amount of bonus pay received last year.

function

A mathematical formula where one or more input variables produce a single numerical output.

full model

In statistical questions, when independent variables are added to a question, it is important to ask how much those independent variables contribute to your understanding of the data. For example, if you want to know whether training affects sales, you might re-ask the question as:

> Does adding the variable "training" to my question tell me more about sales than simply knowing the average sales figures?

To phrase this question in a very mathematical way, does the model:

> Sales = Average Sales + Training + Random Variation (Full Model)

tell me more than:

> Sales = Average Sales + Random Variation (Reduced Model)

The Full Model is the version of the question that contains the independent variable of interest, whereas the "Reduced Model" is the one that does not. The F-statistic and the p-value allow us to compare whether the added complexity of the full model really provides us with much better information. If training was really useful, we would expect to be able to better predict a salesperson's performance if we knew whether he or she was trained (which would lead to a higher F-value and a lower p-value). If training was of no use, the extra variable would not provide a better guess (and, hence, we would get a low value for F and a high value for p).

general linear model
A statistical test that answers whether a single dependent variable is a function of one or more independent variables. The independent variables may consist of a mixture of continuous and categorical variables.

granularity
In a data point for a metric or an intervention, the precision of the time measurement (e.g., monthly, yearly, daily).

independent variable
In a statistical question, a factor, or a variable, such as training, that affects the value of a dependent variable. For a single dependent variable, there may be multiple independent variables.

interaction
Interaction in a statistical model indicates that two or more of the independent variables have a synergy between them. Interaction requires that the values of both variables be understood. As an example, suppose that the sales figures for all representatives in a sporting goods company were measured. Further assume that two independent variables were also recorded: (1) whether the sales representative had participated in training,

and (2) the region of the country. It may be the case that the training had an overall positive effect and also that the different regions of the company sell different amounts on the average.

In the following examples, trained salespeople have an average sales figure that is $20,000 higher than untrained salespeople, and the Southern region is noticeably higher than other regions.

Condition	Average
Trained	$191,231
Untrained	$171,231

Region	Average
North	$191,231
East	$199,456
West	$197,256
South	$222,789

It may be the case that the regions of the country are not affected in the same way by training. For example, perhaps sales representatives in the South are reaching the limit of how many sales the warehouses in that region are able to ship, and additional training will not improve sales in that region. As another example, suppose that the training focused on some aspect of selling sporting goods that does not apply equally to all regions of the country; perhaps the instructor provided a great deal of information about how to sell hockey or skiing equipment that was of less use to representatives in the South. Another possible scenario might be that the South has a higher concentration of expert sales representatives who have little extra to learn from the training offered. Figure G.1 illustrates these hypothetical situations. Note that the lines for each of three other regions show a noticeable improvement between "trained" and "untrained," whereas the South shows a relatively flat, unsloped line, indicating little improvement from training.

When such situations occur, they are said to be interactions and may tell you very interesting things about your data.

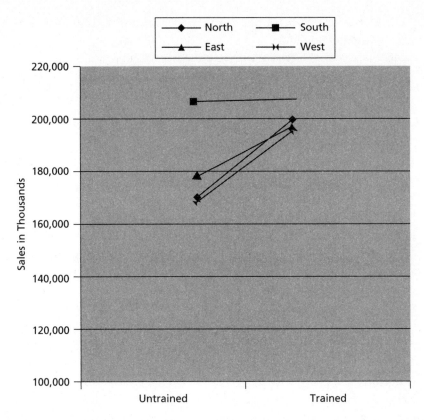

Figure G.1   Regional Sales by Trained versus Untrained

intercept
In an equation, the value on the *y*-axis that corresponds to $x = 0$.

internal rate of return (IRR)
The internal rate of return (IRR) method determines the interest rate required to make the present value of the cash flow equal to zero. It represents the maximum rate of interest that could be paid if all project funds were borrowed and the organization had to break even on the projects. The IRR considers the time value of money and is unaffected by the scale of the project. It can be used to rank alternatives and to accept/reject decisions on a project. It assumes returns are invested at the same internal rate of return. It may make alternatives with high rates of return look particularly good and those with low rates of return look particularly bad.

IRR is calculated by setting net present value (NPV) to 0 and back-solving the equation for NPV.

For one year, the closed-form solution is:

$$\text{IRR} = 100 \times \left(\frac{\text{Gross Benefit}}{\text{Cost}} - 1.0 \right)$$

The answer is calculable for two years and more. A closed-form solution using the quadratic equation is available at two years; a simpler solution is to use a bisection algorithm or some other numerical solution (such as Newton's method) for values 2 and higher.

interval variables
These allow us not only to rank order the items that are measured, but also to quantify and compare the sizes of differences between them. For example, temperature, as measured in degrees Fahrenheit or Celsius, constitutes an interval scale. We can say that a temperature of 40 degrees is higher than a temperature of 30 degrees, and that an increase from 20 to 40 degrees is twice as much as an increase from 30 to 40 degrees. Compare to *ratio variable* and also to *nominal* and *ordinal*.

isolation
Any technique that allows the effect of an investment to be measured accurately and separated from selection bias and other factors that muddy the water.

key performance indicator (KPI)
An important metric that measures one of your business processes.

level
For a categorical variable, a value that it can take on.

Likert scale
A numerical scale that a survey respondent uses to give a response. For example, "On a 5-point scale, with 1 being the worst, and 5 being the best, how would you rate your customer experience?"

linear regression
A statistical technique that describes the relationship between a dependent variable and one or more independent variables. Both the dependent and the independent variables must be continuous numeric values or

ordered categorical variables. The technique involves fitting the best line through the set of data points to minimize the difference between their actual distance from the line and their predicted difference from that line. Linear regression produces a parameter estimate that describes how much each unit of an independent variable adds to the value of the dependent variable.

main effect

A single independent variable is said to have a *main effect* if the dependent variable shows a clear and reliable trend based on that independent variable. For example, if the independent variable is categorical with levels of true and false, a main effect is said to exist if the average value of the dependent variable for true items differs significantly from that of false items. Main effects may occur without an interaction, and vice versa.

mean

The average of a set of data.

Measurement Map™

A depiction of the measureable causal chain of evidence between an investment in human capital and business outcomes typically created in collaboration between learning and development staff and business stakeholders.

median

In a set of data, the median is the value below which 50 percent of the values fall; the midpoint. Medians are preferable to averages in data where a few extreme values might skew the average.

net present value

A way of quantifying discounted cash flow:

$$NPV = CF_0 + \frac{CF_1}{(1+i)^1} + \frac{CF_2}{(1+i)^2} + \ldots + \frac{CF_n}{(1+i)^n}$$

where C_{ij} is the cash flow at time t_i and i is the interest rate.

net profit margin

The percentage of net income generated by each dollar of sales. It can be used as retained earnings or is distributed to shareholders as dividends. Compare to *gross profit margin*.

nominal variables
A type of variable that allows only qualitative classification. That is, they can be measured only in terms of whether the individual items belong to some distinctively different categories, but those categories cannot be quantified or even rank ordered. For example, all we can say is that two individuals are different in terms of variable A (e.g., they are of different race), but we cannot say which one "has more" of the quality represented by the variable. Typical examples of nominal variables are gender, race, color, city, type of degree, and so on. We use the phrase *categorical variable* synonymously.

ordinal variables
These allow us to rank order the items we measure in terms of which has less and which has more of the quality represented by the variable, but still they do not allow us to say how much more. A typical example of an ordinal variable is the socioeconomic status of families. For example, we know that upper-middle is higher than middle, but we cannot say that it is, for example, 18 percent higher. Also, this very distinction between nominal, ordinal, and interval scales itself represents a good example of an ordinal variable. For example, we can say that nominal measurement provides less information than ordinal measurement, but we cannot say how much less or how this difference compares to the difference between ordinal and interval scales.

***p*-value**
In a statistical model, the measure of surety for the model. The *p*-value, formally stated, is the chance that random variation in the data accounts for the patterns seen just as well as the proposed question. Note that *p*-values are typical written as

$$p < 0.05$$

which is read as "the probability that we reached such a conclusion incorrectly is less than 5 percent." This level (5 percent) is regarded as an adequate standard of proof in most situations.

Note that the *p*-value is the inverse of the certainty:

$$C = 1 - P$$

percentile
A way of ranking participants on some value. Percentile value gives the percentage of other participants who scored lower than the given participant

on that value. For example, if the participant is in the 22nd percentile, it means that 22 percent of the participants in the data set had a lower value for the metric (and 77 percent of participants had a higher value).

Performance map
A performance-based task analysis for a particular job function that starts with a definition of measurable success, as defined by high performers in that job. Each task is written using observable, action-oriented verbs. For each task, the map also includes inputs, outputs, tools, frequency, risk, and difficulty to learn. Performance maps often form the foundation for a curriculum plan and can be the basis for a gap analysis.

R
A popular open-source programming language for statistics and graphics. R is particularly notable for having hundreds of separate packages written by its user community that cover almost every conceivable analysis technique.

R-squared
Also called R^2 or the coefficient of determination. Informally, this is a number ranging between 0 and 1 that describes how much of the variation in the dependent variable data is accounted for by the independent variables specified in a statistical model or question. A value of 0 indicates that the independent variables have no influence at all on the data; 1.0 indicates that if the values of the independent variables are known, the value of the dependent variable is known with no error at all. R-squared is formally defined as

$$R^2 = \frac{SSR}{SST}$$

where SSR is the sum of squares in the full model and SST is the total sum of squares. By the sum of squares, we mean the sum of squared deviations between actual values and the mean (SST), or between predicted values and the mean (SSR).

random selection
A technique for selecting participants in an intervention where any participant in the pool of participants has an equal chance of selection. Methods used to implement random selection might include drawing the name out of a hat, flipping a coin, or using a computer program designed for random number selection. In contrast to random selection, many corporate training programs select participants based on high or low performance, tenure

with the company, geographic location, or other factors. Random selection is always preferable from an experimental design and statistical point of view because prior performance need not be taken into account.

ratio variables

Very similar to interval variables; in addition to all of the properties of interval variables, they feature an identifiable absolute zero point, thus they allow for statements such as x is two times more than y. Typical examples of ratio scales are measures of time or space. For example, as the Kelvin temperature scale is a ratio scale, not only can we say that a temperature of 200 degrees is higher than a temperature of 100 degrees, we can correctly state that it is twice as high. Interval scales do not have the ratio property. Most statistical data analysis procedures do not distinguish between the interval and ratio properties of the measurement scales.

reduced model

The opposite of a *full model*.

return on investment (ROI):

For an investment, the percentage return one receives from it. ROI is calculated as:

$$ROI = \frac{\text{Gross Benefit} - \text{Cost}}{\text{Cost}}$$

where Cost is the cost of training or other intervention, and Gross Benefit is the amount of increase seen in a business metric. Unless otherwise specified, the assumption is that cost is incurred a single time, and that benefits are calculated for one full year. If more than a one-year ROI calculation is specified where the ROI is requested for n years, the percentage returned is

$$ROI = \frac{1}{n} - \frac{\sum_{y=1}^{n} \text{Gross Benefit}_i - \text{Cost}}{\text{Cost}}$$

where Cost is incurred a single time.

SAS

A popular statistics analysis package. It is considered the gold standard for statistical analysis but requires significant expertise to program and interpret the results.

selection bias

Selection biases are systematic differences that occur in selecting people for an investment. For example, in many companies there is a selection bias that high performers are more likely to be chosen for training. When surveys are used and there is a low return rate, selection bias is a major concern. Note that self-selection bias is just a specific case of a selection bias.

self-selection bias

A self-selection bias occurs when people volunteer for some experience, such as training, and those people differ in particular ways from nonvolunteers. For example, we often see that people who seek out training are usually already performing at a higher level.

significant

In a statistical model, an independent variable is said to be *significant* if there is a high likelihood that the variable influences the dependent variable. The significance is usually expressed as a percentage, such as "$p < 0.05$." The number indicates the percentage under which the values seen in the data set might have occurred by pure chance. In the example of $p < 0.05$, there is a 5 percent chance (1 in 20) of such a likelihood. In most statistics, if something is said to be "significant," it is understood that there is less than a 5 percent chance of the data values producing this result by coincidence. Put another way, a significance of 95 percent means that 95 percent of the time the experiment or event recurs, the conclusion would be the same.

slope

See the definition of *intercept* for an explanation of slope.

standard deviation

A measure of how widely the data points tend to diverge from the mean. A small standard deviation indicates most values are close to the mean, and a large standard deviation indicates they are much more or much less than the mean. The basic idea is that you'd like to sum up how different the individual data points are from the average. You could just sum up the individual differences, but what about the fact that some are less than the mean and others are greater? That would tend to make them cancel out. The way to get around that is to square the differences, because any time you square a number, the result is positive. Later, after we have added them together, we take a square root, to reduce the value down to something more manageable and reasonable. That's all there is to it. The equation for the standard deviation is:

$$\sqrt{\frac{1}{n-1}\sum_{i=1}^{n}\left(x_{\mu}-x_{i}\right)^{2}}$$

Note that squaring the difference and then taking the square root of the sum cancels out the sign of the difference. The distribution, as previously noted, also gives a lot of feeling to what's going on in the data. There are several ways to measure "central tendency," or how tightly clustered the values are around the center. The best known is standard deviation. The letter sigma (Σ) is used to indicate a set of values added together, and the "mu" (μ) is the standard notation for the "mean."

In most normal distributions, you can take a quick rule of thumb that if you travel one standard deviation in each direction from the mean, then that range contains 90 percent of the data. If you go two standard deviations in either direction, 95 percent of the data falls in that range. Three standard deviations in each direction contain 99 percent of the data. There are many cases where this does not work, of course, but it is a good rule to help you generalize.

statistical paradox

A case where the data set produces one conclusion when analyzed in a simple way and another conclusion when analyzed in another way. Here's an example: Several years ago, Stanford University decided to analyze whether gender biases existed in its graduate admissions. One set of statistics showed women were rejected at a *much* higher rate than men; another showed that men were rejected at a slightly higher rate than the women. How are both of these conclusions possible? The first set of statistics simply looked at the entire graduate student application pool and showed that women were rejected at a higher rate. The second set of statistics broke down the applicant pool by school (medicine, law, business, and so on). No single school showed bias; indeed, women were slightly more likely to be admitted than men in some programs. The crucial fact is that women were more likely to apply to the extremely competitive medical and law schools. Thus, although no single department was biased, the distribution of the applicants to the different schools was responsible for the apparent difference.

trend line analysis

A technique for presenting and analyzing data. Trend lines typically simplify a graph where different values are shown as dots occurring over time as a scatter plot. Figure G.2 shows daily high temperatures recorded

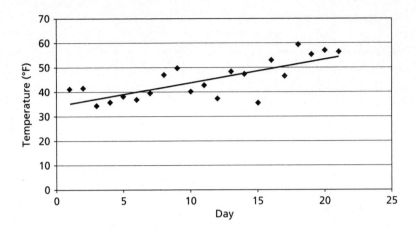

Figure G.2 High Temperatures Recorded over One Month

over a month, with the trend line illustrating the average increase. Trend lines are typically a single straight line derived by using linear regression techniques. It is possible to use higher-degree polynomials when a more curved line that fits the data more tightly is desired. Trend lines are useful in illustrating overall trends in data. Sometimes trend lines are used to identify and estimate the impact of various events. Although it is a simple technique that does not require a control group or expertise, it cannot definitively separate out the effects of other events.

type I error

This is an incorrect conclusion in which one does not accept a correct hypothesis; for example, if training did benefit participants, but the conclusion was that there were no statistically significant differences between trained and untrained participants. Common causes of type I errors are insufficient sample size, very high variance, or an effect too small to be detected with the sample size and the variances.

type II error

This is an incorrect conclusion in which one accepts an incorrect hypothesis; for example, if training did *not* benefit participants, but the report concluded that there was evidence of a benefit. The p-value for a given conclusion represents the chance of a type II error; for example, using $p < 0.05$ implies a 5 percent (1 in 20) chance of a type II error. A hidden and often misunderstood cause of type II errors is a "fishing expedition," wherein a very large set of slightly different post hoc hypotheses or data transformations are used until a desired result is obtained.

type III error

This is an incorrect conclusion in which one accepts a logically opposite conclusion from the actual one. For example, suppose that training, for some reason, hurt the performance of the participants. A type III error would be to accept the hypothesis that training benefits the participants. Type III errors are fairly rare.

type IV error

Type IV errors indicate that the researcher has correctly accepted the hypothesis that a difference does in fact occur, but he or she has incorrectly assumed that the cell mean differences are the actual differences. For example, suppose that it is known that a given training improves performance by 10 percent (assume that 10,000 participants were used, and this is the entire population). Consider a group of only 100 participants who were used as a sample. This group has a 12 percent difference because of sampling error, but the hypothesis that trained and untrained groups differ is confirmed at some level of statistical certainty. Assuming that the actual difference is 12 percent is a type IV error. An excellent discussion of this poorly understood problem can be found in scientists Joel Levin and Daniel Robinson's article in *Educational Researcher*.[1]

NOTE

1. Joel Levin and Daniel Robinson, "Rejoinder: Statistical Hypothesis Testing, Effect Size Estimation, and the Conclusion Coherence of Primary Research Studies," *Educational Researcher* 29, no. 1 (2000): 34–36.

About the Authors

Gene Pease

Gene Pease is a pioneer in the field of Workforce Optimization. He is the Founder and CEO of Vestrics, a company helping businesses optimize their human capital investments through cutting-edge software and consulting solutions. He is the co-author of *Human Capital Analytics: How to Harness the Potential of Your Organization's Greatest Asset* and *Developing Human Capital: Using Analytics to Plan and Optimize Your Learning and Development Investments*, both featured in the Wiley and SAS Business Series. Gene speaks regularly at industry events, most recently at the 2014 Conference Board's Performance Management Conference, the 2013 HR Southwest Conference, and the 2012 SAS Analytics Conference.

Under his leadership, Vestrics has been recognized by #hrwins Top 15 HR Companies to Watch in 2014 and by *CIOReview Magazine* as one of the 2013 Top 20 Data Analytics Companies. Vestrics, as Capital Analytics, has also been recognized by Bersin and Associates as a 2012 Bersin Learning Leader, by Gartner as an "On the Rise Vendor," and in the 2009, 2011, and 2013 Hype Cycle for Human Capital Management, and by the ROI Institute as having the Best Innovative Approach to ROI in 2011. Capital Analytics has helped clients such as National Grid, ConAgra Foods, and Chrysler win CLO Learning in Practice awards in the Business Impact category.

Bonnie Beresford

Bonnie Beresford, Ph.D., is an industry-recognized human capital strategist and performance consultant with over 20 years of experience in the field of human performance improvement. Her hallmark is linking investments in people to measurable business outcomes. A seasoned practitioner and consultant, she has led cross-functional client teams

273

through process and performance improvement engagements, including impact and measurement mapping, alternatives evaluation, solutions development, implementation, and measurement. Her work with both Fortune 500 clients and nonprofits has been recognized by *Chief Learning Office* and *T + D* magazines, and has earned American Society for Training & Development's (ASTD) "Excellence in Practice Award" and three "Chief Learning Office - Business Impact" awards on behalf of her clients.

Bonnie's practitioner approach makes her a popular presenter at industry conferences, including the Conference Board, ASTD, Chief Learning Officer Symposiums, International Society for Performance Improvement (ISPI), Corporate University Week, National Fund for Workforce Solutions, and Elliott Masie's Learning conferences. Bonnie holds a Ph.D. in human capital management from Bellevue University, an MBA from Wayne State University, and a BS from Central Michigan University. She supports the development of the field of performance improvement through her involvement with ISPI, serving on both the international and her local board of directors.

Lew Walker

Lew Walker has forged a very successful career in the discipline of Human Resources, serving in many Vice President roles at AT&T and SBC Wireless. Lew played a significant part in supporting several mergers and acquisitions, including Cingular's acquisition of AT&T Wireless, as well as acquisitions of Pacific Bell and Ameritech.

Prior to his current role as Vice President of AT&T Human Resources supporting the offices of the SVP and CFO, Group President, and Chief Strategy Officer as well as the President of Network Operations, Lew was Vice President of AT&T Learning Services. In this capacity, Lew was responsible for initial and continual training and performance development for all AT&T employees and partners across the globe. AT&T received wide recognition, including first place in *Chief Learning Officer* magazine's Inaugural LearningElite Award in 2011 and 2013, and second place in 2012. AT&T also received one of the five Editor's Choice Awards for best business support in both 2011 and 2013. Bersin & Associates recognized AT&T Learning Services in 2012 in three of their Learning Leader categories. In addition, Lew received the 2011 Next Generation Innovation Award from Women in Technology International (WITI).

Index